CHICAGO ON FOOT

CHICAGO ON FOOT

WALKING TOURS
OF
CHICAGO'S ARCHITECTURE

Fifth Edition

Ira J. Bach and Susan Wolfson
Revised and Updated by James Cornelius

CHICAGO
REVIEW
PRESS

Library of Congress Cataloging-in-Publication Data

Bach, Ira J.
    Chicago on foot : walking tours of Chicago's architecture / Ira J.
Bach and Susan Wolfson. — 5th ed. / revised and updated by James
Cornelius.
        p.   cm.
    Includes index.
    ISBN 1-55652-209-6 : $16.95
    1. Architecture—Illinois—Chicago—Guidebooks.   2. Chicago
(Ill.)—Buildings, structures, etc.—Guidebooks.   I. Wolfson, Susan.
II. Cornelius, James.   III. Title.
NA735.C4B32   1994
720'.9773'11—dc20   93-39802
                                                          CIP

Cover photos: upper left, Cobb Hall, University of Chicago Quadrangle;
center left, Harold Washington Library Center; bottom left, Charnley
House (detail); right, NBC Tower. All photos by Leslie Schwartz.

© 1994 by Susan Wolfson

Published by Chicago Review Press, Incorporated
814 North Franklin Street
Chicago, Illinois 60610

Printed in the United States of America

5 4 3 2 1

*To **Muriel**;*
*and to my dear friend **Marshall Holleb**,*
without whose companionship and wit
I might have given up walking long ago.

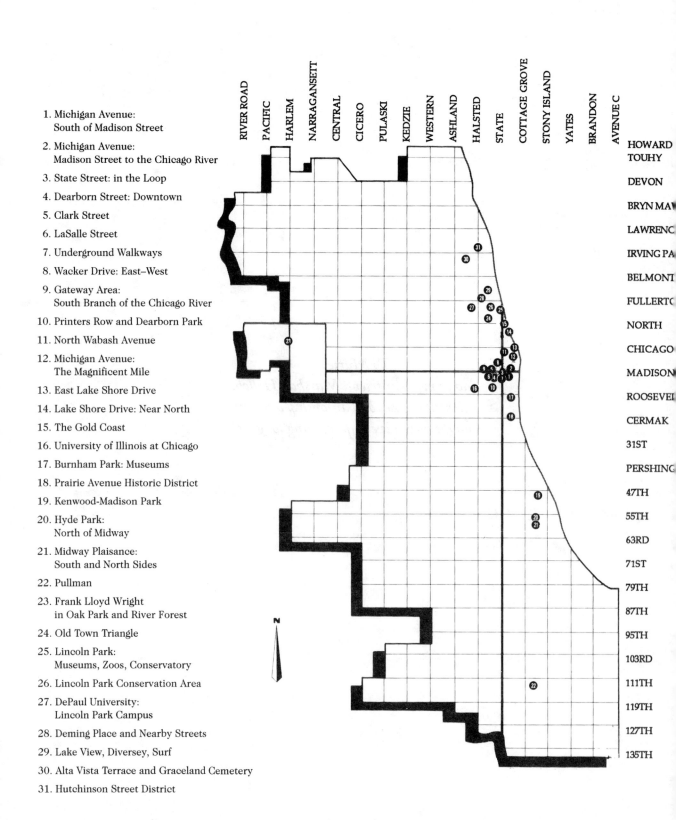

CONTENTS

INTRODUCTION

A continued public response to the fourth edition of this collection of architectural walking tours, combined with major additions to the Downtown and Michigan Avenue areas of Chicago, has prompted its update and revision.

The WALKS proposed here have been selected to present Chicago as a great cosmopolitan city as well as a collection of local communities, tied together by an intricate web of transportation that makes them accessible to the pedestrian for a closer view.

Since Chicago is a vast outdoor museum of great architecture created in about one hundred years, the major focus of the WALKS is architectural. From 1883 to 1893 the "Chicago school of architecture" came into being. During that decade a whole galaxy of buildings appeared, reaching the unprecedented heights of 12, 14, 16, and 23 stories. The architects of the Chicago school employed a new type of construction: the *iron skeleton*, at that time called quite simply *Chicago construction*. They invented a new kind of foundation to cope with the problems of the muddy ground of Chicago: the *floating foundation*. They introduced the horizontally elongated window: the *Chicago window*. They created the modern business and administration building. And around the turn of the century, the so-called *prairie house* came into being here.

Of equal significance is the current work of Chicago architects, often characterized as a continuation of the Chicago school. Its pure forms, horizontally elongated windows, and rugged strength are still to be seen in many of today's buildings. Architects of the present, however, have not hesitated to experiment with their own designs and materials. Though Mies van der Rohe's "glass houses" on North Lake Shore Drive and Helmut Jahn's State of Illinois Building may be considered the ultimate development of certain trends of the Chicago school, the cylindrical towers of Marina City, with their concrete slab construction, circular balconies, and pie-shaped rooms, bear little resemblance. Nor does the facade of the Henry Hinds Laboratory for the Geophysical Sciences Building at the University of Chicago—though the older school of architects would approve the functional origin of the new features.

Complete coverage of buildings worth noting in Chicago cannot possibly be attempted, especially in view of the size of the city. While following the routes proposed here, the pedestrian will many times come across other interesting or beautiful buildings. The frequency with which this may happen is only another tribute to the endless vitality of this tremendous city.

This symbol * appears from time to time throughout the text to indicate buildings and sites that have been officially designated as architectural or historic landmarks. The Commission on Chicago Historic and Architectural Landmarks was created on January 17, 1968 by ordinance of the City Council of the City of Chicago. A predecessor commission, known as the Commission on Chicago Architectural Landmarks, was created in 1957 by Mayor Richard J. Daley. Because broader powers were considered desirable, the legislature and City Council acted to replace the first commission by creating the present one. The new commission now includes the preservation of historic as well as architectural landmarks.

The City of Chicago has been particularly unfortunate in having lost Adler and Sullivan's Garrick Theater in 1961 and the old Stock Exchange Building in 1972. Efforts to save these buildings failed because of inadequate landmarks preservation legislation. Indeed, ineffective landmarks preservation is widespread in the United States, though awareness of the problem is growing.

Chicago is famous for one of the first comprehensive city plans produced on this continent. The pedestrian will become aware of the planning, especially on the lakefront. In 1909 Daniel H. Burnham and Edward H. Bennett enunciated policies that have been instrumental in shaping the city of today. They established, among other things, the city's shoreline for public use only by recommending the extension of lakefront parks, and they set the pattern for the city's system of forest preserves linked by highways.

Chicago's street system is the conventional grid, laid out with major streets at mile and one-half mile spacing. There are also a number of diagonal streets, some of them tracing old Indian trails, that bisect the junctions of major streets of the grid pattern, forming six-spoked intersections—and creating some of the city's most difficult traffic problems.

More recently, a number of expressways have been built in Chicago. These carry traffic to and from the central business district and also serve large columns of north-south and east-west crosstown traffic. The new roads have considerably shortened travel time within the city and have tied the various parts of the metropolitan area more tightly together. They have also helped to improve public transportation by the installation of rapid transit lines in the median strips of the Eisenhower, Stevenson, Dan Ryan, and Kennedy expressways, including a line to O'Hare Airport.

The steet numbering system in Chicago follows the compass, the east-west division marked by State Street and the north-south division at Madison Steet. The city extends about 25 miles north and south and about 15 miles east and west.

Since all the city's topography is flat, walking—said to be one of the best forms of exercise—will not be strenuous. The routes outlined here for most WALKS are designed for daytime enjoyment.

Instructions for each WALK assume that downtown Chicago—the Loop, at the corner of State and Madison streets—is your starting point, and directions to the start of each walk are from that point. Since bus routes and bus numbers change from time to time, the safest way will be to phone the CTA at 836-7000 (or toll-free at 1-800-972-7000) for precise instructions before starting out—or at least ask the bus driver whether the number you are here told to take will still carry you to your destination.

People who would enjoy attending group tours can contact the Chicago Architecture Foundation, whose dedicated staff of young docents conduct many WALKS throughout the year for the benefit of Glessner House and the Landmarks Preservation Council.

This book makes no attempt to advise on places to stay or eat. The city abounds with good hotels and restaurants, lists of which can be obtained from the Chicago Convention and Tourism Bureau (at McCormick Place On the Lake, 567-8500).

1. Grant Park

2. Buckingham Memorial Fountain

3. Chicago Hilton and Towers
   720 S. Michigan Ave.

4. The Blackstone Hotel
   636 S. Michigan Ave.

5. Congress Hotel
   520 S. Michigan Ave.

6. Auditorium Building
   430 S. Michigan Ave.

7. Fine Arts Building
   410 S. Michigan Ave.

8. The Chicago Club
   81 E. Van Buren St.

9. 318 S. Michigan Ave.

10. Britannica Center
    310 S. Michigan Ave.

11. McClurg Building
    218 S. Wabash Ave.

12. Santa Fe Center
    224 S. Michigan Ave.

13. Orchestra Hall Building

14. Borg-Warner Building
    200 S. Michigan Ave.

15. Art Institute of Chicago
    Michigan Ave. at Adams St.

16. Peoples Gas Company Building
    122 S. Michigan Ave.

17. Lake View Building
    116 S. Michigan Ave.

18. 112 S. Michigan Ave.

19. Monroe Building
    104 S. Michigan Ave.

20. 55 E. Monroe Street Building

21. University Club
    76 E. Monroe St.

22. Gage Building
    18 S. Michigan Ave.

23. Chicago Athletic Association
    12 S. Michigan Ave.

24. Willoughby Tower
    8 S. Michigan Ave.

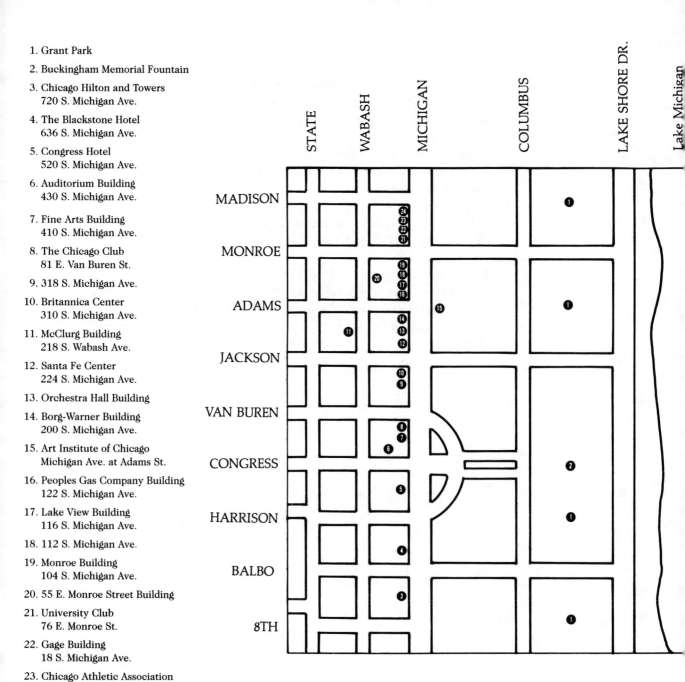

WALK 1 MICHIGAN AVENUE: SOUTH OF MADISON STREET

WALKING TIME: About 2 hours.
HOW TO GET THERE: Take a southbound CTA bus, No. 146 (Marine/Michigan) on State Street. Get off at Balbo Drive (700 S) and Michigan Avenue. Cross Michigan Avenue, and you are in Grant Park.

Chicago's skyline is one of the most exhilarating sights in the world. Day or night the view is magnificent—from an airplane approaching the city, from a boat on Lake Michigan, from a car on the Outer Drive, or from the walkways in Grant Park. It is always impressive.

The section of Michigan Avenue covered in this WALK goes from the Chicago Hilton and Towers on the south, to Madison Street on the north. (WALK 2 goes north from there.) For most of this stretch Grant Park offers a fine contrast to the avenue's strikingly varied architectural styles, through its own rich array of sculpture, gardens, and fountains.

GRANT PARK   Grant Park was no accident. Daniel Burnham designed it as part of the Chicago Plan of 1909. First, the lake was filled from Michigan Avenue east to what is now the Outer Drive, to provide the necessary land space. The park was planned as an immense green expanse following loosely the pattern of Versailles. Burnham's original plan for the park was completed when the Monroe Street parking lot, between Monroe and Randolph streets, was decked over and landscaped. In the spring, when the park's trees and shrubs are in bloom, this is a place of incomparable beauty.

In its midst, southwest of Jackson and Columbus drives, is the magnificent seated Lincoln, the last work of America's most storied sculptor, Augustus St. Gaudens. Chicago is the fortunate possessor of this monument because of a $100,000 bequest for such a statue from John Crerar, who also willed the city the John Crerar Library (see WALK 20).

Flanking Congress Plaza—near Michigan Avenue in Grant Park—are two American Indian equestrians with drawn bows, created by the Yugoslavian sculptor Ivan Mestrovic. Of heroic scale, they make a sweeping entrance to the enormous Buckingham Fountain, just to the east.

BUCKINGHAM MEMORIAL FOUNTAIN

DESIGNERS: *Bennett, Parsons and Frost of Chicago and Jacques Lambert of Paris (1926)*

This fountain, modeled from one of the Versailles fountains, is said to be the largest in the world—about twice as large as its model. It has a great central stream with 133 jets of water, some of which reach about 200 feet in the air. Each night from 9 to 10 during its active season (May through September) the fountain is illuminated, with shifting colors played on it—longer displays on evenings of concerts in the park. The fountain, a popular rendezvous point for visitors to Chicago, was donated to the city of Chicago in 1927 by Miss Kate Buckingham in memory of her brother Clarence.

Start your WALK up Michigan Avenue at the Chicago Hilton and Towers, on the southwest corner of Balbo Drive and Michigan Avenue.

CHICAGO HILTON AND TOWERS
720 S. Michigan

ARCHITECTS: *Holabird and Roche (1927); for the remodeling: Solomon, Cordwell and Buenz (1984–86)*

When built as the Stevens, this hotel was billed as the world's largest—it had 3,000 rooms and a rooftop miniature golf course on grass. It is 25 stories high with a 4-story tower and two to five basements, supported on rock foundations. The $150 million remodeling and renovation slightly reduced the number of rooms to make them larger and more luxurious, many with 2 baths and multiple closets. The hotel's top 3 floors are the Towers, a separate and even more luxurious section with its own added services and separate elevators. The 242,396 square feet of public spaces have been reconfigured, remodeled, or restored. Grand rooms are restored to their original elegance, and new restaurants, lounges, and entertainment areas are designed to harmonize with the older rooms.

An addition to the west contains a porte-cochere entrance, 510-car garage, exhibition space, and health club. It is a state of the art, long-span structure with precast concrete facades detailed to blend with the rusticated cut stone of the existing hotel. The porte cochere becomes the hotel's main covered auto and taxi entrance. There are granite fountains, light fixtures, and paving bricks to carry the design theme of the existing hotel.

On the upper level of the addition is the health club, containing an indoor pool, cushioned running track, saunas, and an outdoor recreation deck. The lower level adds 30,000 square feet of high-ceilinged exhibition space. With the addition and remodeling, the Chicago Hilton boasts the largest single level of exhibition space in any hotel in the world.

Hotel tours may be arranged by advance reservation with the human resources department at 922-4400.

Just north of the Hilton, on the northwest corner of Michigan and Balbo avenues, is the Blackstone Hotel.

* THE BLACKSTONE HOTEL
636 S. Michigan

ARCHITECTS: *Marshall and Fox (1910)*

This hotel, many times the headquarters for a national presidential nominating convention, offers a rather pleasing exterior of French Renaissance architecture. At the time it was built, in fact, it won a gold medal for excellence of design.

Continuing northward on Michigan Avenue, between Harrison Street and Congress Parkway, is another historic hotel building.

CONGRESS HOTEL
520 S. Michigan

ARCHITECTS: *Clinton J. Warren (1893); Holabird and Roche (1902 and 1907); Holabird and Root (1956)*

In contrast with the Blackstone's exterior, the Congress has a facade of rugged gray limestone suggesting the influence of Henry Hobson Richardson. Its "Peacock Alley" off the main lobby was once one of the city's gathering places for outstanding social events. In the last renovation a section of the ground floor, on the north side, was opened up and arcaded, to allow the widening of Congress Street into Congress Parkway. (The south side of the Auditorium Building, across the street to the north, underwent the same kind of change.)

On the northwest corner of Michigan Avenue and Congress Parkway is the Auditorium Building.

* AUDITORIUM BUILDING
430 S. Michigan

ARCHITECTS: *Adler and Sullivan (1889); for the restoration of the Auditorium Theatre: Harry Weese (1967)*

The Auditorium Building, now owned by Roosevelt University, is one of Chicago's most famous cultural and architectural landmarks. Once the tallest tower in the city, its construction was a triumph of the partnership of Louis Sullivan, with his inspired architectural imagination, and Dankmar Adler, with his extraordinary engineering genius.

The Auditorium Theatre, originally surrounded by hotel and office space, has long been justifiably renowned for its large, well-equipped stage and its perfect acoustics. The Chicago Landmarks Commission citation of 1959 reads:

> In recognition of the community spirit which here joined commercial and artistic ends, uniting hotel, office building, and theatre in one structure; the inventiveness of the engineer displayed from foundations to the perfect acoustics; and the genius of the architect which gave form and, with the aid of the original ornament, expressed the spirit of festivity in rooms of great splendor.

Disaster threatened the building in 1929, however, when the Chicago Opera Company, which had used the Auditorium Theatre for many years, moved to the newly completed Civic Opera Building; and it

Auditorium Building
(Philip A. Turner)

became a certainty with the economic depression of the 1930s. By 1940 the Auditorium Building was bankrupt and the theater was closed. From 1942 to 1945 the building was used as Chicago headquarters for the United Service Organization. In 1946 it was purchased by Roosevelt College (now University), and hotel rooms and offices were converted as needed.

The Auditorium Theatre was fortunately left untouched at this time, though all movable contents were sold at auction soon after bankruptcy was declared. Unable to raise the enormous amount of money needed to restore the theater, Roosevelt University nevertheless recognized its value. In 1958 the University established a nonprofit organization, the Auditorium Theatre Council, which in nine years succeeded in raising the $2,250,000 required for restoration. After 26 years of darkness, the

Auditorium Theatre opened once again on October 31, 1967, with the New York City Ballet performing to an audience of 4,200.

The great lobby facing Michigan Avenue was one of the showpieces of the Auditorium Hotel when it opened in 1889, and it still exhibits many of the great architectural elements designed by Sullivan and Adler. The original floor was made of marble tesserae laid in multicolored design motifs. The central columns in the lobby are faced with an imitation marble called scagliola and contain utility plumbing and electrical connections for the upper stories. There is a 6-foot dado of Mexican onyx around the lobby. Originally the lighting was in rosette clusters of filament bulbs and there were stenciled patterns on the ceiling bays and on the undersurfaces of each of the beams. The restoration, including new light fixtures, was close to the original lobby design and color scheme. Plaster ornament was restored by casting replacements in molds taken from existing ornament. Decor was recreated by comparing samples found at the site with early descriptions of the building. Dressing rooms and other service spaces were completely modernized. The restoration of what Frank Lloyd Wright called "the greatest room for music and opera in the world—bar none," is a striking example of adaptive reuse and historic preservation.

Naturally, the upper floors that contain classrooms were modernized for safety but pleasantly designed and planned. The Michigan Avenue stairways, once again the delightful Sullivan brainchild, have been painted to simulate the original copper-plated iron finish on the balustrades; and the stained glass windows were restored with artificial lighting behind. Ascend the stair to the elegant mezzanine for a fine view of Michigan Avenue and the park.

The University also remodeled and modernized the tower. Originally it had 7 floors and now it has 8, and the new 16th floor houses the air conditioning, heating, and other mechanical equipment for the tower offices. Within the main building, facing Michigan Avenue, there are sixteen classrooms, thirty offices, and five laboratories—all remodeled.

A fantastic piece of architectural squeezing was accomplished by constructing the Walter E. Heller Center within the former light and ventilation court. An 11-story and mezzanine structure, 100 feet long and 25 feet wide, was the answer. The connections at each floor to the main building are unobtrusive.

The Herman Crown Center, built by Sullivan on a site 80 feet by 180 feet on Wabash Avenue just north of the Auditorium, is indeed well planned and well conceived. The simple concrete facade with the typical Chicago school windows relates well to its parent building next door. The interior design carries the spirit of Sullivan into another century, to Roosevelt University's credit.

Tours of the Auditorium Theatre may be arranged by calling 431-2354. Groups of 10 preferred.

North of the Auditorium is the Fine Arts Building.

* FINE ARTS BUILDING
410 S. Michigan

ARCHITECT: *S. S. Beman (1885, 1898)*

The Fine Arts Building, built by the Studebaker company to display carriages, has been a center of musical and dramatic events for years; at one time—along with the Auditorium Theatre and the Orchestra Hall—it was *the* performing arts center of Chicago. The facade is rugged and is a good companion for the Auditorium. The 1885 building was 8 stories. In 1898 the top floor was demolished and the upper stories, with a terra-cotta facade and copper cornice, were added. The building now contains four movie theaters and, on the upper floors, high-ceilinged studios and recital halls—from which sounds of hopeful artists can be heard scaling the heights.

Continue north to the corner.

THE CHICAGO CLUB BUILDING
81 E. Van Buren

ARCHITECTS: *Granger and Bollenbacher (1930)*

The site was once occupied by the original Art Institute building designed by Burnham and Root, which was demolished in 1929. The building fronts 90 feet on Van Buren Street and 75 feet on Michigan Avenue. (The original Burnham and Root entrance was reused on the Van Buren Street side.) The building is 95 feet high, including 9 stories and basement, and is made of steel, Connecticut brownstone, and brick. The Italian Romanesque style of the exterior lends dignity to this section of Michigan Avenue.

Continue north.

318 S. MICHIGAN

ARCHITECT: *Unknown (1885); for the restoration: Nagle Hartray and Associates (1982)*

This building originated as the Hotel Richilieu. To convert it to office use, in 1911 a major renovation of the front facade was done and an addition built. It is a heavy-framed timber building with cast-iron columns and masonry exterior. There are 7 stories plus a basement, and an 8th story penthouse.

The 1982 renovations included refacing the first 2 floors in cut limestone, a material compatible with the terra-cotta of the upper floors and with the other architecture on the avenue. The windows were set deep for shadow to give the stone more massiveness, and jointing was revealed for more rustication. The five bays of the building were carried to the ground, with changes in scale and proportion creating a base, middle, and top, representing a conscious continuity of scale and form.

The interior was entirely replaced, bringing it up to the latest building code.

Turn left at Jackson Boulevard and walk to the corner of Wabash.

BRITANNICA CENTER
310 S. Michigan

ARCHITECTS: *Graham, Anderson, Probst and White (1924)*

This building, 21 stories with a tower rising to 28 stories, forms part of what has been called "the Michigan Cliffs." These few blocks were so named because their height is fairly uniform and they appear to drop off to nothingness at the park. The design here is of classical inspiration, though symmetry is lost by using the south bay as the main entrance. Now half occupied by the illustrious encyclopedia publisher, the building was once home to the CNA Corporation, which joined it in back to two modern steel and glass buildings on Jackson and Wabash avenues (see WALK 3).

Walk west on Jackson Boulevard and north on Wabash Avenue. The fourth building on the west side of the street is the McClurg Building.

* McCLURG BUILDING
218 S. Wabash

ARCHITECTS: *Holabird and Roche (1900)*

This landmark building was completed in 1900 and is 9 stories on pile foundations. The famous Chicago windows can be seen, along with the terra-cotta facing of the facade. It is an excellent early example of a simple, straightforward, steel-cage design for an office building. Though the owners and the name of the structure have changed several times, it is still best known as the McClurg Building.

Return to Jackson Boulevard and walk east to Michigan Avenue. On the corner is the Santa Fe Center.

* SANTA FE CENTER
224 S. Michigan

ARCHITECTS: *D. H. Burnham and Company (1903); for the renovation: Metz, Train and Youngren; Frye, Gillan and Molinaro (1984–87)*

The building is 17 stories with a white terra-cotta facing. There is one basement and the structure rests on hardpan caissons. Daniel Burnham maintained his office here on the 14th floor during preparation of the Chicago Plan, completed in 1909. His planning associate, Edward Bennett, also worked with him there.

The renovation and restoration complied with the National Preservation Act while modernizing services, facilities, and office and commercial spaces to attract new tenants. Its unobstructed views, neighboring cultural institutions, and historical significance made it a prominent anchor worth preserving.

The 1st floor and the 2nd floor gallery are restored to their original elegance. A light court, originally designed for lighting and ventilation, ran through the building's center. Modern technology makes this court unnecessary and energy inefficient, so it was converted to an atrium. Open above the second floor to the roof, it is a focal point for all floors and creates visual continuity. Outside, canopies of bronze and glass over the entrance to the Grant Park underground garage complement the adjacent storefronts. The work is a certified rehabilitation project by the National Trust for Historic Preservation. The Chicago Architecture Foundation shop here has much information on local attractions.

* ORCHESTRA HALL BUILDING
220 S. Michigan

ARCHITECTS: *D. H. Burnham and Company (1904); for restoration: Harry Weese (1969); for the rehabilitation and remodeling: Skidmore, Owings and Merrill (1982)*

The building is 9 stories with one basement. The world-famous Chicago Symphony Orchestra, founded by Theodore Thomas in 1891, occupies most of the 9 stories, and the Orchestral Association, a not-for-profit citizens organization, owns the property. Call 435-8141 for information about tours. The facade is composed of Indiana limestone and red brick in a style derivative of the Italian Renaissance. The names of Bach, Mozart, Beethoven, Schubert, and Wagner are made a part of the design over the entrance.

The 1982 rehabilitation and remodeling included new seating, improved acoustics, and increased stage depth. The basement was remodeled to include women's locker rooms and a new rehearsal hall.

BORG-WARNER BUILDING
200 S. Michigan

ARCHITECTS: *A. Epstein and Sons, William E. Lescaze, associate architect (1958)*

This steel-cage building with lake-blue sheathing was the first contemporary structure on Michigan Avenue. It replaced the old Pullman Building designed by S. S. Beman in 1884.

Now cross Adams Street and then Michigan Avenue to view one of Chicago's most prized possessions, the Art Institute of Chicago—the entrance guarded by two large, sculptured lions.

ART INSTITUTE OF CHICAGO
Michigan at Adams

ARCHITECTS: *Shepley, Rutan and Coolidge (1892); for McKinlock Court: Coolidge and Hodgson (1924); for North Wing: Holabird and Root (1956); for Morton Wing: Shaw, Metz and Associates (1962); for East Wing: Skidmore, Owings and Merrill, Walter A. Netsch, partner in charge (1976); for South Wing: Thomas Beeby (1991)*

The original part of the building is French Renaissance in spirit, a style considered appropriate for art museums at the time but quite at variance with the trend of the Chicago school.

The Art Institute houses a theater, an art school, and a film school in addition to its art collections. A section of special interest to architects is

the Burnham Library of Architecture Gallery, created to provide space for exhibits from the Burnham Library Collection—established in 1912 in memory of the great architect and city planner Daniel H. Burnham. In the center of McKinlock Court, which is classical rather than Renaissance, is a fountain with sea creatures sculptured by Carl Milles—a duplicate of one in his native Sweden.

To celebrate its centennial in 1976, the Art Institute added a wing of 216,500 square feet along Columbus Drive and remodeled another 46,000 square feet. The building program included an east entry, dining facilities, auditorium, galleries around McKinlock Court, and an expanded facility for the school of art. The entry arch of the old Stock Exchange Building was re-erected in a garden on Columbus Drive. Also on the Columbus Drive side stands Isamu Noguchi's bicentennial sculpture.

A prominent part of the expansion was the reconstruction of the Trading Room of the former Chicago Stock Exchange building, which stood at 30 N. LaSalle Street from 1894 to 1972. One of the foremost interior spaces created by the architectural partnership of Adler and Sullivan, the room was reconstructed, using original salvaged materials and carefully duplicated missing elements, based on historical photographs and contemporary descriptions. Reopened in 1977, the Trading Room is a masterpiece of architectural form and color, the decorations of which were created by Louis Sullivan in close collaboration with master colorist Louis J. Millet. The stencil patterns on the walls and ceiling contain up to fifty-two colors each.

The Art Institute is open Monday, Wednesday, Thursday, and Friday from 10:30 A.M. to 4:30 P.M.; Tuesday from 10:30 A.M. to 8 P.M.; Saturday from 10 A.M. to 5 P.M.; Sunday and holidays (except Christmas) from noon to 5 P.M. Tuesdays free.

On the west side of Michigan Avenue at Adams Street is the Peoples Gas Company Building.

rt Institute of Chicago
Olga Stefanos)

* PEOPLES GAS COMPANY BUILDING
122 S. Michigan

ARCHITECTS: *D. H. Burnham and Company (1911)*

This gray granite and terra-cotta building is 20 stories, with two basements on hardpan caissons. The exterior walls on the two street fronts, above the monolithic granite columns, are supported on steel cantilever girders. The original main floor featured Pentelikon marble (used for the Parthenon in Athens) and mahogany from the Andaman Islands. The building was the temporary quarters of city offices while City Hall (WALK 5) was being built.

Continue north.

* LAKE VIEW BUILDING
116 S. Michigan

ARCHITECTS: *Jenney, Mundie and Jensen (1906, 1912); for the restoration: Pappageorge Haymes (1985)*

This was originally known as the Municipal Court Building. It was built as a 12-story structure, and 5 stories were added in 1912. The facade has three bays for windows, with white terra-cotta as the exterior material. In 1985 the lobby and facade were restored, the mechanical systems were upgraded, and a roof deck was added.

112 S. MICHIGAN

ARCHITECTS: *Haynes and Barnett of St. Louis (1907); for the addition and renovations: Swann and Weiskopf (1985)*

The Illinois Athletic Club was the original occupant of this building when it was completed in 1907 as 12 stories with two basements on hardpan caissons. The facade of the original building is Indiana limestone with a base of gray granite. Step to the curb and look up to the sculptured frieze at the 11th-floor level, just under the original cornice. The figures portray mythological characters in action. Also note the three heroic figures before fanlight stained-glass windows at the 2nd-floor level. These ornaments add luster to this section of Michigan Avenue.

The 6-story addition and major renovations, completed in 1985 for a hotel, increased the number of rooms from 83 to 180 and added 16,000 square feet of commercial space. The newer construction is of cut limestone and glass, intended to complement the older structure.

MONROE BUILDING
104 S. Michigan

ARCHITECTS: *Holabird and Roche (1912)*

This building is 16 stories with a beige-colored granite facade on the first 2 stories and white terra-cotta above, in a simplified eclectic Gothic and Italian Romanesque design. It has not only a pleasing appearance, but a well-planned series of office floors. Note the way the fluting is carried the full length of the building. The lobby is an excellent example of architectural faience produced by the famed Rookwood pottery.

Around the corner on Monroe Street is a building that extends along the whole east side of Wabash Avenue.

55 E. MONROE STREET BUILDING

ARCHITECTS: *Alfred Shaw and Associates (1972)*

Look up at the 50-story structure, where the eye follows the vertical lines of the aluminum skin over the steel and concrete columns. There is a secondary horizontal series of lines that mark the floors and add rhythm to all three facades. The interior ground floor has been well planned for large pedestrian movements from the garage, street, and elevators to the upper floors. The striking lobby has gray marble floors and walls that set off the aluminum escalators. This building and plaza in the heart of the Loop has been well conceived for the convenience of the public and tenants, and, in addition, it provides parking for guests of the Palmer House across Wabash Avenue.

Back at the northwest corner of Monroe Street and Michigan Avenue is the University Club.

UNIVERSITY CLUB
76 E. Monroe

ARCHITECTS: *Holabird and Roche (1909)*

The Indiana limestone structure of Tudor Gothic design is 14 stories, with 1 basement on pile foundations. If you step across Michigan Avenue, you can see the great cathedral dining hall that occupies 2 stories of the top floors.

Walk around the corner from the University Club and north on Michigan Avenue to come to the Gage Building.

* GAGE BUILDING
18 S. Michigan

ARCHITECTS: *Holabird and Roche; for the decorative facade: Louis Sullivan (1898)*

The citation of the city's first Landmarks Commission speaks of "the imaginative use of original ornament." Although the two buildings to the south of it, at 30 and 24 S. Michigan Avenue, both completely the work of Holabird and Roche, seem more modern in their lack of ornament, they do not equal the quality of design in the Gage Building. The entire citation from the Commission reads:

> In recognition of the fine relations established between piers, windows, and wall surfaces; the excellence of proportions throughout; and the imaginative use of original ornament.

CHICAGO ATHLETIC ASSOCIATION
12 S. Michigan

ARCHITECTS: *Henry Ives Cobb (1893); for the addition at 71 E. Madison Street: Schmidt, Garden and Martin (1906, 1925)*

The building at 12 S. Michigan Avenue was completed in 1893 after experiencing a disastrous fire. It is 10 and 11 stories, with 1 basement, on spread foundations. The adjoining addition at 71 E. Madison is 12 stories (the top 2 of which were added in 1925 by the same architect) with three basements, steel columns, and rock caissons. Step to the curb on Michigan Avenue and note the fascinating way in which Cobb designed the facade in a Venetian Gothic theme. From across the street you may note that the top floors contain a great 2-story dining hall like that at the University Club. Limestone and red brick are the materials used.

WILLOUGHBY TOWER
8 S. Michigan

ARCHITECT: *Samuel N. Crowen (1929)*

Replacing the 8-story Willoughby Building, this 36-story structure on caissons has a gray granite base with an Indiana limestone facade on Michigan Avenue as well as on Madison Street. The mock balcony above the door and the stonework at the 5th floor anchor the building to life at street level.

Santa Fe Center lobby
(courtesy Frye Gillan Molinaro Architects)

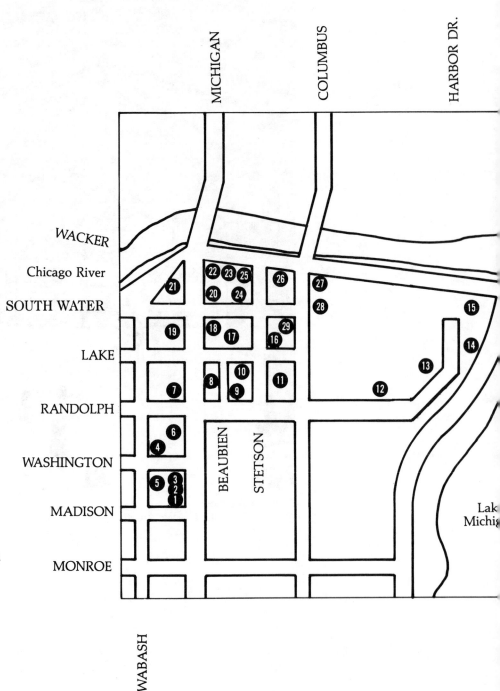

WALK 2 MICHIGAN AVENUE: MADISON STREET TO CHICAGO RIVER

WALKING TIME: About 2 hours.

HOW TO GET THERE: Walk 2 blocks east on State Street to Michigan Avenue and start at the northwest corner.

For many decades Michigan Avenue seemed to be the city's eastern edge of major development. Since the 1960s the focus of this whole area has moved eastward with the river and Randolph Street, and plenty of open land (created by a rerouting of Lake Shore Drive) makes further development likely.

TOWER BUILDING
6 N. Michigan

ARCHITECTS: *Richard E. Schmidt (1899); for addition: Holabird and Roche (1922); for remodeling: Loebl, Schlossman and Bennett (1955)*

The building was formerly known as the Montgomery Ward and Company Building with a frontage of 86 feet on Michigan Avenue and 163 feet on Madison Street. The steel-frame construction rises 12 stories with a tower and 1 basement on wood-pile foundations. The street facade of the lower 3 stories was originally of carved Georgia marble. The upper part of the facade is of umber-colored brick and terra-cotta. Stories 13 to 16 were added later, thus reducing the original prominence of the tower.

A. Montgomery Ward, who occupied the original tower office, was victorious for all Chicagoans in obtaining an opinion from the Supreme Court of Illinois that no building other than the Art Institute be permitted in Grant Park.

ILLINOIS STATE MEDICAL SOCIETY
20 N. Michigan

ARCHITECTS: *Beers, Clay and Dutton (1885, 1892); for rehabilitation and adaptive reuse: Nagle Hartray and Associates (1985)*

This building was originally a Montgomery Ward catalogue warehouse. It was built in three stages: the first, a 5-story building 3 bays wide; the second, an addition of the same size added 3 stories to the extant structure; and in 1892 a third, an 8-story addition 2 bays wide. The building has masonry walls and cast-iron beams and columns at each window.

Long the John M. Smyth Building, it has undergone major renovations. The exterior was restored and a limestone base was added. The building was gutted and all mechanical systems were upgraded with computer-monitored equipment. The windows were replaced. New elevator cabs were installed. A cut-out entry 50 feet into the building created an arcaded entrance, and an 8-story atrium and skylight were added.

30 N. MICHIGAN AVENUE BUILDING

ARCHITECT: *Jarvis Hunt (1914)*

This was originally named the Michigan Boulevard Building when it was 15 stories high with two basements on rock caissons. The base is granite and the facade is terra-cotta. Five stories were added in 1923. The exterior design is a modified Gothic and the lobby carries on this theme pleasingly. Many medical offices are located here.

Walk west on Washington Street. On the northeast corner of Washington Street and Wabash Avenue is the Garland Building.

GARLAND BUILDING
111 N. Wabash

ARCHITECTS: *C. A. Eckstrom (1915, addition 1925); for the remodeling: Solomon, Cordwell and Buenz (1982–85)*

This is a representative brick skyscraper with double-hung windows, typical of its period. With the change in occupancy of the store, the lobby was remodeled, and a new lobby to serve the new office space and the second floor stores was added on Washington Street. Show windows were put on the second floor level.

On the south side of Washington Street is the Pittsfield Building.

PITTSFIELD BUILDING
55 E. Washington

ARCHITECTS: *Graham, Anderson, Probst and White (1927)*

The building is 21 stories with a 17-story tower. A black granite base and terra-cotta facade give this structure a dignified effect. The lobby's ceiling forms an ornate hexagon and diamond pattern in gilded plaster. Medical personnel are the principal occupants of the building.

Across the street, east of the Garland Building, is the Chicago Public Library Cultural Center.

* CHICAGO PUBLIC LIBRARY CULTURAL CENTER
78 E. Washington

ARCHITECTS: *Shepley, Rutan and Coolidge (1897); for the renovation: Holabird and Root (1977)*

Extending a full block along Michigan Avenue from Washington to Randolph streets is the former main building of the Chicago Public Library, now the Chicago Public Library Cultural Center. Though the structure is not at all in the style of the Chicago school of its day, it is an impressive example of revivalist architecture, not only on the outside but throughout the interior as well. The broad marble staircases and the many beautifully colored mosaics that decorate both the walls and the

Chicago Public Library Cultural Center
(Leslie Schwartz)

ceilings are a magnificent sight for any period. The lighting fixtures and mosaics are the work of Louis Tiffany.

The blue Bedford stone, granite, and limestone exterior with large arches and columns is not unlike a Roman gateway. The colonnade is Ionic, with solid piers interspersed. The Washington Street entrance is treated in the Roman style with coffers and ornament, while the Randolph Street entrance is in the Grecian style with Doric columns and entablature. A stone balustrade surmounts the walls. An enormous Grand Army of the Republic Memorial Hall with a statue of a young Lincoln occupies the entire second floor north.

Not now housing books, the Cultural Center includes a broadcasting museum, an exhibition hall, a theater, a Fine Arts Division (music, dance, and art), and Preston Bradley Hall for concerts. After years of obscurity, the two Tiffany domes are again revealed in their full beauty by means of artificial lighting placed outside the stained glass. There is also an interior light court.

Open daily 10 A.M. to 7 P.M.; Friday 10 A.M. to 6 P.M.;
Saturday 10 A.M. to 5 P.M.; closed Sunday and holidays.

Across Randolph Street from the Cultural Center is a building best viewed from a distance in Grant Park.

ASSOCIATES CENTER
150 N. Michigan

ARCHITECTS: *A. Epstein and Sons (1983)*

Oriented to the southeast in a way that makes it prominent on Chicago's skyline, the Associates Center (now home of the Stone Container Corporation) has a curtainwall of alternating bands of glass and metal. The entrance is arranged on an angle, with a passage inviting the pedestrian to cut through the building, or into the shops of the arcade, while turning the corner. The design was conceived to have the base of the building follow the grid of the city (save for an entry niche), while the top is sliced off at an angle to face the park and lake. This device also makes the structure very noticeable along the skyline. A 3-story sculpture by Israeli artist Yaacov Agam, titled *Communication-X9* (1983), changes as you walk around it.

On the east side of Michigan Avenue is Doral Plaza.

DORAL PLAZA
151-155 N. Michigan

ARCHITECTS: *Martin Reinheimer and Architects (1981)*

This multiuse building has alternating Chicago bays with flat areas of metal and glass wall systems, sympathetic with the neighboring buildings to the north. The concrete structure is clearly expressed on the exterior in bands between the bays. The base of the building is a 2-floor enclosed arcade. There are offices above, and apartments on the upper levels.

Walk east on Randolph Street. This 40-story building occupies a square block of choice property facing Grant Park.

ONE PRUDENTIAL PLAZA
130 E. Randolph

ARCHITECTS: *Naess and Murphy (1955); for remodeling: Loebl, Schlossman and Hackl (1985–86)*

This was the first major office building built in Chicago in the twenty years since the Depression and World War II. Unlike buildings of the Chicago school of architecture, the 40 stories of gray Bedford limestone present the appearance of a huge monolith. The Prudential's trademark, the Rock of Gibraltar, is used as the theme for a sculptured west wall of the east wing by Alfanso Ianelli. The styling of the balconied lobby belongs to the jet age.

In 1985, in connection with the addition of Two Prudential Plaza, the building underwent renovations and cleaning and was linked with the

Underground Walkway system (see WALK 7). An annex to the north was torn down to make way for the new office tower.

TWO PRUDENTIAL PLAZA
180 N. Stetson

ARCHITECTS: *Loebl, Schlossman and Hackl (1990)*

This 59-story office building of polished granite is the fourth tallest building in Chicago (after the Sears Tower, the John Hancock Center, and the Amoco Building). The first 9 floors adjoin its parent building to the southwest. An indoor winter garden overlooks the rather windswept one-acre plaza on its west. Dramatically lit peaked setbacks make the building especially visible on the night skyline.

AMOCO BUILDING
200 E. Randolph

ARCHITECTS: *Edward D. Stone and the Perkins & Will Partnership (1974); for addition: Perkins & Will (1985)*

The Amoco Building, containing the corporate headquarters of the Amoco Oil Company of Indiana, is at 80 stories the third tallest in the city. With a strongly vertical facade composed of light-gray marble, and facing Grant Park on the south, the building can be seen for miles around.

The design of the slender steel tower is based on the tube principle. It incorporates an outside wall of 5-foot windows separated by 5-foot triangular sections that are part of the building frame. This permits window walls to be flush on the inside and the bulk of mechanical services, such as utilities and air conditioning, to be supplied through the triangular sections.

The tower, occupying only 25 percent of the site, is 194 by 194 feet and set back 140 feet from Randolph Street. It rises to a height of 1,136 feet, with a gross area of 2.7 million square feet.

In 1985 a formal entrance was added at the north end of the building, and Lake Street was closed. Ornamental pedestrian entrances were added along Stetson Avenue and Columbus Drive. In 1992–93 the building's marble exterior was entirely replaced and its front plaza refurbished, completing the effort to lend the entire site a more sculpted feeling.

Continue east on Randolph Street.

(The next four stops, all high-rise residences, are well to the east. You can skip to stop 16 instead by stepping north now on Stetson Avenue.)

BUCKINGHAM PLAZA
360 E. Randolph

ARCHITECTS: *Fujikawa Johnson and Associates (1982)*

This 44-story building has 375 apartments. It is a concrete structure with infilled glass panels. The pool at the top of the building is covered by a skylight with outdoor decks on both sides.

The next building to the east, still called Outer Drive East, is, of course, no longer east of the Outer Drive now that the highway has been rerouted to the east.

OUTER DRIVE EAST
400 E. Randolph

ARCHITECTS: *Martin Reinheimer and Architects (1962)*

This T-shaped building of condominiums has its major facade oriented south. It has infill panels of glass contrasting with white brick curtain-walls. Note the domed recreation area containing the swimming pool.

Continue east to Harbor Drive.

HARBOR POINT
155 N. Harbor

ARCHITECTS: *Solomon, Cordwell and Buenz (1978)*

The building is 50 stories tall. Its structure is evident at the first floor arcade. Because of the advantages of its site, the architects wanted to design a tower, instead of a slab building. Influenced by the design of their recently built Edgewater Plaza triangular building, and the success of the triangular slab to provide exceptional views in all directions, this building started with the same inner design. The freer form of the articulated multicurved bays of the exterior glass curtainwall (possibly influenced by Lake Point Tower in WALK 14, which can be seen to the north) provides both spectacular views in all directions and interesting reflections of light and the city to the observer on the ground.

175 N. HARBOR

ARCHITECTS: *Fujikawa Johnson and Associates (1988)*

This complex of 55 stories contains 600 apartments. A separate building of similar scale at 195 Harbor Drive shares its approach.

Walk west on Randolph, back to Columbus Drive. Turn north and walk under the archway behind the Amoco Building to Stetson Avenue.

ATHLETIC CLUB ILLINOIS CENTER
211 N. Stetson

ARCHITECTS: *Kisho Kurokawa; associate architects, Fujikawa Johnson (1990)*

The Japanese architect's first U.S. building, this is a fanciful gesture sited amid many stern skyscrapers. The nearly transparent structure, attached to its neighbor, allows the athletes inside to be seen from outside. The constructivist frame of 4 stories above grade and 2 below is painted white and carries to the roof in 4 objects that look like steel box kites, revolving almost free of attachment. This motion above mimics the motion within, where athletes run, jump, stretch, even rappel.

Walk west on Lake Street.

BOULEVARD TOWERS NORTH
225 N. Michigan

ARCHITECTS: *Fujikawa Johnson and Associates (1981)*

BOULEVARD TOWERS SOUTH
205 N. Michigan

ARCHITECTS: *Fujikawa Johnson and Associates (1985)*

Boulevard Towers function as an entranceway from Michigan Avenue to the Illinois Center complex. Both towers are of steel with glass curtainwalls, a continuation of the original Illinois Center buildings' design. The complex was built in stages. First came the 24-story north tower and the 19-story link between the towers. When the 44-story south tower was added, the complex was connected; the link gave it structural strength and provided various options in tenant space. Under the north tower is the Illinois Central South Water commuter station, serving about 15,000 riders each day. The south building is an entrance to the Underground Walkway system (see WALK 7).

CARBIDE AND CARBON BUILDING
230 N. Michigan

ARCHITECTS: *Burnham Brothers (1929)*

This Art Deco structure is 40 stories with two basements on rock caissons. It is distinguished for the gold and very dark green terra-cotta tower, dark green terra-cotta facade, and black granite and gold base. The gold, of course, is glazed on the terra-cotta and metal. The Burnham brothers were the sons of the noted architect and city planner Daniel H. Burnham.

Continue north.

OLD REPUBLIC BUILDING
307 N. Michigan

ARCHITECTS: *Vitzhum and Burns (1925)*

The original name of this structure was the Bell Building. It is 24 stories on hardpan caissons. The base is a beige-colored granite and a light gray, terra-cotta facade—typical of the commercial school of architecture of the 1920s—with much Greek-influenced decoration.

320 N. MICHIGAN

ARCHITECTS: *Booth/Hansen and Associates (1983)*

This very narrow building makes the best use of a small site. Note how all the windows face east and west, because of the close property lines on both sides. It is a highly articulated concrete structure with an arcade and entrance marked by two round columns and an interesting penthouse structure on top.

333 N. MICHIGAN AVENUE BUILDING

ARCHITECTS: *Holabird and Root (1928)*

This building is representative of the distinguished work of the equally distinguished firm of architects for the golden period of the late 1920s. The building can be seen from the full length of Michigan Avenue north of the Chicago River. The entrance was remodeled in 1969, but the balance of the building retains that fascinating design quality of the 1920s sometimes referred to as Art Moderne. The elevator doors carry

One Illinois Center and 333 North Michigan
(Architectural Camera)

Tower of the Carbide and Carbon building
(Allen Carr)

sculptured figures in relief by Edgar Miller. The building's base is a gray marble and the entire facade is a gray limestone.

Walk east on Wacker Drive.

ILLINOIS CENTER   Also known as the Illinois Central Air Rights Development, Illinois Center is constructed on air rights over the Illinois Central railroad yards. The Center's business and residential towers, hotels, and parks, with below-plaza shopping concourse and parking facilities, have been developed on 83 acres of land. The Center extends east of Michigan Avenue to the lake and south of the Chicago River to Randolph Street. In the early 1990s the traditional urban land development pattern was updated as an athletic center and a 9-hole golf course and a driving range—some of this winterized—were built. It was the nation's first downtown golfing facility.

ONE ILLINOIS CENTER
111 E. Wacker

ARCHITECT: *Ludwig Mies van der Rohe (1970)*

One Illinois Center is an office tower consisting of 29 office floors and a lobby floor on a landscaped plaza overlooking the Chicago River. Lobby escalators lead below plaza level to a concourse bordered by retail shops and restaurants. Below the concourse are 3 levels of parking for more than 300 cars. The building contains approximately 1 million square feet of office space and 35,000 square feet of retail shops. The structure is reinforced concrete. The curtainwall is dark bronze aluminum and bronze-tinted glass.

Walk through the plaza east of One Illinois Center to view Two Illinois Center.

TWO ILLINOIS CENTER
233 N. Michigan

ARCHITECT: *Ludwig Mies van der Rohe (1973)*

A twin of the One Illinois Center building, its concourse and parking areas are an extension of the levels provided under the other. The buildings function as a unified development. Two Illinois Center is built partially over the lower and intermediate levels of E. South Water Street.

The next building east on Wacker Drive is the Hyatt Regency Chicago.

HYATT REGENCY CHICAGO
151-201 E. Wacker

ARCHITECTS: *A. Epstein and Sons (1974, 1980)*

Directly east of One Illinois Center is the Hyatt Regency Chicago. This hotel of more than 2,000 rooms is built of brick and glass.

The addition, in the same style and materials as the original building, is joined by a glass-enclosed pedestrian bridge. The hub of the complex is a glass winter garden. Above the first floor is an angled, mirrored surface that creates an unusual reflection of the cars and pedestrians below. The brick of the complex stands in pleasant contrast to the glass and steel of the surrounding structures and bespeaks the privacy of a hotel.

Walk east on Wacker Drive.

COLUMBUS PLAZA
233 E. Wacker

ARCHITECTS: *Fujikawa Johnson and Associates (1980)*

This 47-story building has 552 apartments. It is of exposed reinforced concrete, with an infill of dark bronze aluminum, and tinted double-insulated glass. There are two parking levels below and a solarium and sundeck on the penthouse level. It is connected to the concourse system.

On the southeast corner of Wacker Drive and Columbus Drive is Three Illinois Center.

THREE ILLINOIS CENTER
303 E. Wacker

ARCHITECTS: *Fujikawa Johnson and Associates (1980)*

This 28-story building has a refined bronze-painted aluminum and tinted glass curtainwall in the Miesian tradition and a reinforced concrete frame. Note the restrained use of materials. There are 40,000 square feet of retail space as part of the concourse level.

Attached to the south is a fire station.

FIRE STATION CF-21
Columbus and S. Water

ARCHITECTS: *Fujikawa Johnson and Associates (1981)*

This fire station sits on a very tight site, tucked partially beneath Three Illinois Center. It is clad in dark aluminum and glass, harmonizing with the neighboring building. It is 14,000 square feet on 2 stories. There are an apparatus room for the fire engines and equipment, drying rooms, hose tower, exercise room, offices, kitchen, lounge, and dormitories for men and women. The station serves all levels of the Illinois Center complex and the adjoining Loop area.

Across Columbus Drive is our last stop.

FAIRMONT HOTEL
200 N. Columbus

ARCHITECTS: *Hulmuth, Obata and Kassabaum (1987)*

This hotel of warm gray granite has 692 rooms on 37 floors and is connected to the Amoco and Prudential buildings via the concourse. The main entry faces northeast, away from the city, to provide an access drive for cars and an overhanging lounge above for patrons. The lobby is unusually intimate for a hotel of this size.

Preston Bradley Hall, Chicago Public Library Cultural Center
(Kathy Richland, courtesy Marshall Holleb)

1. Harold Washington Library Center
   400 S. State St.

2. One Congress Center
   401 S. State St.

3. DePaul Center
   333 S. State St.

4. CNA Center
   55 E. Jackson Blvd.
   325 S. Wabash Ave.

5. 14 E. Jackson Boulevard

6. Home Federal Building
   201 S. State St.

7. 1 Quincy Court
   220 S. State St.

8. Singer Building
   120 S. State St.

9. Amalgamated Bank Building
   100 S. State St.

10. Palmer House
    17 E. Monroe St.

11. Carson Pirie Scott
    1 S. State St.

12. Chicago Building
    7 W. Madison St.

13. Wieboldt's Department Store
    1 N. State St.

14. Stevens Store Building
    17 N. State St.

15. 32 N. State St.

16. Marshall Field Store
    111 N. State St.

17. Chicago Theater
    175 N. State St.
    Page Brothers Building

18. ABC Building
    190 N. State St.

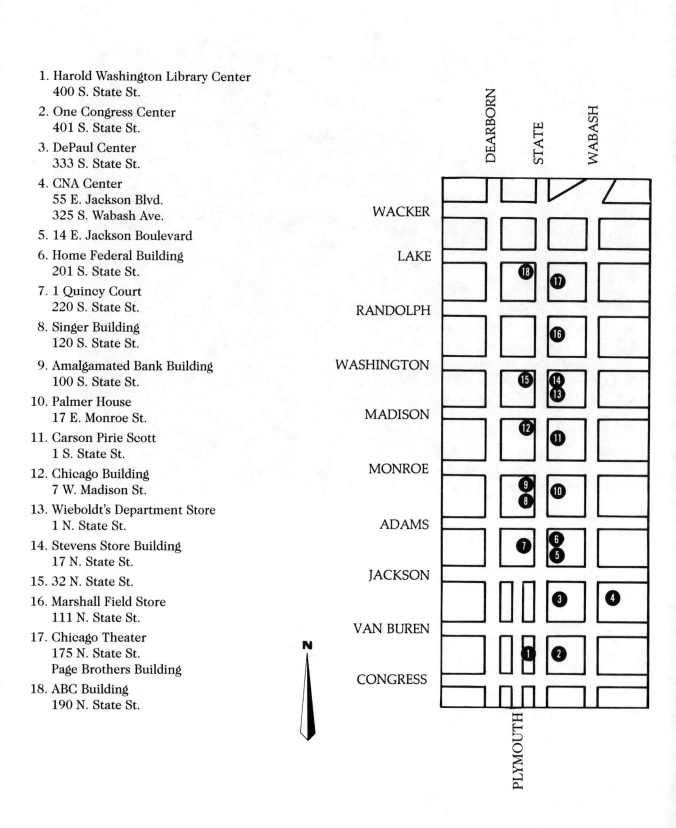

WALK 3 STATE STREET: IN THE LOOP

WALKING TIME: About 1½ hours.

HOW TO GET THERE: Walk to Congress Parkway, 5 blocks south of Madison Street; or take any southbound CTA bus on State Street south of Randolph Street, and get off at Congress (500 S). (Check with the driver to be sure the bus will not leave State Street before then.)

State Street—"That Great Street," as the song goes!—is a part of Chicago's central business district. State Street offers economic advantages provided nowhere else in the entire Midwest. It has long been a market for buyers and sellers from all over the nation and the world, and this fact alone gives it special distinction. In addition, State Street displays some architectural gems along the way as it stretches through the Loop from the Congress Parkway to the Chicago River—the extent of this WALK.

Since the 1970s there has been a repositioning of State Street. No longer a mile-long shopping district, it has escaped the fate of other major urban downtown areas plagued by disinvestment. With the establishment of the State Street Mall, there has been major reinvestment in older buildings, converting some from retail to office space. Once also a theater and entertainment strip, at night State Street was Chicago's Great White Way, as a result of its unusually large and brilliant lights. With the rehabilitation of the Chicago Theater in 1986, State Street again attracts people in the evening.

Its first role still dominates. Nowhere in the nation was there such a concentration of retail department stores. Starting at the south end with the former Sears store, there was one large building after another. The main entrances were on State Street, augmented by the former carriage entrances on the side streets as well as on Wabash Avenue. The linear relationship of the buildings made it convenient for the shopper to go on foot from store to store—or be driven to the nearest side street. Sears, Wieboldt's, and the Montgomery Ward stores have been lost (though the buildings remain), and there has been downsizing of some of those that remain, but much renovation has also been done.

Starting the WALK at the northwest corner of Congress Parkway, you see the new anchor of the street's ongoing vitality, the public library.

Harold Washington Library Center
(Leslie Schwartz)

HAROLD WASHINGTON LIBRARY CENTER
400 S. State

ARCHITECT: *Hammond Beeby and Babka (1991)*

Twenty years before Mayor Richard Daley dedicated this building on October 4, 1991, the city had outgrown its former central library at 78 E. Washington Street (see WALK 2). Getting it planned and built ignited prolonged civic debate, but the result has made Chicago proud.

Named for the city's first black mayor, a known book-lover, this 10-story structure is a palace for reading; filling its whole block, this is the largest municipal library building in the nation. The design picks up several themes in Chicago's architectural heritage, including a rusticated stone base and the vast arching entryway that pays homage to Louis Sullivan's Transportation Building at the 1893 Columbian Exposition. The door faces south, to the city's often neglected half. Polished red granite covers the facade, save for a pediment of steel and glass that acknowledges Chicago's reputation as a city of factories. Curvaceous iron ornaments enliven the street-level view.

Inside, the reading areas are well lighted and comfortable. Printed matter gives way to much space for audio-visual materials and public artwork, which found no home in the library's cramped temporary quarters in a former warehouse. Open space, in fact, is often the rule here, particularly in the elegant top-floor Winter Garden used for public and private events. For tours, ask at the information desk.

Cross to the east side of State Street.

* ONE CONGRESS CENTER
401 S. State

ARCHITECT: *William LeBaron Jenney (1891); for renovation: Louis Arthur Weiss (1985–86)*

The building extends a whole block—from Congress north to Van Buren Street. At the time it was built it was the tallest steel frame construction building. In its very early days this was known as the Leiter Building II. Levi Z. Leiter, once a partner of Marshall Field, had already done business on his own at another location. (The first Leiter Building, also designed by Jenney, stood at Wells and Monroe streets.) Although the present building was originally constructed as an investment property for still another company, Leiter took it over after a very short time. In later years, it was operated as a cooperative store as Leiter Shops. Just under the cornice of the State Street facade remains this inscription: L. Z. LEITER, MDCCCXCI.

This 8-story building, with three facades of white Maine granite, was designed by one of the pioneers in the Chicago school of architecture, William LeBaron Jenney. He had produced the first example of typical Chicago construction in his Home Insurance Building of 1885 (no longer standing), and here he continued the development of the Chicago school. Jenney allowed the steel skeleton, only recently introduced at that time, to determine the outward characteristics of the building—its division into enormous square sections, each filled with many large windows. During renovation, it was found that Jenney had intended two open light wells, which were never built. The fire escapes on the north and south sides have been removed to improve the building's appearance. The lower level, first floor, and mezzanine are retail space; floors 2–8 are offices. The building is now a national landmark.

Cross to the northeast corner of State and Van Buren streets.

* DePAUL CENTER
333 S. State

ARCHITECTS: *Holabird and Roche (1912); for adaptive reuse: Daniel P. Coffey and Associates (1992–93)*

In this building's long history it was first known as Rothschild's, later as the Goldblatt's Store; once meant to be the public library, it was renovated to be the downtown campus of DePaul University. The building is 10 stories, with three basements. The adaptation involved opening an atrium space through floors 1–3 in the center of the building, installing new elevators, and replacing all windows in a style in keeping with the original design. One key part of the interior work was to strip the column capitals to reveal their original egg and dart ornamentation.

Walk east on Jackson Boulevard to Wabash Avenue.

CONTINENTAL NATIONAL AMERICAN CENTER
55 E. Jackson

ARCHITECTS: *C. F. Murphy and Associates (1962)*

325 S. WABASH

ARCHITECTS: *Graham, Anderson, Probst and White (1972)*

Both buildings are painted a rich red, uniting them thematically and bringing color into the downtown area. The first building has very wide bays at 42 feet, extending this frequent component of Chicago design to a new width. The building on Wabash also embodies the strength of the sleek steel-and-glass structures. At 45 stories it stands high above its predecessor and is virtually the tallest building in the southeast portion of the Loop. The facade has a deep sculptured appearance. Here the ¼-inch-thick steel plates that sheath the building reflect the shape of the structural members. The windows, which are twice as wide as those in the first building, are set back and free from all metal surrounds. The window mullions are bold, and the structural columns exposed on the exterior clearly express the large uninterrupted interior spaces.

Return to the northeast corner of Jackson Boulevard and State Street.

14 E. JACKSON

ARCHITECTS: *Marshall and Fox (1913)*

This building formerly contained the Lytton Store and is now retail and office space. It is 19 stories with 3 basements on caissons—a graceful, well-designed structure for its time. Note the gilded window surrounds on the first 3 stories.

Continue north to the corner.

HOME FEDERAL BUILDING
201 S. State

ARCHITECTS: *Skidmore, Owings and Merrill (1966)*

At the southeast corner of Adams Street is the Home Federal Building. In this handsome structure of 16 stories the vertical lines are accented by the stainless steel mullions. The entire building is enveloped in dark glass panels. To make way for this building, an earlier one of considerable architectural merit—the Republic Building designed by Holabird and Roche (1905)—was demolished.

Cross State Street and backtrack south a bit.

ONE QUINCY COURT
220 S. State

ARCHITECT: *J. L. Kesner (1912–13)*

State Street has few skyscrapers. It was historically a street lined with multistory buildings of moderate height, occupied by stores of long-established companies. One exception is this 22-story steel-frame office tower, originally the Consumers Building. Its facade of terra-cotta was cleaned in 1992, revealing an attractive Gothic design newly back in fashion. Cream-colored marble adorns the lobby and stair. The building's unusual narrowness proves that "sliver" style construction did not begin with the boom of the 1980s.

* SINGER BUILDING
120 S. State

ARCHITECTS: *Mundie and Jensen (1926)*

This 10-story building was built for the Singer Sewing Machine Company. That it is even narrower—just 3 windows wide!—than One Quincy Court is testimony to land speculation fever in the late 1920s.

Continue north.

AMALGAMATED BANK BUILDING
100 S. State

ARCHITECTS: *A. Epstein and Sons, Inc. (1972)*

This steel cage, 5-story bank building is a remodeled former department store structure. The Amalgamated Bank itself, founded in 1922 by labor union locals, moved in shortly after construction. A tapestry by Picasso and an American folk-art quilt hang in the banking area.

Walk east on Monroe Street.

PALMER HOUSE
17 E. Monroe

ARCHITECTS: *J. M. Van Osdel, then C. M. Palmer (1874); Holabird and Roche (1925)*

On the east side of State Street just south of Monroe Street is the west entrance to the popular shopping arcade of the Palmer House. The arcade connects State Street with Wabash Avenue and with the Monroe Street entrance of one of the most distinguished hotels in Chicago. Through the Egyptian-revival lobby pass many important visitors to the city.

The Palmer House preceding this one was a real Chicago pioneer, for it was erected only a few years after the Great Fire of 1871—a still earlier Palmer House having been opened just two weeks before the fire and then completely destroyed. The 1875 building is said to have been the first fireproof hotel and the first to provide its residents with electric lights, telephones, and elevators. It was built at a time when the Chicago school of architecture was making great strides in improving the construction and facilities of hotels and apartment buildings.

State and Madison is the intersection famed as the "World's Busiest Corner." Here stands the architecturally most notable of Chicago's department stores, and the one always most noticed by the infrequent visitor to State Street—the Carson Pirie Scott Store.

* CARSON PIRIE SCOTT STORE
1 S. State

ARCHITECTS: *Louis Sullivan (1899, 1903);*
D. H. Burnham and Company (1905); Holabird and Root (1960);
for the restoration: John Vinci (1979)

Entrance to Carson Pirie Scott
(Allen Carr)

What you see today is the result of several stages of construction, so that the total building is probably less unified than it would otherwise have been. Fortunately, however, the architects of 1905 and 1960 had such deep respect for Sullivan's original design that they followed the pattern closely in their additions. Here you have one of the best illustrations of the effectiveness of the horizontally elongated Chicago window. The ornamentation decorating the windows of the first 2 stories is in pleasant contrast with the clean, unadorned precision of the window lines above them.

Originally occupied by the Schlesinger and Mayer Company, for whom it had been constructed in 1899 and enlarged in 1903, it was purchased later in 1903 by Carson Pirie Scott. The first and easternmost section, of only 3 bays and 9 stories, faced only Madison Street. The 1903 enlargement was made possible by the demolition of two older adjacent buildings. The addition, which rose 12 stories, included 3 more bays on Madison Street and extended around the corner, with 7 bays on State Street. Sullivan was the architect for both the original building and the extension. His love of incorporating ornamentation even in commercial buildings is expressed here in the intricate intermingling of leaf and flower designs that decorate the main entrance at the corner, as well as the windows of the lower stories. This rich but delicate pattern gives an unusually luxurious effect to an entrance already distinguished by its semicircular shape and its location at the corner of the building.

The third unit, extending the building still farther south on State Street, was designed by Burnham in 1905; and the extension of that long facade, by Holabird and Root in 1960, still follows Sullivan's original plan. The result is therefore a true Sullivan masterpiece, no matter what other architects were involved.

Sigfried Giedion, who did much to call attention to the Chicago school, wrote of this building (*Space, Time and Architecture*, Sixth Edition. Cambridge: Harvard University Press, 1946, p. 311):

The front is designed to fulfill its indispensable function, the admission of light. Its basic elements are the horizontally elongated "Chicago windows," admirably homogeneous and treated to coincide with the framework of the skeleton. The whole front is executed with a strength and precision that is matched by no other building of the period.

And Frederick Koeper remarks, (*Illinois Architecture*. Chicago: The University of Chicago Press, 1968, p. 64):

> In this design Sullivan has afforded us those dual pleasures of architecture: an involvement with decoration as well as the satisfaction of discipline and order.

The 1979 restoration work included the stripping of layers of paint from the ornamental iron on the base of the building to reveal the original red and green finish, which simulated patinated bronze. The terra-cotta on the upper stories was cleaned and repaired. The corner entrance vestibule was stripped and later alterations (the dropped ceiling and the formica paneling) were removed, and all was restored to the original mahogany finish.

On the southwest corner of State and Madison streets is the Chicago Building.

* CHICAGO BUILDING
7 W. Madison

ARCHITECTS: *Holabird and Roche (1905)*

This building is 15 stories with 2 basements on rock caissons. It is an excellent example of Chicago school commercial architecture, with large windows dominating the storefronts. The projecting bays give it a prismatic look.

Cross diagonally to the former Wieboldt's Store.

WIEBOLDT'S DEPARTMENT STORE
1 N. State

ARCHITECTS: *Holabird and Roche (1900, 1905, 1912); for the remodeling: Barancik and Conte (1978)*

A colorful character of the 1920s was Colonel Leon Mandel, the titular head of an old Chicago merchant family. This building, formerly Mandel Brothers Store Building and still best known as Wieboldt's, was built in three main sections and today is divided into two main sections. The Wabash Avenue building is 12 stories and the State Street building 15 stories. They cleverly span the loading docks in between.

STEVENS STORE BUILDING
17 N. State

ARCHITECTS: *D. H. Burnham and Company (1912)*

This building is 19 stories over 2 basements on hardpan caissons. Lerner of New York, a women's specialty store, now occupies the lower floors and basements. Small shops and offices occupy the balance of the building.

Cross back to the west side of State Street. On the southwest corner of State and Washington streets is 32 N. State Street.

* 32 N. STATE

ARCHITECTS: *for ground floor: Burnham and Root (1890); for the rest of the building: D. H. Burnham and Company, Charles Atwood, designer (1894–95)*

This Architectural Landmark was once known as the Reliance Building. The original granite base was replaced by the terra-cotta and limestone base, which contrasts markedly with the glass and white terra-cotta of the towering 15-story structure above. Speaking of the Reliance Building, Sigfried Giedion comments that "... although its glazed white tiles have become encrusted with dirt, its airiness and pure proportions make it a symbol of the Chicago school." He continues, pointing out that the Reliance was built nearly 3 decades before Mies van der Rohe envisioned his glass-and-iron skyscraper as a kind of fantasy in 1921, "but it may be that this Chicago building is something more than an incentive for fantasy: an architectonic anticipation of the future." (*Space, Time and Architecture*, Sixth Edition. Cambridge: Harvard University Press, 1946, p. 310.)

The citation by the Architectural Landmarks Commission reads:

> In recognition of the early and complete expression, through slender piers, small spandrels, and the skillfully restrained use of terra-cotta with large areas of glass, of the structural cage, of steel that alone supports such buildings.

The North Loop Development Program will soon rebuild the block on the west side of State Street between Washington and Randolph streets. The plans are to include a huge atrium running east and west to bring people from the west into State Street.

Cross the street diagonally. The WALK up State Street should include the interior of Marshall Field's. You can walk through from State Street to Wabash Avenue or from Washington Street to Randolph Street, for the building occupies the entire block.

* MARSHALL FIELD STORE
III N. State

ARCHITECTS: *D. H. Burnham and Company (1892, 1902, 1904, 1906–1907, 1914)*

The original Marshall Field Store was built at the corner of State and Washington streets. This was the site of three previous buildings that had been used by the Field and Leiter partnership—the first building had been destroyed by the Chicago Fire a few years after it was erected. The rest of this famous store was constructed in sections between 1892 and 1907 and the former Marshall Field men's store, at the southwest corner of Wabash Avenue and Washington Street, was added in 1914.

At the Washington and Randolph street ends of the store are open courts, surrounded by grilled railings at each floor and covered by

Marshall Field
(Olga Stefanos)

skylights. The one at the south end of the store (Washington Street) is a slightly arched dome of colored mosaic at the level of the fifth floor ceiling. The other is a plain glass skylight at the top of the building. The Randolph Street court is a perfect setting for the enormous Christmas tree that has delighted Marshall Field's customers for years.

Walk north past the alley. You are now standing in front of the Chicago Theater.

* CHICAGO THEATER
175 N. State

ARCHITECTS: *Rapp and Rapp (1921); for the restoration: Daniel P. Coffey and Associates, Ltd. (1986)*

* PAGE BROTHERS BUILDING

ARCHITECTS: *J. M. Van Osdel (1872); for remodeling and addition: Hill and Woltersdorf (1902); for adaptive reuse: Daniel P. Coffey and Associates, Ltd. (1986)*

The landmark Chicago Theater and the Page Brothers Building were restored by an ad hoc group committed to protecting them. The theater reopened on September 10, 1986, with a gala performance by Frank Sinatra, who opened his show singing *My Kind of Town.* Take a look in the theater's Grand Lobby. Also restored was the Grand Staircase and the Grand Promenade, which leads to the Lake Street exit.

The Beaux-Arts facade of the Chicago Theater is ornamental terracotta; the Grand Arch exhibits a Tiffany stained-glass window with the Balaban and Katz crest. B & K built it as a movie house, and this was their national headquarters. The Marquee (the symbol of the theater, and in many eyes the symbol of the City) has been restored with slightly lowered side panels so as not to obscure the view of the arch.

The Page Brothers Building is on the National Register of Historic Places because the cast-iron facade on its Lake Street side is reputedly the last surviving example in the Loop. Through an innovative structural system, the entire interior was replaced with new fireproof concrete construction. Interestingly, this is in keeping with the history of the building, because a sixth story was added and the State Street facade was replaced in 1902 when Potter Palmer redirected Chicago's major commercial street from Lake Street to State Street.

Across State Street is the ABC Building.

ABC BUILDING
190 N. State

ARCHITECTS: *Rapp and Rapp with G. Albert Lansburgh (1917); for the remodeling: Skidmore, Owings and Merrill (1982–87)*

This was formerly the State-Lake Building. Starting in 1982, the 13-story building underwent major upgrading. The entry was relocated one bay to the south; the terra-cotta facade was refurbished and cleaned; all windows were replaced; and a new storefront was installed. An interior atrium and penthouse were added, and the interior office space was reorganized.

The El tracks bring this WALK to a close. Or, one block north of you is Wacker Drive, the topic of WALK 8.

Chicago Theater
(Olga Stefanos)

1. Manhattan Building
   431 S. Dearborn St.

2. Old Colony Building
   407 S. Dearborn St.

3. Fisher Building
   343 S. Dearborn St.

4. Chicago Bar Association
   321 S. Plymouth Ct.

5. Standard Club
   320 S. Plymouth Ct.

6. Monadnock Building
   53 W. Jackson Blvd.

7. Union League Club
   65 W. Jackson Blvd.

8. John C. Kluczynski Federal Building
   230 S. Dearborn St.

9. Everett McKinley Dirksen Federal Building
   219 S. Dearborn St.

10. Marquette Building
    140 S. Dearborn St.

11. Xerox Centre
    55 W. Monroe St.

12. Inland Steel Building
    30 W. Monroe St.

13. First National Bank Building and Plaza
    One First National Plaza

14. Three First National Plaza
    70 W. Madison St.

15. Citibank Building
    7 S. Dearborn St.

16. 33 N. Dearborn Street Building

17. 69 W. Washington St.

18. Richard J. Daley Center and Plaza
    55 W. Washington St.

19. Delaware Building
    36 W. Randolph St.

20. Oliver Typewriter Co.
    159 N. Dearborn St.

21. Dearborn Cinemas
    170 and 186 N. Dearborn St.

22. Marina City
    300 N. State St.

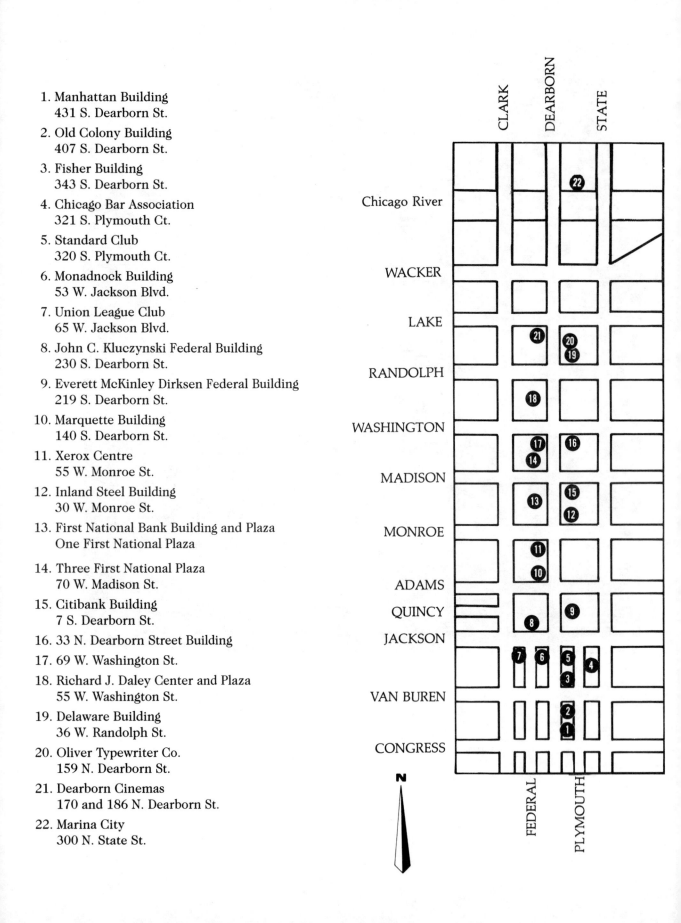

WALK 4 **DEARBORN STREET**

WALKING TIME: About 1½ to 2 hours.
HOW TO GET THERE: Take a southbound CTA bus No. 29 on State Street and get off at Congress Parkway (500 S). Walk west across Plymouth Court to Dearborn Street (36 W), which runs parallel to State Street.

This WALK offers a virtual history of the modern skyscraper, which had its beginnings here in Chicago—one of the results of the tremendous architectural development that rebuilt the city after its almost total destruction by fire in 1871.

* MANHATTAN BUILDING
431 S. Dearborn

ARCHITECTS: *Jenney and Mundie (1889–91); for the rehabilitation: Wilbert R. Hasbrouck (1981)*

Designed by the man who has often been called the father of the steel skyscraper, William LeBaron Jenney, the Manhattan is now the oldest tall office building to have used skeleton construction throughout. At the time it was built, it was also the tallest building in the world. The second Rand McNally building, designed by Burnham and Root in the same year, also used skeleton construction throughout but was demolished in 1911.

The building has been restored to its original condition. The ground floor is now retail space. The interior had been adapted into 105 apartments. At the time of the conversion, it was the largest commercial building in Chicago converted to residential use.

Walk north to the southeast corner of Dearborn and Van Buren streets.

* OLD COLONY BUILDING
407 S. Dearborn

ARCHITECTS: *Holabird and Roche (1894)*

This building, named for Plymouth Colony, is 210 feet high, with 17 stories and a basement. It fronts on three streets—Plymouth Court and Dearborn and Van Buren streets. It is built with tower bays at the corners and presents a well-designed appearance. The first 4 stories are of light-blue Bedford stone and the upper part pressed brick and white terra-cotta. This was the first building to employ portal arches against the wind, a technique borrowed from bridge construction.

Cross Van Buren Street. On the northeast corner stands the Fisher Building, an Architectural Landmark.

Manhattan Building
(Tom Yanul courtesy
Hasbrouk/Hunderman)

Fisher Building
(Allen Carr)

Monadnock Building
(Richard Nickel)

* FISHER BUILDING
343 S. Dearborn

ARCHITECTS: *D. H. Burnham and Company (1896); for addition: Peter J. Weber (1907)*

The steel frame skeleton, which was also used here, is by no means disguised by the rather elaborate, even fanciful, Gothic ornamentation. The architect for this building was the same Daniel Burnham who is world famous for his Chicago city plan. His frequently quoted admonition, "Make no little plans; they have no magic to stir men's minds," seems to have been heeded by Chicago architects, and Dearborn Street is one of the results. The 1907 north addition is taller than the original part of the building but follows the style of the older building.

Walk east on Van Buren Street a short block to Plymouth Court and proceed north on it.

CHICAGO BAR ASSOCIATION
321 S. Plymouth

ARCHITECT: *Tigerman McCurry (1990)*

A cast-aluminum statue of Justice surmounts the doorway of this 16-story building. The rusticated base pays homage to century-old neighbors around the corner. Matching gray speckled granite rises from this base, and many spires ornament the setbacks and top. Inside, the steel elevator doors are elaborately etched.

STANDARD CLUB
320 S. Plymouth

ARCHITECT: *Albert Kahn of Detroit, Michigan (1926)*

This elegant 10-story private club building follows a general design pattern of the Italian Renaissance. Bedford limestone and pressed brick are the materials used on both the Plymouth Court and the unassuming Dearborn Street facade.

Walk north to Jackson Boulevard and turn west.

* MONADNOCK BUILDING
53 W. Jackson

ARCHITECTS: *north half: Burnham and Root (1891); south half: Holabird and Roche (1893)*

The Monadnock Building was internationally famous as the world's largest office building at the time of construction and is still known as the highest commercial building (16 stories rising 197 feet high) with outside walls of wall-bearing construction. Some of the walls at the base are 6 feet thick to support the tremendous weight. The north half of the building, however—the part that has outside walls of masonry only—does use steel for the interior columns and floor supports; the south half, built two years later, used a full steel frame.

Originally this building had 4 separate entrances to 4 separate sections, each named after a New England mountain, according to the fancy of the four branches of the New England family that owned it. Jackson Street was the original entrance. When the south half of the building was added, a more impressive entrance was put on Van Buren Street. From the time of its opening, the building was popularly known as the Monadnock (although each section had a name) and over the years the separation of the entrances and the other names were forgotten.

The Monadnock's files tell of an early test of the building's ability to withstand Chicago's winds despite its unusual height and lack of wind braces. When a near hurricane, with winds reaching the velocity of 88 miles per hour, struck Chicago, experts in engineering rushed to the building with some trepidation and conducted a pendulum experiment from the top floor. A plumb bob that was swung down through the stairwell to the lobby floor, to measure the structure's vibrations at the height of the storm, marked a small pattern not more than $5/8$ inches by $3/8$ inches. The experiment reassured everyone who had feared what high winds might do to this building!

The citation of the Monadnock Building as an Architectural Landmark reads:

> In recognition of its original design and its historical interest as the highest wall-bearing structure in Chicago. Restrained use of brick, soaring massive walls, omission of ornamental forms, unite in a building simple yet majestic.

Continue west on Jackson Boulevard.

UNION LEAGUE CLUB
65 W. Jackson

ARCHITECTS: *Mundie and Jensen (1926)*

Just to the west of the Monadnock Building is this 22-story club building with a granite base and pressed-brick facade in the style of the late Italian Renaissance. The club maintained a separate entrance and elevator "for the ladies" until the board of directors voted a rules change on February 15, 1972, and marked the end of an era. This private club was once famous as the citadel of the Republican Party of Chicago.

Crossing Jackson Boulevard on Dearborn Street, going north, means jumping from the late 19th to the middle 20th century at two buildings of the Chicago Federal Center.

JOHN C. KLUCZYNSKI FEDERAL BUILDING
230 S. Dearborn

EVERETT McKINLEY DIRKSEN FEDERAL BUILDING
219 S. Dearborn

ARCHITECTS: *Ludwig Mies van der Rohe; Schmidt, Garden, and Erikson; C. F. Murphy and Associates; A. Epstein and Sons (1964; 1975)*

On the east side of Dearborn Street stands a spectacularly modern 27-story structure of steel and glass, the Everett McKinley Dirksen Building, part of a complex of buildings in Chicago's Federal Center. The Center extends from Jackson Boulevard north to Adams Street, occupying both sides of Dearborn Street and extending west to Clark Street. The equally striking John C. Kluczynski Building of more than 40 stories is at the south end of the complex, and adjacent is a post office in a low-rise building. These two structures, completed in 1975, are actually one building—they share the same basements. All three structures face a large open plaza, the entire design being a strong statement of the genius and influence of the great architect Mies van der Rohe.

A stabile by Alexander Calder, 53 feet in height, made of carbon steel and painted a special shade of red, presides at the center of the Plaza, making Dearborn Street a great area of plazas, architecture, and sculpture. Calder's bright red steel *Flamingo* is a worthy addition to the Picasso, in the Richard J. Daley Plaza, and the Chagall, in the First National Bank Building Plaza. Later in this WALK you will see these two other great plazas surrounded by first-rate buildings.

The style of those decades, toward more open space around skyscrapers, sits in marked contrast with the canyon effect so often developed in the past, and revived in the 1980s for reasons of economy and design. Dearborn Street is indeed a street of overwhelming architecture, in space as well as in time.

Just to the east on Adams Street is the Berghoff restaurant—an eating and meeting institution throughout the 20th century.

At the northwest corner of Dearborn and Adams streets is the Marquette Building.

* MARQUETTE BUILDING
140 S. Dearborn

ARCHITECTS: *Holabird and Roche (1894); for restoration: Holabird and Root (1980)*

In this National Historic Landmark, the influence of Louis Sullivan can be seen in the ornamental design, which marks off the bottom two stories and the top three, distinguishing these clearly from the rest. The wide windows and the obvious response of the pattern to the skeleton structure are characteristic of the Chicago school.

In 1980 major restoration work was done. The exterior terra-cotta was restored and cast-aluminum storefronts, replicating the original work, were made. A new corridor, connecting the interior storefronts between the Marquette lobby and the Commonwealth Edison Building to the west, was created with the same cast aluminum. The bronze friezes over the entrance doors and inside (designed by well-known sculptor J. A.

Xerox Centre
(Keith Palmer and James Steinkamp
courtesy Murphy/Jahn)

Inland Steel Building
(Allen Carr)

MacNeil) were restored; they commemorate Marquette's journey in the
Mississippi River Valley and the people he met. The Tiffany mosaics
that decorate the mezzanine balcony, unquestionably the best in the city,
were restored and properly lighted for the public's enjoyment. They were
designed by J. A. Holzer, who was Tiffany's chief mosaicist; he came to
Chicago to execute the Tiffany Chapel at the World's Columbian
Exposition of 1893. They depict scenes from Chicago history. You will
want to go inside this building to see them.

Continue north.

XEROX CENTRE
55 W. Monroe

ARCHITECTS: *Murphy/Jahn (1980)*

This most elegant, straightforward design is a 40-floor office building with 900,000 square feet of rental space and commercial space on the ground floor and mezzanine level. It was originally designed for a bank.

Emphasis was put on optimum relationship to the First National Bank and Plaza, the historic Marquette Building, and the remaining structures along Monroe Street. The building is set back on Dearborn, curved at the corner, and slightly slanted toward the existing structures. It touches at the lower level to the fit in the existing urban fabric and continues the plantings of the trees from the First National Plaza. The curved front facade of the building turns the two planes into a single front on the building. On the west facade the building is set back from the property line, anticipating the future development of the adjacent site.

Xerox Centre has concrete construction with columns based on 20-foot by 20-foot bays. The exterior wall is enameled aluminum painted white. The varying amounts of double-glazed clear glass, responding to the views and orientation, are floor-to-ceiling on the north facade and cover 50 percent of the surface on the rest of the building. The glass at street level is in scale with the pedestrian, and the rounded corner invites pedestrians to hug the site as they pass.

Diagonally across the corner is the Inland Steel Building.

INLAND STEEL BUILDING
30 W. Monroe

ARCHITECTS: *Skidmore, Owings and Merrill (1957)*

The Inland Steel Building is appropriately constructed of stainless steel and glass. In the lobby is a stunning piece of wire sculpture by Richard Lippold, executed for the site.

This 19-story building was one of the first to use only external steel columns for support, also one of the first to build a separate structure (to the east) for elevators and stairs, and to use steel and glass as the chief building materials. The result is a striking, first-rate design.

Across Dearborn Street is a multibuilding complex.

FIRST NATIONAL BANK BUILDING and PLAZA
One First National Plaza (between Monroe and Madison, Dearborn and Clark)

ARCHITECTS: *C. F. Murphy Associates and Perkins & Will Partnership (Building 1969, Plaza 1973)*

This is one of the great plazas in the Loop. The first object to capture the eye is the building itself. The sweeping lines of this A-shaped, 60-story structure creates an exhilarating sight. The steel frame has a skin of light-gray granite. The granite is carried out not only on the sidewalks and plaza, but in the 2-story banking room and mezzanine as well.

The architects have stated that the form of the bank building evolved quite naturally from the space-need program. From a broad banking base, where the lower floors accommodate all the bank's equipment and staff, the tower tapers upward in a sweeping curve to narrower floors for tenants. Thus, form follows function.

The bank's upper-floor offices contain distinguished works of art from all over the world. This excellent collection was made under the direction of Katherine Kuh, former Curator of Modern Art at the Art Institute of Chicago.

The exciting 2-level plaza covering a half a city block has restaurants, landscaping, and a major work of Marc Chagall called *The Four Seasons.* The massive architectural mosaic, measuring 70 feet long, 14 feet high, and 10 feet wide, has more than 3,000 square feet of bright glass murals, specially designed as a gift to the people of Chicago by the world-renowned artist, who personally supervised each step of its realization. The donors for the cost of construction were Mr. and Mrs. William Wood Prince of Chicago. The Chicago Chagall occupies an open terrace at the east end of the plaza and overlooks an illuminated fountain of changing water columns in a park-like setting of trees, plants, and flowers.

Walk through or around the bank, heading north, and cross to the north side of Madison Street.

THREE FIRST NATIONAL PLAZA
70 W. Madison

ARCHITECTS: *Skidmore, Owings and Merrill (1982)*

This 75-story office tower has commercial space on the first two levels. There is a 9-story glass-enclosed lobby, designed to respond to the heavy pedestrian traffic of the area. The bay windows were chosen to relate to Chicago's architectural heritage, such as in the Monadnock Building. In the lobby here is a Henry Moore sculpture, *Large Upright Internal/External Form* (1983), in the lobby. There is a sky bridge to the First National Bank Building, and both also connect to the underground walkway system. (The bank's second building is described in WALK 5.)

Before continuing north, look back across Dearborn Street to the former Tribune Building, now used by Citibank.

CITIBANK BUILDING
7 S. Dearborn

ARCHITECTS: *Holabird and Roche (1902); for south wing: Holabird and Root (1958)*

This structure housed The Chicago Tribune before the move to its present location on North Michigan Avenue. The building is 18 stories high and reputed to be the first in Chicago with 2 basements (another first for the city). Granite facing was added to the lower four stories.

Walk north 1 block to the southeast corner of Dearborn and Washington streets.

33 N. DEARBORN STREET BUILDING

ARCHITECTS: *Skidmore, Owings and Merrill (1966)*

This glass structure stands light and lean on its steel frame. Though it was designed by the same firm of architects as the next building, the two are in striking contrast with each other. They are a tribute to the versatility of the architects' inventiveness and illustrate the wide variety of modern building materials and forms.

Walk west on Washington Street.

69 W. WASHINGTON

ARCHITECTS: *Skidmore, Owings and Merrill, partner in charge: Myron Goldsmith (1964)*

Though more recently constructed, the heavy concrete wall surfaces here are reminiscent of the Monadnock Building. Both are massive, though in this case marble-clad piers support the upper stories of poured concrete. From the lower concourse of this building you can reach other downtown buildings by an underground walkway.

On the north side of Washington Street is the great plaza of the Richard J. Daley Center, a focal point of city and county government activity. This immense open space offers the visitor an exciting visual treat and a chance to sit and rest in the midst of otherwise crowded city streets.

RICHARD J. DALEY CENTER and PLAZA
Between Washington and Randolph, Dearborn and Clark

ARCHITECTS: *C. F. Murphy and Associates; Loebl, Schlossman and Bennett; Skidmore, Owings and Merrill (1964)*

The Daley Center, 31 stories of offices and courtrooms, covers the north half of the plaza. This building was highly controversial at first, especially before the steel of its walls had oxidized to its present russet brown. Cor-Ten steel was chosen as the material for the building because it requires no upkeep and becomes more attractive as it ages. (A special virtue of Cor-Ten steel is its resistance to atmospheric corrosion, so that it is not worn away by weathering, even though its color is changed.) The horizontal bays are 89 feet wide, which makes this distinguished building one of great strength and vigor.

The power and the scale of this contemporary structure are overwhelming; the older, shorter buildings around the plaza come into focus only later, though many were most impressive when erected. They are a phenomenon of contrasts, one with another.

With fountain, flags, and trees, the plaza is dominated by the huge Picasso sculpture, also in Cor-Ten steel. The design of Chicago's Picasso was a gift to the city from the sculptor himself, and the original model is in the Art Institute. Like many of Picasso's creations, this was the subject of much controversy. People disagreed about whether it represents the great head of a woman, the soaring wings of an enormous bird, a strange

Picasso sculpture in Daley Plaza
(Ira J. Bach)

composite animal, or—as one facetious newspaper columnist would have it—the head of Picasso's pet basset hound! Controversy aside, this is a powerful work of art. It has been erected in an especially appropriate setting, which allows viewers to walk around it freely and consider it from all angles and various distances—from each of which it presents a different effect.

Cross to the northeast corner of Randolph and Dearborn streets.

* DELAWARE BUILDING
36 W. Randolph

ARCHITECTS: *Wheelock and Thomas (1871); for the addition: Holabird and Roche (1889, 1894, 1904); for the restoration: Wilbert R. Hasbrouck; base building architects: Bernheim, Kahn and Lozano (1982)*

This is the oldest building in the Loop, and the first built after the Chicago Fire that still survives. Built as the Bryant Building (it was later known as the Real Estate Board Building), the structure was 6 stories tall. Two stories were added before 1890, and later changes by Holabird and Roche gave it the appearance it has today. The facade of the first 2 stories is glass and cast iron; the next four stories are precast concrete; and the top 2 floors are of pressed metal.

In the rehabilitation, the exterior was restored exactly to its appearance in 1900. The interior public and office spaces, including the interior atrium, were also restored.

Delaware Building
(Ron Gordon courtesy
Hasbrouck Hunderman)

*** OLIVER
TYPEWRITER CO.**
159 N. Dearborn

ARCHITECTS: *Holabird and Roche (1907)*

After a much-needed facelift, the cast-iron facade is gorgeous again, announcing on the spandrels the original occupant. The decoration on the ground floor is among the Loop's finest. Note that the 6th and 7th stories are an addition, in 1920 by the same architects. The brick piers are continued from below, but keystones adorn the windows here.

Cross to the west side of the street.

*** DEARBORN
CINEMAS**
170 and 186
N. Dearborn

ARCHITECTS: *Crane and Franzheim (1923); for the renovation: Bertrand Goldberg and Associates (1956)*

Originally the Harris and the Selwyn, these twin theaters represent the best of their time. The exterior design is English Renaissance of the Edwardian period, when many similar small theaters were built in London. The exterior skin is a white terra-cotta. The wood paneling and spacious proscenium arches of both auditoriums created just the right climate for good, live performances and appreciative audiences.

Continue north to the river.

MARINA CITY
300 N. State

ARCHITECTS: *Bertrand Goldberg and Associates (1964)*

Although the official address of Marina City is State Street, you have an excellent view of these twin towers from Dearborn Street and Wacker Drive. This exciting, world-famous complex has its many functions in a highly concentrated space—apartments, garages, restaurants, offices, bank, bowling alley, marina (and at one time a television studio and an ice rink). The parking space is a continuously rising circular slab throughout the first 18 stories of each tower. Pie-shaped residences (condominiums since 1977) take up the rest of the 62 stories. The cantilevered balconies of the residences give these cylindrical towers their scalloped forms.

Marina City marked a departure from the glass-and-steel skeletons that had been so popular at the time. Once the tallest concrete building in Chicago, 62 stories rising more than 580 feet in the air, they use virtually no structural steel. These are towers of slab construction, circular disks resting on columns. Marina City also demonstrates excellent application of core-and-cantilever construction, which was first used by Frank Lloyd Wright.

As you cross the Dearborn Street drawbridge, read the plaques. They summarize the history of the bridge and quote the citation presented to it as the "Most beautiful steel bridge—movable span," by the American Institute of Steel Construction in 1963–64. (Also see information on the Ira J. Bach Walkway at the beginning of WALK 8—Ed.)

First National Bank Building
(Philip A. Turner)

1. Chicago Title Tower
   161–171 N. Clark St.

2. County Building
   118 N. Clark St.
   City Hall
   121 N. LaSalle St.

3. Chicago Temple Building
   77 W. Washington St.

4. Chicago Title and Trust Building
   111 W. Washington St.

5. Avondale Centre
   20 N. Clark St.

6. St. Peter's Church and Friary
   110 W. Madison St.

7. Chicago Loop Synagogue
   16 S. Clark St.

8. Two First National Plaza
   20 S. Clark St.

9. Bell Federal Savings Building
   79 W. Monroe St.

10. Commonwealth Edison Building
    72 W. Adams St.

11. Bankers Building
    105 W. Adams St.

12. Continental Illinois Bank Building
    231 S. LaSalle St.

13. Ralph H. Metcalfe Federal Building
    77 W. Jackson Blvd.

14. William J. Campbell
    United States Courthouse Annex
    Van Buren and Clark St.

LASALLE CLARK FEDERAL DEARBORN

WACKER

LAKE

RANDOLPH

WASHINGTON

MADISON

MONROE

ADAMS

QUINCY

JACKSON

VAN BUREN

CONGRESS

N

WALK 5 **CLARK STREET**

WALKING TIME: 1 to 1½ hours.
HOW TO GET THERE: Walk west on Washington Street to Clark Street (77 W), 2 blocks west of State Street.

This WALK starts on the east side of Clark Street, opposite the State of Illinois Center.

CHICAGO TITLE TOWER
161-171 N. Clark

ARCHITECTS: *Kohn, Pedersen and Fox (1992)*

This large insurance company, formerly headquartered in another building on this WALK, adds to the North Loop Redevelopment Program with a bold, even futuristic, design. The structure is slender at 50 stories but humanized by the addition of a 13-story annex on the north. The exterior is aluminum painted white, its noticeability enhanced by a metal awning above the door; the awning for the annex is wave-shaped. Near the roof a projecting grille pierces the sky but does not blend well with the rest of the tower.

The State of Illinois Center across Clark Street is featured in WALK 6. Now, cross diagonally to a landmark dual building.

* COUNTY BUILDING
118 N. Clark

ARCHITECTS: *Holabird and Roche (1907)*

* CITY HALL
121 N. LaSalle

ARCHITECTS: *Holabird and Roche (1911)*

These twin buildings are the City Hall–County Building, dating to the days when machine politics neared its zenith. The two cover an entire city block; the lobbies and their terrazzo floor are connected and appear as one. Both buildings are designed on sturdy classic revivalist lines with heavy Corinthian columns across the facade. In the county building lobby is an entrance to the Underground Walkway system.

Free tours are available through the Mayor's Office of Inquiry and Information, Room 100, or phone 744-5000. Reservations are required. Tours include the City Hall, City Council, Mayor's office, Daley Center courts, and the State of Illinois Center. Tours take 1½ hours.

On the southeast corner of Clark and Washington streets is the Chicago Temple Building.

County Building and City Hall
(Philip A. Turner)

CHICAGO TEMPLE BUILDING
77 W. Washington

ARCHITECTS: *Holabird and Roche (1923)*

This 21-story church stands 550 feet high, including an elaborate 8-story spire and a basement on rock caissons. This provides space for offices and a downtown Methodist church. Except for a short time after the Great Fire of 1871, this site has been occupied continuously by a downtown church. (Ten stained-glass windows set in the wall behind the Miro sculpture tell the story.) The gray Indiana limestone in French Gothic style offers an interesting pattern of intricate design as opposed to the bold, plain design of the modern office building to the east.

We will soon visit two additional religious structures—a Roman Catholic Church and an Orthodox Jewish Synagogue. These three major churches representing the Protestant, Catholic, and Jewish faiths are located within a 1-block radius, making it convenient for Loop workers to worship during daytime hours.

Now cross to the west side of Clark Street to a building that long housed nearly all of abstract and real estate property insurance for metropolitan Chicago and many other regions of the United States.

* CHICAGO TITLE AND TRUST COMPANY BUILDING
111 W. Washington

ARCHITECTS: *D. H. Burnham and Company (1913);*
for the remodeling: Holabird and Root (1947); for the renovations:
Jack Train and Associates (1984)

Known as the Conway Building when it was built as an investment by Marshall Field, the structure was purchased in 1947 and remodeled. At that time the interior court was filled to a height of 6 stories. An indoor pedestrian walkway system connects with the adjacent American National Bank Building and One North LaSalle Street Building.

This white terra-cotta building, 21 stories and completely modernized, commands a strategic location near City Hall–County Building and the Daley Center. At one time probably more business deals were made in its lobby than in the offices above.

The 1984 work included updating the building without destroying the original design. The effect of the light court was recaptured, and it was brightened substantially with the installation of bay windows. The utilization of the building was improved, including the roof terrace.

Walk south.

AVONDALE CENTRE
20 N. Clark

ARCHITECTS: *A. Epstein and Sons (1980)*

This 36-story office building on the corner of Clark and Madison streets has a smooth-planed facade that allows for the maximum utilization of interior floor space and gives the structure a clean look. The building has a curtainwall of flame-cut Aswan red granite, bronze aluminum, and reflective glass. The spacious lobby of marble and wood is enhanced by a vividly colored sculpture created by Israeli artist Yaacov Agam.

Walk west on Madison Street.

ST. PETER'S CHURCH and FRIARY
110 W. Madison

ARCHITECTS: *K. M. Vitzhum and J. J. Burns (1953)*

St. Peter's Church is a 5-story, marble-covered Roman basilica, consisting of the main church, two chapels on the second floor, and living quarters on the other three floors for the Franciscan priests in charge. The facade is overwhelmingly dominated—as the designers intended it to be—by a gigantic crucified Christ, 18 feet high and weighing 26 tons. This extraordinarily expressive figure, the work of the Latvian sculptor Arvid Strauss, hangs above the entrance in front of the only window of the building, a Gothic arch of stained glass. The church, built on the site of the old LaSalle Theatre, was planned as a religious center for Catholic visitors to the city and the many thousand Catholics who work in the Loop.

Backtrack east across Clark Street and turn south.

CHICAGO LOOP SYNAGOGUE
16 S. Clark

ARCHITECTS: *Loebl, Schlossman and Bennett (1957)*

As you approach the Loop Synagogue, just a few doors south of Madison Street, you will be struck by the unique metal sculpture above the entrance—*The Hands of Peace,* by Israeli sculptor Henri Azaz. Symbolically outstretched hands are surrounded by irregularly spaced letters, in both English and Hebrew, spelling out a Biblical benediction.

From the visitors' balcony inside you can see the well-conceived plan of this structure, which has made optimum use of its narrow lot. The seating arrangement, running at right angles to what is expected, achieves a special effect of spaciousness. And the entire wall opposite the street entrance is composed of a gloriously colored stained-glass design on the theme "Let there be light!"—the work of Abraham Rattner of New York.

TWO FIRST NATIONAL PLAZA
20 S. Clark

ARCHITECTS: *C. F. Murphy and Associates and The Perkins & Will Partnership (1971)*

This is the second structure of the First National Bank complex that faces on the First National Bank Plaza (see WALK 4). There are 30 stories above grade. The exterior columns and spandrels are fireproofed with poured-in-place concrete and faced with pointed steel panels. Enclosures at street level are clear glass in steel frames with bronze doors. Upper floors have solar bronze double glazing in steel frames with plastic thermal break for air circulation.

The granite paving on the sidewalks and interior floor areas at street level match the One First National Plaza. Note the narrow walkway along the building's north side, connecting with Arcade Place and thence to LaSalle Street. The walkway has been in this location for decades and continues the tradition of linking the city's largest bank with its main banking street.

Cross to the southeast corner of Clark and Monroe streets.

BELL FEDERAL SAVINGS BUILDING
79 W. Monroe

ARCHITECTS: *Jarvis Hunt (1906); for the south addition: Holabird and Roche (1924)*

This structure of 13 stories and 1 basement was formerly known as the Chicago Title and Trust Building. Up-to-the-minute weather reports are available in the lobby and outside by the bell. Also, monthly construction reports covering the Chicago metropolitan area are produced upstairs.

Continue south to the northeast corner of Clark and Adams streets.

COMMONWEALTH EDISON BUILDING
72 W. Adams

ARCHITECTS: *D. H. Burnham and Company (1907)*

Located at the northeast corner of Clark and Adams streets, this 18-story structure has two basements and contains the principal offices and control center of the local utility company. Although the executive offices are located nearby in the First National Bank Building, nearly all of the consumer services are located here. There is a pedestrian walkway connecting the adjacent Marquette Building that contains shops and restaurants.

Cross Clark Street to the southwest corner.

BANKERS BUILDING
105 W. Adams

ARCHITECTS: *Burnham Brothers (1927)*

This structure was designed by the Burnham Brothers, who followed in the footsteps of their illustrious father, Daniel H. Burnham. The building is 41 stories with 1 basement on rock caissons. The lobby is richly covered in red marble faced with carved oak columns. Outside, pebbled concrete is imaginatively molded up to the 4th story.

At this point it should be worth looking across the street to one of the three great open plazas that you encountered in WALK 4—the Federal Center Plaza. Note the low post office structure at the corner in contrast with the two tall structures and the excellent site plan that provided the open area for the plaza.

Backtrack to Clark Street and turn south.

CONTINENTAL ILLINOIS BANK BUILDING
231 S. LaSalle

ARCHITECTS: *Graham, Anderson, Probst and White (1924)*

On Clark Street is the eastern facade of this huge bank building that is included in WALK 6. It was formerly known as the Illinois Merchant's Trust Building. The massive building is 19 stories with two basements on rock caissons.

Cross diagonally to the southeast corner of Clark Street and Jackson Boulevard.

RALPH H. METCALFE FEDERAL BUILDING
77 W. Jackson

ARCHITECTS: *Fujikawa Johnson and Associates (1991)*

This sleek building fits well with yet avoids mimicking the other federal government buildings to its northeast (see WALK 4). The windows are flush to the surface, not set between protruding piers as in the style of Mies van der Rohe.

Ralph Metcalfe (1910–78) was an Olympic sprinter in 1936 who went on to become a civil rights leader, a Chicago city alderman, and a U.S. Congressman.

(WILLIAM J. CAMPBELL) UNITED STATES COURTHOUSE ANNEX
Van Buren between Clark and Federal

ARCHITECTS: *Harry Weese and Associates (1975)*

This skyscraper detention center stands on a square block. The 27-story triangular tower and 7-story garage recognize the Loop in scale, geometry, and form. The triangular tower plan maximizes perimeter space for exterior windows, and minimizes corridor lengths. Corners function as stairwells and elevator service cores. One of three Metropolitan Correctional Centers in the country, this federal correction center offers more humanitarian prison conditions. Administration and social services comprise the lower half; federal detainees awaiting trial and prisoners are housed in the upper half, which includes a landscaped rooftop exercise yard.

Based on program guidelines, each multipurpose core space serves 44 people. Each module contains inmates' rooms, exercise, lounge, kitchenette, dining, and visitors space. The size of each module allows for separation of men from women, old from young, and first-time offenders from repeaters. The 5-inch vertical windows are the maximum opening allowed by the Bureau of Prison Standards, and almost completely hide the bars from view.

Near this point you can begin either WALK 4 or WALK 10. To start, walk 1 block south to Congress and 2 short blocks east to Dearborn Street.

St. Peter's Church
(Allen Carr)

1. Loop Transportation Center
   203 N. LaSalle St.

2. 200 N. LaSalle St.

3. State of Illinois Building
   160 N. LaSalle St.

4. State of Illinois Center
   100 W. Randolph St.

5. Randolph Tower
   188 W. Randolph St.

6. Bismarck Hotel
   171 W. Randolph St.

7. Savings of America Tower
   120 N. LaSalle St.

8. 100 N. LaSalle St.

9. American National Bank Building
   33 N. LaSalle St.

10. One N. LaSalle Street Building

11. Chemical Plaza
    10 S. LaSalle St.

12. Paine Webber Tower
    181 W. Madison St.

13. Madison Plaza
    200 W. Madison St.

14. Northern Trust Company
    50 S. LaSalle St.

15. Harris Trust and Savings Bank
    111 W. Monroe St.

16. AT&T Corporate Center
    227 W. Monroe St.

17. 200 W. Adams St.

18. 190 S. LaSalle St.

19. LaSalle Bank Building
    135 S. LaSalle St.

20. The Rookery Building
    209 S. LaSalle St.

21. 208 S. LaSalle St. Building

22. Federal Reserve Bank
    230 S. LaSalle St.

23. Continental Illinois Bank Building
    231 S. LaSalle St.

24. Board of Trade Building
    141 W. Jackson Blvd.

25. LaSalle Atrium Building
    401 S. LaSalle St.

26. Exchange Center
    440 S. LaSalle St.

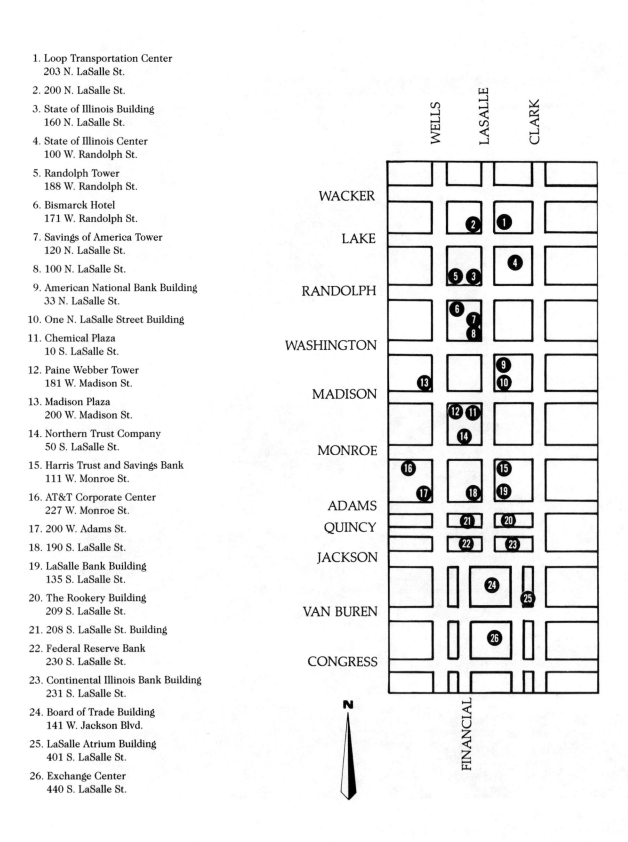

WALK 6 LaSALLE STREET

WALKING TIME: 1½ to 2 hours.

HOW TO GET THERE: Walk west on Wacker Drive to LaSalle Street (140 W), 3 blocks west of State Street.

Be sure to take this WALK on a weekday during business hours, when the rhythm of Chicago at work is best felt. LaSalle Street in the Loop is the Wall Street of the Midwest. From Wacker Drive the street looks like a canyon, with skyscraper office buildings and banks along each side and the 45-story Board of Trade Building like a towering mountain at the south. Here, in a corridor roughly bounded by Randolph Street and Congress Parkway, are clustered Chicago's major banks; here is the Chicago Stock Exchange; and here, straddling LaSalle Street, stands the overpowering Board of Trade Building with the statue of Ceres at its top. Activities inside some of these buildings send political and economic waves across the world.

This WALK starts at the northeast corner of LaSalle and Lake streets. This is the cornerstone of the North Loop Redevelopment Project.

LOOP TRANSPORTATION CENTER
203 N. LaSalle

ARCHITECTS: *Skidmore, Owings and Merrill (1986)*

The 27-story Loop Transportation Center was designed to integrate numerous transportation and travel services with office and retail facilities. The multiuse structure has two distinct elements: one is composed of travel and retail services and 10 levels of self-parking spaces; the office portion of the building rises from the 13th through the 27th floor.

The exterior is painted precast concrete with silver reflective glass on the north and south facades and a combination of silver reflective and green tinted insulated glass on the east and west facades. Along Clark Street, the east side, 3 glassed-in elevators provide highly visible transportation for those traveling to and from the garage.

200 N. LaSALLE

ARCHITECTS: *Perkins & Will, Wojciech Madeyski, partner in charge (1984)*

This is one of a new generation of office buildings which breaks from the stereotype of the box, making the building more open to the environment. The impressive serrated plan opens the corners and steps back to create corner offices (ten to a floor) with views of neighboring buildings. The 2-way access from the corner leads to a monumental, 4-story lobby. Both lobby and exterior are clad with insulated clear glass panels to break the claustrophobic feeling of some buildings, and to allow the occupants to feel a participation in city life.

Walk south on LaSalle Street.

**STATE OF
ILLINOIS
BUILDING**
160 N. LaSalle

ARCHITECTS: *Burnham Brothers (1924); for the renovation and addition: Holabird and Root (1992)*

This building, 20 stories with 1 basement, was known as the Burnham Building until its purchase by the State of Illinois in 1946. During years of renovation, what had been a U-shaped court above the 5th floor was infilled to the roof, using blue-tinted glass in 4 setbacks; a limestone-clad penthouse was added. The new skylit lobby also blends well with the original structure.

Across LaSalle Street is the State of Illinois Center.

**STATE OF
ILLINOIS CENTER**
100 W. Randolph

ARCHITECTS: *a joint venture of Murphy/Jahn and L. B. Knight & Associates (1980)*

The State of Illinois Center (restyled the James R. Thompson Center in 1993) was designed to make several statements; some about the building's use and others in relationship to buildings nearby. The southeast portion of the block is sliced away to form a sloped, setback configuration and open the space at the corner in response to the Dearborn-Clark corridors, City Hall–County Building, and the Civic Center, without losing the spatial closure of the street. The continuous, but stepped-back, west facade of the building rises from the street line to reinforce its relationship to LaSalle Street. An indentation of the skin at the lowest two floors creates a covered arcade, which continues along both LaSalle and Clark streets as well as along the curved southeast wall. The arcade provides a zone of spatial transition into the rotunda.

Along Randolph and Clark streets, the granite screen wall of the arcade continues to define the open space, but diminishes gradually in deference to the entry. The plaza thus created is a free composition of water, paving, and trees. The Lake Street elevation is a straight wall along the building line that gives a clear reading of the setbacks on the other exposures.

The building, in its large scale and urban monumentality, is also a statement of the importance and the dignity of state government. The truncated glass cylinder projects above the building's mass, creating a top and making a clearly identifiable shape on the skyline of the city. This cylinder suggests the tradition of domed government buildings throughout the history of the building arts. The State of Illinois Center breaks with tradition by making the central space visible from outside. This openness is continued along the curved facade by the 5-story atriums that follow the setbacks.

State of Illinois Center, exterior and interior
(James R. Steinkamp courtesy of Murphy/Jahn)

A glazed skin encloses all surfaces of the building. Opaque glass colored blue-gray-white is used with silver and clear glass to create various degrees of transparency and reflection, and to give the monumental shape a painted quality on the surface.

Across Randolph Street to the south looms the bulky, massive City Hall–County Building with its heavy pillars, designed under the old belief that government buildings should be monumental in size and style. (See WALK 5). Free tours are available of all the government buildings by calling 744-5000.

Walk west 1 block on Randolph Street.

RANDOLPH TOWER
188 W. Randolph

ARCHITECTS: *Vitzhum and Burns (1930)*

Long neglected before a facelift in 1993, this 45-story office building with many setbacks and Gothic appointments is once again a notable presence on the skyline. Cream-colored terra-cotta, brick, and stone trim form the exterior. The Steuben Club originally occupied the top floors, and its swimming pool remains.

BISMARCK HOTEL
171 W. Randolph

ARCHITECTS: *Rapp and Rapp (1926)*

Built as part of the Eitel Block along with a theater and office building now gone, the hotel retains some of its pre-Depression aura. The interior has been renovated and modernized. The terrazzo floor and starburst plaster ceiling in the lobby are well preserved, and the Walnut Room is certainly worth a visit.

Return to LaSalle Street and walk south.

SAVINGS OF AMERICA TOWER
120 N. LaSalle

ARCHITECT: *Helmut Jahn (1990)*

At 38 stories this is a very slender building, made more humane by various means. The developers commendably paid for a large mosaic mural by Roger Brown of Chicago to cover the curving entry roof. From the 7th story to the top the curtainwall springs out in a similar curve as if on a hinge, with the windows braced by a granite ladder. The same motif in granite is carried at the 2nd story for the length of the alley to Wells Street. In the mural, called "The Flight of Daedalus and Icarus," two mythic figures wearing wings soar aloft, just as the entryway does.

100 N. LaSALLE

ARCHITECTS: *Graven and Maygen (1929); for the remodeling: Joel Scheckerman (1985)*

This 25-story brick and steel building was constructed in 36 days in 1929. It has undergone changes over the years, the most recent in 1985. At that time the first 40 feet of the facade were refaced in granite, leaving only partially revealed the original carved-stone windows.

South of Washington Street, at 30 N. LaSalle Street, a 43-story blue paneled and glass office building now occupies the site of the old Stock Exchange Building designed by Adler and Sullivan, completed in 1894 and demolished in 1972. The trading room of the Stock Exchange has been incorporated in the Columbus Drive wing of the Art Institute of Chicago; its entry arch now stands in the Art Institute's Grant Park Garden (see WALK 1).

Cross to the east side of the street.

AMERICAN NATIONAL BANK BUILDING
33 N. LaSalle

ARCHITECTS: *Graham, Anderson, Probst and White (1929)*

The building was originally known as the Foreman National Bank Building. It is 38 stories with 2 basements on rock and hardpan caissons. The exterior materials are a granite base and Bedford limestone. The first 18 floors, occupied by the bank, were completely remodeled in 1971 in the Williamsburg style.

Continue south.

ONE N. LaSALLE STREET BUILDING

ARCHITECTS: *Vitzhum and Burns (1930)*

This Bedford limestone building is 49 stories on rock caissons. Hammered brass ornament fills the lobby. The majority of tenants are law firms, as are those in the American National Bank Building, both buildings representing the powerful growth of the banking business just prior to the Great Depression.

Diagonally across LaSalle Street is our next stop.

CHEMICAL PLAZA
10 S. LaSalle

ARCHITECTS: *Holabird and Roche (1909); Holabird and Root (1985)*

This bank center is built atop the partially demolished 1909 structure. The bottom four floors of generously sculpted granite seem to have a blue glass tube inserted for support, but this is the launching of the upper 35 floors of steel with tinted glass.

Across the street is the genteel little arch for Arcade Place, a bit of Old London tried in roughneck Chicago.

Go through Chemical Plaza's lobby to the back door for a glimpse of a tiny urban canyon, and continue into the next building.

PAINE WEBBER TOWER
181 W. Madison

ARCHITECTS: *Cesar Pelli and Associates with Shaw and Associates (1990)*

The main lobby is cavernous, vaulted like a train depot. Outside, the off-white granite rises in strongly vertical fashion to 50 stories on narrow piers and mullions. The steps are covered by a screen-like awning on six supports. This was the Argentinean architect's first Chicago building.

Cross to the northwest corner of Madison and Wells streets.

MADISON PLAZA
200 W. Madison

ARCHITECTS: *Skidmore, Owings and Merrill (1982)*

This 45-story office building has a glass front elevation in a sawtooth form, which rises from the plaza to the sloped roof of the 39th and 44th floors. The steel tube structure is clad with bands of silver reflective glass and light gray polished granite. By setting the building back from the street, a triangular elevated entry plaza was formed as a buffer from the heavy street traffic and the adjacent El tracks. This plaza also provided an appropriate setting for a major public sculpture by Louise Nevelson. The lobby is finished in statuary Bettogi marble with polished stainless steel trim. Stainless steel elevator doors are etched with a subtle grid. The elevator interiors are mahogany wood paneled with a custom ceiling of stainless steel and luminous panels. The building envelope contains highly reflective glazing to minimize winter heat losses and summer solar heat gains, while maintaining acceptable office window area. These elements won the building an energy efficiency award.

Walk south on Wells Street. On your left is one door of the Northern Trust Bank. Look at the refreshing change from the city canyon of LaSalle Street—a landscaped space with fountains, providing a drive-in section for hurried or late customers.

Walk through the banking area to LaSalle Street.

NORTHERN TRUST COMPANY
50 S. LaSalle

ARCHITECTS: *Frost and Granger (1906); for addition: Frost and Henderson (1928); for addition: C. F. Murphy Associates (1967)*

The Northern Trust Company presents a face of massive granite topped by columns. Its adjoining structure along Monroe Street lightly updates this aspect.

A plaque on the bank's southeast corner notes that all elevations in Chicago are measured from here.

Diagonally across the street is another evolving bank headquarters.

HARRIS TRUST AND SAVINGS BANK
111 W. Monroe

ARCHITECTS: *Shepley, Rutan and Coolidge (1910); for the additions: Skidmore, Owings and Merrill (1957, 1975)*

Note the lion friezes; the same firm designed the Art Institute. The original 20-story building of red granite and brick is now framed by 2 stunning steel additions. The first is 23 stories and fronts on the southwest corner of Monroe and Clark streets; the second is 38 stories, fronting on the southeast corner of Monroe and LaSalle streets. All 3 buildings are connected at the banking floor levels and make up a complex a full block long.

An unusual feature of the building farthest east is its recessed floor halfway up, which holds mechanical equipment usually found on the roof or in the basement. The stainless-steel mullions and the tall, narrow window pattern are especially effective.

A bronze-sculpture fountain in a granite basin by Russel Secrest is located on the bank's public plaza. Water flows over the seven petal-like pedestals.

Walk 2 blocks west on Monroe Street past Wells Street.

AT&T CORPORATE CENTER
227 W. Monroe

ARCHITECTS: *Skidmore, Owings and Merrill, partner in charge Robert Diamant (1989)*

This is in fact two buildings, linked by a 16-story base. The northern one of 60 stories houses AT&T. To the south, through the 40-foot vaulted lobby—look for the skylight midway—is the 43-story quarters of the USG corporation, which left its signature building on Wacker Drive to move here. Little expense was spared in the marble, granite, or elaborate Gothic setbacks with decorative top. The aluminum spandrels were emblazoned using a new photographic technique.

Emerging from the door at 222 W. Adams Street, walk east to the corner of Wells Street.

200 W. ADAMS   ARCHITECTS: *Fujikawa Johnson and Associates (1985)*

The structural design of this 30-story building was new to Chicago. To facilitate construction, the concrete core was poured in its entirety, with steel erection following. The steel provides large spans and the concrete core braces the high-rise structure. The cladding is silver metallic aluminum, with blue-tinted reflective insulating glass.

Continue east to LaSalle Street.

190 S. LaSALLE   ARCHITECTS: *John Burgee Architects with Philip Johnson of New York City (1986)*

This 42-story office tower has 900,000 gross square feet. It is a concrete core, steel framed building with cladding of Spanish pink granite in a flame finish and grey-tinted glass. It has two different window systems, punched and the more typical glass curtainwall. The granite on the 5-story base is a flame finish, and the accent bands around the entrance and horizontal bands around the windows are a honed finish. The building has a copper roof and six gables topped by an ornate bronze cresting.

All buildings from this point south to the Board of Trade are at least 60 years old. The design here for the gabled rooftop and for the base of the building drew on elements seen in John W. Root's Masonic Temple (built in the early 1890s), which stood at State and Randolph streets. Johnson and Burgee also drew on design elements of the nearby Rookery and paid homage to it in this building.

There are 5-story lobbies off both LaSalle and Adams streets. The handsome LaSalle Street lobby is 180 feet long, 40 feet deep, and 55 feet tall and has a floor of a black and off-white botticino marble; the walls are clad in the same botticino marble and a red alicante marble up to a height of 33 feet. The fluted columns with Corinthian capitals are in matching red alicante marble. The recessed lighting in the red alicante marble crown molding, which wraps around the entire lobby, shines onto the barrel-vaulted ceiling, painted in gold leaf. The wainscotting is of the same alicante marble; the rest of the walls are in the botticino. The lobbies are retail-free, an unusual occurrence in today's buildings. By all means look at the large wool tapestry by Helena Hernmarck, a representation of Daniel Burnham's 1909 Plan for Chicago.

Cross LaSalle Street.

LaSALLE BANK
BUILDING
135 S. LaSalle

ARCHITECTS: *Graham, Anderson, Probst and White (1934)*

This bank's original home (it expanded into number 120 during the 1980s) was formerly known as the Field Office Building. It was carried out in two sections, one on Clark Street and one facing LaSalle Street. The building is 23 stories with a 19-story tower and 3 basements on rock caissons.

This is the site of the famous Home Insurance Building (demolished in 1931), the world's first skeleton steel-and-iron building. It was designed in 1884 by the father of such construction, William LeBaron Jenney.

Cross Adams Street to see one of the city's great treasures.

* THE ROOKERY
BUILDING
209 S. LaSalle

ARCHITECTS: *Burnham and Root (1886–88); for the inner lobby: Frank Lloyd Wright (1905); for elevators and lobby: William Drummond (1932); for remodeling of ground floor: Graham, Anderson, Probst and White (1972); for renovations: Booth/ Hansen and Associates (1986–87); for restoration: McClier Corporation (1988–92)*

Here is an architectural landmark, an extraordinary building called The Rookery. This quaint name is a holdover from the temporary city hall located on the site from 1872 to 1884, which had been nicknamed The Rookery because it seemed to be the gathering place of both birds and politicians! The city hall had been built around an iron water tank, the only remnant after the Fire of 1871 of the reservoir building serving the south side. While the temporary city hall was here, Chicago's first public library stored its books in the old water tank.

The present Rookery, one of the oldest precursors of the modern skyscraper, is distinguished in its own right. It was designed to be the most modern and amenable office building of its day. The architects used masonry bearing walls for the exterior facades of the building and iron framing for the walls of the interior light court and atrium. Through this design, both inner and outer offices received a maximum amount of natural light. The public spaces of the building were also carefully designed and ornamented with marble, glass, and cast iron, some in Moorish elements. The sturdy yet ornamental exterior is partly of skeleton structure, partly wall-bearing, and the building as a whole has an appearance of enormous vitality. The powerful columns, alternating with piers, arches, and stonework, make a dramatic contrast with the lobby inside—unique in its elaborate but delicate ornamentation. The glass-and-iron tracery of the domed skylight above the second floor of the lobby court (now restored and protected by an upper skylight added in the restoration) harmonizes with the extensive grillwork used around the first- and second-floor balconies and along the sides of the two-winged

LaSalle Bank Building
(Allen Carr)

Details of the Rookery
(Allen Carr)

suspended stairway at the west side. The main stairway by Root, uncon-
nected with this one, starts at the second floor and runs to the top of the
building. A cylindrical staircase, it projects beyond the east wall into the
light court, requiring an additional, semicircular tower to enclose it. In
the restoration, cracked walnut shells aided in removing 20 coats of black
paint over the copper plating.

The gold-and-ivory decorations of the lobby court are the work of
Frank Lloyd Wright, who remodeled this part of the building in 1905.

The result was a splendid integration of new materials carefully blended with the old lobby design. The citation from the Landmarks Commission reads:

> In recognition of its pioneering plan in providing shops and offices around a graceful and semi-private square and further development of the skeleton structural frame using cast iron columns, wrought iron spandrel beams, and steel beams to support party walls and interior floors.

In 1986–92 the building underwent major restoration of the exterior and public spaces. Work began with a complete inspection of the exterior facades, documented with written and illustrative data and video photography. Sample material was removed and laboratory tested to assist in the development of the long-term masonry repairs. This led to the cleaning of the brick, terra-cotta, and granite facades, including appropriate repairs. The second phase of the project involved the restoration and preservation of the designated historic features of the building, and the rehabilitation of the tenant spaces, including Burnham and Root's 11th-floor office, its library now restored. The historic areas of the building include the light court, lobbies, entrances, and stairways. The Rookery is now on the National Register of Historic Places, and is also a Chicago Historic Landmark.

208 S. LaSALLE STREET BUILDING

ARCHITECTS: *D. H. Burnham and Company (1914)*

Across LaSalle Street is the former City National Bank and Trust Building, 20 stories with 2 basements on rock caissons. A huge monolith extends west to Wells Street, from Adams to Quincy streets. It has a Bedford limestone base with terra-cotta above and formed one of the first canyon walls of LaSalle Street.

Directly south on LaSalle Street is another bank building. (As you cross Quincy Street, look west at the El station in relief against the Sears Tower.)

FEDERAL RESERVE BANK
230 S. LaSalle

ARCHITECTS: *Graham, Anderson, Probst and White (1922);*
for addition: C. F. Murphy and Associates (1960)

This bankers' bank for the 7th Federal Reserve District has 3 basements on rock caissons and faces on LaSalle, Jackson, and Quincy streets. The original structure's entrance on LaSalle Street has Roman Corinthian columns and pediment. All facades are of a light Bedford limestone. The addition facing on Jackson and Quincy streets is 25 stories.

Cross LaSalle Street.

CONTINENTAL ILLINOIS BANK BUILDING
231 S. LaSalle

ARCHITECTS: *Graham, Anderson, Probst and White (1924, 1975); for the remodeling: Skidmore, Owings and Merrill (1981)*

In the giant, block-square building of the Continental Illinois National Bank and Trust Company, you have revivalist architecture again. The design is said to have been taken from some early Roman baths. Inside, take an escalator to the enormous open banking floor, where tall Ionic columns stress again the pseudo-classic style. In 1981 the lobby was redesigned and the vast frieze and entablature cleaned.

The Continental Illinois claims to be Chicago's oldest bank, the result of many mergers and changes of name dating back to 1857. It got its present name with a national charter in 1932.

* BOARD OF TRADE BUILDING
141 W. Jackson

ARCHITECTS: *Holabird and Root (1929); for the addition: Murphy/Jahn; Shaw and Associates; Swanke, Hayden and Connel (1979–82)*

The focal point of this entire WALK has been the Board of Trade Building, with its commanding location at the foot of LaSalle Street, on Jackson Boulevard. From Randolph Street this towering structure seems to block LaSalle Street at its southern end, but at Jackson Boulevard you discover that the north-south street merely jogs a bit to the east and continues southward. At the top of the 45 stories stands a statue of Ceres, Greek goddess of grain. The 32-foot figure topping the 526-foot skyscraper is by John Storrs. A mural of Ceres once decorated the trading room. When the addition was built, it was moved to the 12th floor atrium.

Step into the lobby and enjoy the interior Art Deco design by Gilbert Hall, former chief designer of Holabird and Root. The school of design known as Art Deco flourished from the mid-1920s to the outbreak of World War II (and was revived in the late 1980s). The style is forceful and direct, emphasizing rectilinear rather than voluptuously curving lines. It was an upbeat, inspiring type of art, featuring sunrays, rainbows, large leafy plants, and well-muscled young people at work or at some athletic pursuit.

The lobby, upper lobby, trading room, elevator doors, and lighting fixtures are exceptionally high caliber Art Deco. The contrast of the black and light color marbles is fascinating and pleasant to view. The enormous room of the grain exchange, which was the largest in the world, was divided horizontally to create a financial-instruments trading room.

If you are fortunate to be here before 2 P.M. on a weekday, you can go to the visitors' gallery of the Trading Room on the 5th floor. A 20-minute video is shown at 9:15, 10, 11, noon, and 12:30, Monday through Friday. Call 435-3590 for information. To the uninitiated, the sights and sounds from the trading pit seem like bedlam. On both sides are several pits,

Board of Trade with addition
in foreground
(Keith Palmer courtesy
Murphy/Jahn)

each a circle of traders interested in buying or selling a particular item—wheat, corn, soybeans, soybean meal, corn, sugar, oil, foreign currencies, government bonds, and others. Shouts and hand signals in the bidding are clear to those involved, and the constantly changing prices are recorded on a big board immediately for all to see. Messengers run back and forth between the bidders with messages telephoned or wired from firms or individual customers in all parts of the world. Five minutes before trading ends, microphones are turned up to let visitors hear the often-wild closing action. The men and women trading here represent more than 1400 members of the Board of Trade. Traders, messengers, and staff of the exchange are distinguished by the color of the jackets they wear. The Board of Trade is indeed a tremendous marketplace, although the actual goods that change hands here are far away.

Walk through or around to the addition facing Van Buren Street. Providing more than a half million gross square feet, it responds functionally and formally to the existing Art Deco landmark structure. The first twelve floors are large bulk spaces housing the trading floor and support spaces corresponding to similar spaces in the existing structure. Above, the office floors are designed as U-shaped spaces around a central atrium that adjoins the existing structure. To provide the required trading floor area, the building projects 20 feet beyond the existing structure to the street curb, creating a covered pedestrian arcade along LaSalle Street.

The addition derives its formal characteristics from an abstracted, literal duplication of the Art Deco style of the existing building. The device used is a glass wall, wrapping the highly articulated planes of the wall and the roof. This taut membrane slips behind limestone "screen walls" on both sides, recalling the dominant expression and the material of the old building. The glass elevators in the atrium, through their movement, add a dynamic element to the central open space.

At the southeast corner of LaSalle and Van Buren streets is a handsome former hotel.

* LaSALLE ATRIUM BUILDING
401 S. LaSalle

ARCHITECTS: *Holabird and Roche (1914); for the restoration: Booth/Hansen and Associates (1983–85)*

This 17-story building, once the Fort Dearborn Hotel, was transformed into office space. The masonry and terra-cotta exterior and the mahogany-laden lobby are restored to their original grandeur. The original decorative plaster ceiling, ornate bronze and iron work, murals, and marble floors were also restored. A skylighted atrium extends from the lobby to the roof, surrounded on all sides by office space. It stands in pleasant contrast in this mostly modern precinct.

Continue south.

EXCHANGE CENTER
440 S. LaSalle

ARCHITECTS: *Skidmore, Owings and Merrill (1983–84)*

Exchange Center is a complex composed of three elements: the Chicago Board Options Exchange, the Chicago Stock Exchange, and the One Financial Place office tower. (The first uses a separate address of 141 W. Van Buren Street.) The exterior cladding on the buildings is Imperial red polished granite with reflective, bronze-tinted, double pane, insulating glass.

Two covered exterior arcades and a ground-level interior concourse link the three elements of the complex. The pedestrian concourse, part of the Underground Walkway system (see WALK 7) joins the three structures to the Chicago Board of Trade Building and Annex. There is a Rock Island commuter station at the south end of the Exchange Center complex.

CHICAGO BOARD OPTIONS EXCHANGE

This is a 7-story building with a 44,000 square-foot trading floor, including an electronic display system. The trading floor has a raised floor system to allow for the cabling requirements between the trading posts. The building was planned to place all core elements at the perimeter so the center is an open and uninterrupted space. The central area is a high clerestory-lit space, which serves as open offices. There is a bridge linking this building at the 4th floor to the Chicago Board of Trade.

ONE FINANCIAL PLACE

This 40-story office tower, a steel frame structure with cladding to match the other structures in the complex, is joined to the Chicago Stock Exchange building. It was dubbed one of the first "intelligent" office buildings in the world, providing special communication needs to serve the modern-day business tenant. It also contains one of the largest in-house computer facilities in the city of Chicago.

The much-appreciated plaza on the west, gently stepped from Van Buren Street, culminates at a large bronze statue of a horse, "San Marco II," by Ludovic de Luigi, inspired by statues in Venice.

CHICAGO STOCK EXCHANGE

The nation's second city has had a stock market since 1882; from 1949 to 1993 it was called the Midwest Stock Exchange before retaking its original name. This building is 6 stories tall and houses the 19,000-square-foot trading floor as well as a sports club. It may appear smaller than 6 stories because two broadly arching windows address the two lanes of traffic underneath—for like the main Post Office ½ mile west, it straddles Congress Parkway without interrupting traffic.

Call 663-2183 to arrange free group tours; individuals may visit without reservations.

Subway entrance, under the Richard J. Daley Center
(Allen Carr)

WALK 7 UNDERGROUND WALKWAYS

WALKING TIME: 2 hours or more
(if you don't stop along the way to shop).
HOW TO GET THERE: Start at State and Madison streets.

An all-weather underground walkway system in Chicago's Loop, continually being expanded, is available for a walking tour, or at least exploration. Parts of the system date from the 1950s, and above-ground skywalks began to catch on in the early 1990s. Some of the grander plans for linking most Loop buildings met with security and cleaning problems, while others met with the more mundane obstacle of cost. Some private tunnels afford such convenience as underground mail delivery within the Federal Center and a link from the General Post Office to Union Station. This tour will focus on the public thoroughfares.

Because of the outdoor connotation of the term "walking tour," the suggestion for a subterranean walk may seem odd. Yet one of Chicago's fascinations is this underground walkway system (also called Pedways), on a scale that is rare today in American urban centers. There are several segments that will take you a surprising distance out of the rain, cold, or wind.

To begin, enter the Howard–Dan Ryan subway station at State Street north of Madison Street. From there you can enter the Wieboldt's Building at 1 N. State Street. Turning west instead takes you on a long route into the Walgreen's store at 4 N. State Street, the One North Dearborn Building, and next door into 33 N. Dearborn. Continuing west, descend into the Congress-Douglas subway station on Dearborn Street between Washington and Madison streets, turn south past Trattoria No. 10 at 10 N. Dearborn, and into Three First National Plaza at 70 W. Madison Street (where a wall map guides you).

At this point there are two options: you can cross the skywalk (the city's oldest) south to the First National Bank at One First National Plaza, then back underground to Two First National Plaza at 20 S. Clark Street, or up to the Street-Side Restaurant on the bank plaza.

The second option is to walk north from Three First National Plaza to the vast concourse under 69 W. Washington Street, and continue north to the Daley Center concourse between Washington and Randolph streets and Dearborn and Clark streets. If you have taken the second option, you have two more choices: you can walk west through the Daley Center, to the County Building–City Hall at 118 N. Clark Street and 121 N. LaSalle Street, then continue west to 120 N. LaSalle Street, through which you can emerge on Wells Street. Or, from City

1. H-DR Subway
   State & Madison St.

2. Wieboldt's Store
   1 N. State St.

3. Walgreen's
   4 N. State St.

4. One N. Dearborn Building

5. 33 N. Dearborn Building

6. C-D Subway
   Dearborn & Washington St.

7. Three First National Plaza
   70 W. Madison St.

8. First National Bank
   One First National Plaza

9. Two First National Plaza
   20 S. Clark St.

10. Trattoria No. 10
    10 N. Dearborn St.

11. 69 W. Washington St.

12. Richard J. Daley Center
    50 W. Washington St.

13. County Building–City Hall
    118 N. Clark St.

14. 120 N. LaSalle St.

15. State of Illinois Center
    100 W. Randolph St.

16. Chicago Title Tower
    161 N. Clark St.

17. H-DR Subway
    State & Washington St.

18. Marshall Field Store
    111 N. State St.

19. Wabash-Washington Shops
    25 E. Washington St.

20. Chicago Public Library Cultural Center
    78 E. Washington St.

21. Associates Center
    150 N. Michigan Ave.

22. Metra Electric Randolph Street Station
    Michigan & Randolph/South Water St.

23. North Grant Park Underground Garage

24. One Prudential Plaza
    130 E. Randolph Dr.

25. Two Prudential Plaza
    180 N. Stetson Ave.

26. Amoco Building
    200 E. Randolph St.

27. Fairmont Hotel
    200 N. Columbus Dr.

28. Boulevard Towers North & South
    205 & 225 N. Michigan Ave.

29. Two Illinois Center
    233 N. Michigan Ave.

30. One Illinois Center
    111 E. Wacker Dr.

31. Hyatt Regency Chicago
    151 E. Wacker Dr.

32. Hyatt Regency Chicago Annex
    201 E. Wacker Dr.

33. Columbus Plaza
    233 E. Wacker Dr.

34. Three Illinois Center
    303 E. Wacker Dr.

35. South Grant Park Underground Garage

36. Metra Electric Van Buren Street Station
    Columbus & Van Buren St.

37. H-DR Subway
    State & Adams St.

38. C-D Subway
    Dearborn & Adams St.

39. Board of Trade Building & Annex
    141 W. Jackson Blvd.

40. Exchange Center
    440 S. LaSalle St.

41. LaSalle Street Station

42. Union Station
    210 S. Canal St.

43. MidAmerica Commodity Exchange
    444 W. Jackson Blvd.

44. 222 S. Riverside Plaza

45. Northwestern Atrium Center
    500 W. Madison St.

46. Riverside Plaza Building
    2 N. Riverside Plaza

47. C-D Subway
    Clark & Lake St.

48. Loop Transportation Center
    203 N. LaSalle St.

49. R. R. Donnelley Center
    77 W. Wacker Drive

50. Leo Burnett Building
    35 W. Wacker Dr.

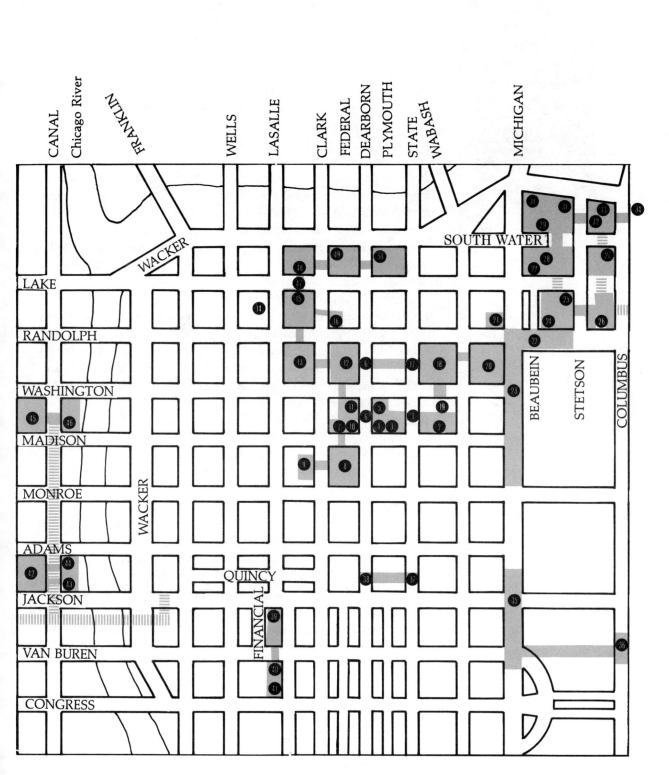

Outside entrance to the
Daley Center Concourse
(Olga Stefanos)

Hall walk underground north to the State of Illinois Center at 100 W. Randolph Street, then cross east into the Chicago Title Tower at 161 N. Clark Street.

From the lower level of the State of Illinois Center you can enter the Congress-Douglas subway at Clark and Lake streets; or go into the Loop Transportation Center at 203 N. LaSalle Street. From there skywalks lead you eastward: across Clark Street into the shops behind the R. R. Donnelley Center at 77 W. Wacker Drive and the 200 N. Dearborn Apartments; then across Dearborn Street to the ground level of the Leo Burnett Building at 35 W. Wacker Drive, behind the Stouffer Riviere Hotel, to emerge at State and Lake streets.

Back at the Daley Center you can walk east through the Congress-Douglas subway tunnel, to the Howard–Dan Ryan subway station, and then to the Marshall Field building at 111 N. State Street. At this point you again have two options: from Field's basement you can walk south into the Wabash-Washington Shops at 25 E. Washington Street, where it dead ends; or you can continue east to the 139 N. Wabash Building (the old Blackhawk restaurant), up via a shiny gold elevator into the Chicago Public Library Cultural Center at 78 E. Washington Street, or on to the Associates Center at 150 N. Michigan Avenue, and to the Metra Electric Randolph Street station.

From this station you again have two options: you can enter the North Grant Park Underground Garage; or you can walk east to One Prudential Plaza at 130 E. Randolph Drive, then to Two Prudential Plaza at 180 N. Stetson Avenue. You may continue east to the Amoco Oil Building at 200 E. Randolph Street, then north into the Fairmont Hotel at 200 N. Columbus Drive.

A separate path begins across Lake Street in Boulevard Towers South and North, respectively, at 205 and 225 N. Michigan Avenue. Down below is the South Water end of the Metra Electric Randolph Street station. Or, proceeding north, you reach Two Illinois Center at 233 N. Michigan Avenue, One Illinois Center at 111 E. Wacker Drive, and to the east the Hyatt Regency Chicago at 151 E. Wacker Drive. Here both a skyway and an underground walkway take you east across Stetson Avenue into the Hyatt's Annex and Columbus Plaza. Still moving east, you reach the terminus of this route on the other side of Columbus Drive in Three Illinois Center at 303 E. Wacker Drive (from which you can also reach Fire Station CF-21 at Columbus Drive and South Water Street).

Back nearer the Loop, a few short underground segments may yet spawn more arms. From S. Michigan Avenue, enter the South Grant Park Garage at Adams, Jackson, or Van Buren streets to reach the Metra Electric station at Van Buren Street east of Michigan Avenue.

Another segment links the Howard–Dan Ryan subway station under State Street, through a long tunnel, to the Congress-Douglas Adams Street station, emerging at the Federal Center.

Something more akin to a city-within-a-city than to a walkway begins at 141 W. Jackson Boulevard, the Board of Trade Building. This is attached on the south to the Board of Trade Annex, and from the 4th floor there you can walk over the bridge to the Exchange Center at 440 S. LaSalle Street, which is 3 contiguous buildings; the Chicago Board Options Exchange, the Chicago Stock Exchange, and the One Financial Place office tower, as well as the Rock Island Railroad's LaSalle Street terminal.

Access to train stations accounts for the other two links as of this writing. To reach Union Station, enter the MidAmerica Commodity Exchange at 444 W. Jackson Boulevard, on the west bank of the Chicago River; proceed west through the station's Great Hall, emerging on Clinton Street. Or, enter through another building on the river, 222 S. Riverside Plaza. The large and attractive concourse under this entire site was refurbished in 1991. Passengers may also enter and exit the station's platforms two blocks to the north, at Madison Street, although the noise and smoke along the tracks do not invite casual exploration.

Kitty-corner from those Madison Street stairs is the Chicago & Northwestern Atrium, 500 W. Madison Street. It is reached via skywalk from the river as well, by entering the Riverside Plaza Building at 2 N. Riverside Plaza. For walkers, this passage is among the most modern of all of the shopping arcade/lunch stop/commuter paths that Chicago has to offer.

1. 360 N. Michigan Ave.

2. Lincoln Tower Building
   75 E. Wacker Dr.

3. Executive Plaza Hotel
   71 E. Wacker Dr.

4. Seventeenth Church of Christ, Scientist
   55 E. Wacker Dr.

5. 35 E. Wacker Dr.

6. 1 E. Wacker Dr.

7. Leo Burnett Building
   35 W. Wacker Dr.

8. Combined International Insurance Building
   55 W. Wacker Dr.

9. R. R. Donnelley Center
   77 W. Wacker Dr.

10. 225 W. Wacker Dr.

11. 333 W. Wacker Dr.

12. Merchandise Mart
    350 N. Wells St.

13. City of Chicago Central Office Building
    325 N. LaSalle St.

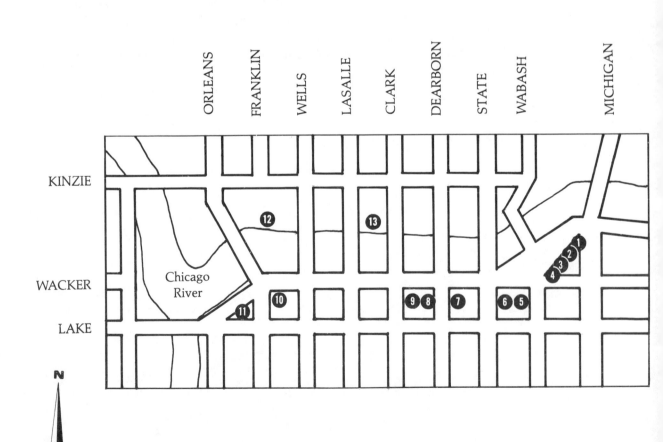

WALK 8 WACKER DRIVE: EAST–WEST

WALKING TIME: 1½ hours.

HOW TO GET THERE: Take a northbound CTA bus No. 11, No. 146, No. 147, or No. 151 on State Street. Get off at Michigan Avenue and Wacker Drive (300 N). Or walk east to Michigan Avenue, turn left and walk north to Wacker Drive.

This WALK begins at the intersection of East Wacker Drive and North Michigan Avenue, the spot where from 1803 to 1812 stood Fort Dearborn, one of the military outposts established by President Thomas Jefferson. Plaques on both sides of the street are the only reminders of this historic fact. If you stand near the Michigan Avenue bridge and look west, you can see an exciting panorama of today's Chicago along the banks of the Chicago River, where that primitive fort was once the only settlement. The array of contemporary architecture—vertical, horizontal, round, and square—would surely have astonished those early settlers, no matter how ambitious their visions for the future may have been.

The Chicago River, along which you walk, is famed as the river that runs backwards. In order to make it serve more adequately the commercial and sanitary needs of metropolitan Chicago, engineers reversed its current in 1922, so that it now flows from Lake Michigan to the Des Plaines River via canal, and on to the Mississippi River, rather than into Lake Michigan as nature intended. With the opening of the St. Lawrence Seaway in June 1959, the character of the boats seen on the river changed. Seagoing vessels from distant ports were sometimes anchored here—from England, Denmark, Sweden, Italy, and other far countries—along with the barges and pleasure boats still seen.

Wacker Drive, named for Charles Wacker, first chairman of the Chicago Plan Commission, was constructed in 1925, following up the Burnham Plan of 1909. The cluttered old South Water Street produce market was demolished to make way for this vast improvement.

Wacker Drive and North Michigan Avenue, along with the Michigan Avenue bridge, are double-decked, with a seemingly different life going on at the lower level. A double-decked ring road around the Loop had been proposed as part of the Burnham Plan of 1909, but the Wacker Drive segment was the only portion to be completed. Few stoplights slow the traffic on this lower level.

As you walk along the south river bank on Upper Wacker Drive between Franklin Street and Michigan Avenue, you will be on the Ira J. Bach Walkway.

A resolution adopted by the City Council of the City of Chicago reads:

Dedication of the Ira J. Bach Walkway
(Peter Schulz courtesy Elizabeth Hollander)

Whereas, the City of Chicago has been the beneficiary of the dedication, expertise, and commitment of Ira J. Bach for many years; and

Whereas, Ira J. Bach started his distinguished career in the public sector in 1946 when he was appointed Director of Planning for the Chicago Housing Authority; and

Whereas, Ira J. Bach has continually served the public as Executive Director of the Cook County Housing Authority, Executive Director of the Chicago Land Clearance Commission, the first Commissioner of Planning for the City of Chicago, Executive Director of the Chicago Dwellings Association, Administrator of the Illinois-Indiana Bi-State Planning Commission, Senior Projects Advisor and then Director of City Development for the Mayor Byrne administration and presently was reappointed Director of City Development by Mayor Harold Washington; and

Whereas, he has voluntarily participated in numerous organizations such as the Northeastern Illinois Planning Commission, the Commission on Chicago Historical and Architectural Landmarks; and

Whereas, he is a noted author having written numerous books on the architecture and landmarks of the Chicago metropolitan area . . . (which) have greatly improved our understanding of the beauty and importance of our City; and . . .

Whereas, Ira J. Bach has always been a person of quite unassuming humility, he has also been a very meticulous public servant; . . .

Be it resolved that the Mayor of City of Chicago and the Members of its Council duly assembled on this 25th day of April, 1984, hereby designate the walkway along Upper Wacker Drive between Franklin Street and Michigan Avenue bordering the Chicago River the "Ira J. Bach Walkway," a permanent expression of the City of Chicago's appreciation, acknowledgment, and gratitude to Ira J. Bach for his past, present, and future contributions to our City . . .

At the southwest corner of East Wacker Drive and North Michigan Avenue is the first stop on this WALK.

360 N. MICHIGAN　ARCHITECT: *Alfred S. Alschuler (1923)*

First the London Guarantee Building, then the Stone Container Building, it is especially well known for the replica of a Greek temple on its roof. Obviously, the designers were not following the standards of indigenous art that were developed by the late 19th-century architects of the Chicago school.

A few hundred feet west is the 24-story Lincoln Tower Building (formerly known as the Mather Tower), with its pseudo-Gothic ornamentation in terra-cotta.

LINCOLN TOWER BUILDING
75 E. Wacker

ARCHITECT: *Herbert H. Riddle (1928)*

This narrow structure is distinguished primarily by the fact that it has the smallest floor space per story of any commercial building in Chicago! Immediately to the west is our next stop.

EXECUTIVE PLAZA HOTEL
71 E. Wacker

ARCHITECTS: *Milton M. Schwartz and Associates (1960)*

This was designed as a high-quality hotel with special appeal to the business traveler—an appeal that has proved highly successful. The aquamarine-colored glass echoes the color of the river without matching it.

To the west is the handsome Seventeenth Church of Christ, Scientist.

SEVENTEENTH CHURCH OF CHRIST, SCIENTIST
55 E. Wacker

ARCHITECTS: *Harry Weese and Associates (1968)*

This church fits very well the wedge of land it occupies on a prominent corner of Heald Square. The bronze and glass street-level lobby, which leads to the auditorium one level above and the Sunday School one level below, serves as a reading room, sheltered from passersby and traffic by a sunken garden, which admits natural light to the Sunday school. The auditorium, seating 925, is the dominant element of the structure, and its semicircular geometry, with seats encircling the reader's platform, is expressed on the exterior in the curved travertine marble facade that turns the corner. The convex curve of the ceiling defuses organ sounds and rises to a domed lantern directly over the platform. Tours of the auditorium are available. The adjacent office wing accommodates space for meetings and committee work as well as mechanical equipment.

Amid the traffic outside the church is an area called Heald Square.

* HEALD SQUARE
E. Wacker and
N. Wabash

A block west of Michigan Avenue lies Heald Square, holding The Children's Fountain on one side and a sculpture of three figures from the American Revolutionary War on the other—Robert Morris, George Washington, and Haym Salomon. The square was named for Captain Nathan Heald, ill-fated commandant of Fort Dearborn at the time it was ordered evacuated. He was advised that the Indians would permit safe passage of the soldiers and their families. But as the group of 95 left the fort on August 15, 1812, they were attacked near what is now East 18th Street and South Prairie Avenue, and 53 were killed. (See WALK 18.)

On the south side of Heald Square is our next stop.

35 E. WACKER

ARCHITECTS: *Giaver and Dinkelberg,*
with Thielbar and Fugard as Associates (1926)

First known as the Jewelers Building and then as the North American Life Insurance Building, this building is topped with a neoclassical temple on each of the four corners, surrounding a huge central tower that rises to 523 feet. Not following any single architectural style, the designers, it may be said, have used an eclectic design, though the term Baroque would be more appropriate. The clock overhanging the corner weighs six tons.

Proceed west.

ONE E. WACKER

ARCHITECTS: *Shaw, Metz, and Associates (1962)*

This 41-story structure of white marble, built for the United Insurance Company, was once the tallest marble-faced commercial building in the world. The strongly vertical lines contrast sharply with the circular towers of Marina City across the river.

Continue west one block.

LEO BURNETT BUILDING
35 W. Wacker

ARCHITECTS: *Kevin Roche–John Dinkeloo and Associates (1989)*

Both vertical and horizontal accents, as well as imaginative use of color, add variety to this 50-story Constructivist design. Note how the copper-colored tiles on the roof of the arcaded entry continue into the lobby. Windows are deeply recessed throughout the greenish granite facade.

Cross Dearborn Street.

COMBINED INTERNATIONAL INSURANCE BUILDING
55 W. Wacker

ARCHITECTS: *C. F. Murphy and Associates (1968)*

This structure of beige-tinted concrete has vertical striations to emphasize its height. The rugged, heavy quality gives an effect of tremendous mass, too, especially in the upper section extending by cantilever construction beyond the lower part.

R. R. DONNELLEY CENTER
77 W. Wacker

ARCHITECTS: *Ricardo Bofill Arquitectura/Taller U.S.A., with DeStefano/Goetsch Ltd. (1992)*

For this noted Spanish architect's first U.S. building, he chose a classically inspired design with an exterior of polished granite and a curtainwall of silver-tinted glass. A small courtyard to the east is contained by a classical balustrade of molded concrete. The lobby features walls of polished white marble and a pink ceiling for a Mediterranean atmosphere, while reflective chrome elevators and sconces add a touch of art deco. Although the great amount of glass would seem to provide floor-to-ceiling windows for many offices, the floor construction on the 50 stories is conventional except at the top. There, the triangular pediment on all 4 sides, visible from afar or just across the street, creates very tall peaked conference rooms.

Continue west 3 blocks.

225 W. WACKER

ARCHITECTS: *Kohn, Pedersen and Fox; associate architects: Perkins and Will (1989)*

After the great acclaim for this team's building across the street at 333 W. Wacker, they designed this one as a counterpoint to the first. Its 31 stories of exterior masonry contrast with the glass next door, and round windows above the first floor echo a theme set by the grille ornaments next door at a similar height. Otherwise, the pair are too easily distinguished by this one's rooftop Gothic styling and its rather narrow lot.

333 Wacker Drive
(Barbara Karant courtesy Perkins and Will and Kohn Pederson Fox Associates)

333 W. WACKER

ARCHITECTS: *Kohn, Pedersen and Fox; associate architects: Perkins and Will (1983)*

This 36-floor granite and glass office building is one of the finest recent additions to Chicago's downtown area. It has a lobby with retail spaces and a colonnade at the bottom and office space above. The base is marble and granite, richly detailed with stainless steel. The well-detailed reflective glass curtainwall, along with granite, marble, and stainless steel create a striking view from the street. The lobby is granite, marble, stainless steel, and terrazzo. The curved facade reflects the bend in the river; the other facades, which are geometric, reflect the grid of the Loop.

Cross the Chicago River by the Franklin Street bridge to reach the Merchandise Mart.

MERCHANDISE MART
Merchandise Mart Plaza (about 350 N. Wells)

ARCHITECTS: *Graham, Anderson, Probst and White (1930); for the restoration: Graham, Anderson, Probst and White (1986–88)*

On the north side of the Chicago River, between Wells and Orleans streets, where the CTA elevated lines cross the river, looms the massive Merchandise Mart. Although its architectural design is hardly as distinguished or praiseworthy as it was thought to be at the time of construction, this building is nevertheless not to be missed. For many years the largest building in the world, the Merchandise Mart is still the world's largest wholesale marketing center and one of its largest commercial buildings. Its floor space amounts to about 4 million square feet, where more than 5,000 manufacturers and designers display their products, chiefly furniture and other home furnishings. Twice a year wholesale buyers from all across the country come to Chicago to the home furnishings show held here. The restoration involved repairing stone work, roof ornament, and terra-cotta, and installing about 4,000 new windows.

On the river side of the plaza stand tall columns with the busts of those retailers who have been elected to the "Merchandise Mart Hall of Fame": Julius Rosenwald, Frank Winfield Woolworth, Marshall Field, John Wanamaker, George Huntington Hartford, Edward A. Filene, Robert E. Wood, and A. Montgomery Ward.

The complex to the west, of steel and precast concrete cladding, opened in 1976. One tower is the Apparel Mart, an addition to the parent structure; the taller one contains exhibition space and a hotel. The Mart is owned by the Kennedy family, who bought it in 1945 from the Marshall Field family.

Although not all floors of the Mart are open to the public, there are tours of the building. The tours are given on Monday, Wednesday, and Friday at 10 A.M. and 1:30 P.M. and last approximately 1½ hours. Children under 16 years old are not allowed on the tours. Call 644-4664 for information.

Walk east along the river bank.

* CITY OF CHICAGO CENTRAL OFFICE BUILDING
325 N. LaSalle

ARCHITECT: *George C. Nimmons (1913)*

West of Clark Street, still on the river front, is the City of Chicago Central Office Building, holding a traffic court and other city offices. Formerly the Reid, Murdoch and Company Building, it was leased, then sold, to the city. This is a clean, straightforward structure in red brick—its 320-foot-long facade of 8 stories is topped off at the center with a prominent clock tower of 4 more stories. The brick work and contrasting terra-cotta accents give this structure a pleasing effect.

To return to State Street, cross to the south bank of the Chicago River and walk east 2 blocks on the Ira J. Bach Walkway.

View of Wacker Drive, with the Stone Container Building and the Ira J. Bach walkway along the bottom
(Robert Thall courtesy Commission on Chicago Landmarks)

1. 311 S. Wacker Dr.

2. MidAmerica Commodity Exchange
   444 W. Jackson Blvd.

3. Union Station
   210 S. Canal St.

4. 222 S. Riverside Plaza Building

5. 150 S. Wacker Drive Building

6. 200 S. Wacker Dr.

7. Sears Tower
   233 S. Wacker Dr.

8. The Northern Building
   125 S. Wacker Dr.

9. U.S. Gypsum Building
   101 S. Wacker Dr.

10. Harris Trust and Savings Bank
    111 W. Monroe St.

11. The Chicago Mercantile Exchange
    10 and 30 S. Wacker Dr.

12. Hartford Building
    100 S. Wacker Dr.

13. 120 S. Riverside Plaza Building

14. 10 S. Riverside Plaza Building

15. 500 W. Monroe St.

16. Presidential Towers
    555, 575, 605, and
    625 W. Madison St.

17. Social Security Administration
    Great Lakes Program Service Center
    600 W. Madison St.

18. Northwestern Atrium Center
    500 W. Madison St.

19. Riverside Plaza Building
    2 N. Riverside Plaza

20. Morton International Building
    100 N. Riverside Plaza

21. 1 S. Wacker Dr.

22. Civic Opera Building
    20 N. Wacker Dr.

23. 101 N. Wacker Dr.

24. 123 N. Wacker Dr.

25. Illinois Bell Telephone Building
    225 W. Randolph St.

WALK 9 GATEWAY AREA: SOUTH BRANCH OF CHICAGO RIVER

WALKING TIME: About 2 hours.
HOW TO GET THERE: Walk east 2 blocks to Michigan Avenue. Take a southbound CTA bus No. 1. Get off at Jackson Boulevard (300 S) and Wacker Drive (348 W).

Wacker Drive, which here runs north and south, intersecting Van Buren Street, is the same street you followed from east to west in WALK 8. The change in direction took place just after the end of that WALK, where Wacker Drive follows a bend in the Chicago River and then turns directly south, at Lake Street, to follow the South Branch of the river.

Daniel Burnham, in his plan for Chicago back in 1909, saw Wacker Drive as part of a ring of roads surrounding the Loop. Incidentally, Burnham also anticipated the need for a highway comparable to the Eisenhower Expressway. With this plan in mind, the architects designed the Central Post Office building in the 1920s with a large opening in the center at street level. Subsequently, the Eisenhower Expressway passed through and under the building with a minimum of inconvenience to the Post Office.

This section of the city is sometimes referred to as the Gateway area, since Wacker Drive and the South Branch of the Chicago River are in fact a gateway to the near west. South Wacker Drive, formerly the wholesale garment section of the city, lost hundreds of tenants to the Merchandise Mart when that building was constructed, in 1930 (see WALK 8). This change forecast in a way the Drive's ongoing redevelopment.

311 S. WACKER ARCHITECTS: *Kohn, Pedersen and Fox with Harwood K. Smith and Partners (1990)*

For almost 20 years people approaching the city from the west saw the Sears Tower looming nearly alone on the skyline; this quirky building joins the shapely Sears in marking the southwest edge of the downtown area. With a 65-story tower, flanked by 51-story wings, it is the largest reinforced-concrete structure in the world (surpassing Water Tower Place). The top sports two turrets reminiscent of the old Water Tower, while the rest of the exterior consists of 3 colors of granite (polished and not) and 5 shades of marble, as well as aluminum framing around 5 styles of windows.

311 S. Wacker
(courtesy Lincoln Property Company)

At street level the building fills its lot facing Franklin Street but a Winter Garden projects from the main structure some 200 feet to Wacker Drive. This barrel-vaulted glass arcade soars 100 feet and contains palm trees, a sunken garden cafe, and a balcony connected to passageways that daringly combine steel I-beams and marble in their design. Dominating the atrium is a 24-foot bronze fountain with a 15-foot water wall, "Gem of the Lakes," by Raymond Kaskey, depicting Neptune on a clamshell. The landscaping on the building's northwest is generous, but the southwest is a parking lot.

Walk west on Jackson Boulevard, crossing the river.

**MIDAMERICA
COMMODITY
EXCHANGE**
444 W. Jackson

ARCHITECTS: *Skidmore, Owings and Merrill (1972)*

Supported by four huge columns over air rights of the Union Station, this distinctive dark green glass building is skillfully engineered. A combination of columns, crisscross girders, and walls transfers the entire load of the roof and floor to the four main columns to make possible a column-free interior. The dimensions are 225 feet facing Jackson and 100 feet facing the Chicago River. The height of the old trading room is 60 feet. (Trading activities have since moved to LaSalle Street.)

Walk west to Canal Street and turn north.

UNION STATION
210 S. Canal

ARCHITECTS: *Graham, Anderson, Probst and White (1925)*

Union Station formerly covered two square blocks instead of one, yet it remains one of the few enormous railway terminals in existence. The section fronting the river was razed in 1970 and replaced by the 222 S. Riverside Plaza and 444 W. Jackson buildings; the concourse levels of these buildings now serve as the main corridors for entering and departing passengers.

The closing of other south Loop railway terminals brought several lines into Union Station, leaving four terminals in the Loop area (the others are the Northwestern Station, LaSalle Street Station, and the Illinois Central under Michigan Avenue). In addition to Amtrak's long-distance riders, Union Station serves commuters from western and northwestern suburbs.

In the early 1990s the Station's lower facade was cleaned and the interior extensively remodeled. The cavernous, classical-pillared Great Hall remains, an architectural focal point seen by few of the passengers hurrying elsewhere.

Continue north.

**222 S. RIVERSIDE
PLAZA BUILDING**

ARCHITECTS: *Skidmore, Owings and Merrill (1972)*

This 35-story building—constructed on air rights of the railway tracks—was the third office building of the Gateway Center complex. The project's 80,000 square-foot plaza provides all pedestrian and vehicular entrances to the office tower and railroad.

The superstructure was a composite structural system consisting of structural steel interior framing and reinforced concrete, exterior-bearing wall. The exterior of the building has a light-colored architectural concrete finish, complementing the steel buildings of the Gateway Center.

Walk east on Adams Street, across the river to Wacker Drive.

150 S. WACKER DRIVE BUILDING

ARCHITECTS: *Skidmore, Owings and Merrill (1971)*

The Hartford Plaza has been extended to form a platform for this 33-story office building by the same owners and architects as the Hartford Building. The lower concourse connects the two structures and provides space for a complex of restaurants and shops.

This building's reinforced concrete bearing walls are clad in black granite. From the 10th floor down, alternate columns transfer vertical loads to spandrels of increasing depth to form the major column system at plaza level.

200 S. WACKER

ARCHITECTS: *Harry Weese and Associates (1981)*

This 38-story building has an unusual plan, designed to fit the small site and the angle of the river. The building is an asymmetrical four-sided polygon composed of a right triangle joined at the hypotenuse with its mirror image. The 3-story, glass enclosed lobby is set back from the building's perimeter to create a pedestrian arcade at street level and downstairs along the river. Two partial mezzanines, which float within the lobby, provide commercial space. The extensive use of glass brings natural light to these spaces. There is a 2-story health club below street level. The facade is of reinforced concrete and glass; the tower is sheathed in a curtainwall of painted aluminum panels and tinted insulating glass and reflective spandrel glass.

SEARS TOWER
233 S. Wacker

ARCHITECTS: *Skidmore, Owings and Merrill (1974, 1984–85)*

Upon completion in 1974, Chicago's Sears Tower became the largest private office complex in the world. The total development contains a gross area of 4.4 million square feet with 101 acres of floor space. The daily population is 16,500 people.

The Sears Tower itself is the world's tallest structure, enclosing 3.9 million gross square feet of floor area rising 110 stories or 1454 feet above its grade, 12 feet more above Chicago City datum. It is 100 feet higher than the twin towers of New York's World Trade Center and approximately 325 feet higher than the roof of the John Hancock Center.

The tower consists of a structural-steel frame bolted in place on the site. The fireproofed frame is clad in a black aluminum skin and bronze-tinted, glare-reducing glass. The exterior sloping plaza has a granite surface. The space below the plaza has 3 full levels, which include a cafeteria and tenant storage space.

In 1984 major renovations were undertaken by the original firm. A striking 4-story, glass-enclosed, domed entrance was added on Wacker Drive; extending from the street, it shelters visitors from the weather. In 1993 an ornamental arcade was added to the south plaza.

The 103rd-floor Skydeck affords spectacular views of Chicago and environs. It is open every day from 9 A.M. to 11 P.M. in March–September and 10 A.M. to 10 P.M. the rest of the year. Call 875-9696 for information. Call 875-9447 for reservations.

Cross Adams Street.

THE NORTHERN BUILDING
125 S. Wacker

ARCHITECTS: *The Perkins & Will Partnership (1974)*

This 30-story structure, on the northeast corner of Wacker Drive and Adams Street, has an attractive exterior that consists of granite-faced columns with an infill of anodized aluminum that frame the dark glass windows. The floor plan has an off-center utility core that is not visible from the street.

Walk north on Wacker Drive.

U.S. GYPSUM BUILDING
101 S. Wacker

ARCHITECTS: *The Perkins & Will Partnership (1961)*

At the southeast corner of Monroe Street and Wacker Drive is the U.S. Gypsum Building. Its placement on the building lot—at a 45-degree angle from the street lines—caused some consternation among the adherents of the Chicago school of architecture. Many of them felt that this departure from the usual procedure insulted the unity of the buildings that Chicago school architects had developed in the Loop over more than half a century. Many others, however, admired the arrangement and the building itself, designed as a trademark to symbolize the company and the materials the company mines. For example, the triangular character of the plazas and the shape of the building itself (note that each of the 19 stories has 8 corners!) were designed to represent the crystalline mineral in gypsum. The soberness of the slate panels and gray glass is offset by the columns of white Vermont marble, which also give the building a sweeping vertical effect. The company outgrew these quarters and moved a block east in 1992 (see WALK 6).

Walk east on Monroe.

HARRIS TRUST AND SAVINGS BANK
111 W. Monroe

ARCHITECTS: *A. Epstein and Sons, Inc. (1973)*

Just east of the U.S. Gypsum Building, on the southwest corner of Franklin and Monroe streets, is this 15-story structure that houses the bank's data processing and computer departments. There is a complete banking facility on the main floor and a drive-through bank. The structure is a modular design with a tinted-glass and granite-exterior facade.

Backtrack west to Wacker Drive and turn north.

THE CHICAGO MERCANTILE EXCHANGE
10 and 30 S. Wacker

ARCHITECTS: *Fujikawa Johnson and Associates (1984–86)*

The Chicago Mercantile Exchange trading floors form a focal point and connecting base for twin towers, each containing 1.1 million square feet of office space. The exteriors are clad in Carnelian granite and solar-gray tinted glass. The trading floors of the south tower were completed in 1984 and the north tower in 1986.

In order to achieve the required amount of floor space in the office towers, without infringing on the clear spanned space of the two trading floors, the top 34-stories of each tower had to be cantilevered 32 feet over the low-rise building. Site constraints led to the design of the serrated corners, which allow sixteen corner offices per floor.

The two trading floors contain a total of 70,000 square feet. The main trading room measures 215 feet by 90 feet by 30 feet high and contains 40,000 square feet of clear span trading space. The expansion trading floor is located immediately above the main floor and has 30,000 square feet of clear span space.

The facility also has retail space and a 4-level parking garage below. A public promenade along the Chicago River, connecting Madison and Monroe streets, affords an excellent place to rest and view the river.

Cross to the south side of Monroe Street.

HARTFORD BUILDING
100 S. Wacker

ARCHITECTS: *Skidmore, Owings and Merrill (1961)*

On the southwest corner of Wacker Drive and Monroe Street is the Hartford Building—of the Hartford Fire Insurance Company. Here the architects exaggerated the old Chicago school belief that the facade of a building should disclose its interior structure. The 21-story concrete skeleton becomes more than a framework: it serves as sunshades for the interior and gives the building a constantly changing pattern of light and shadow during the day.

Walk west on Monroe Street.

120 S. RIVERSIDE PLAZA BUILDING

ARCHITECTS: *Skidmore, Owings and Merrill (1974)*

10 S. RIVERSIDE PLAZA BUILDING

ARCHITECTS: *Skidmore, Owings and Merrill (1968)*

Union Station and its concourse soon gave way to development of nearby Gateway Center. These first two buildings, on either side of Monroe Street and just north of the station's concourse exit ramp on Adams Street, were built on air rights over the tracks leading to Union Station. In extending the business center west of the Chicago River, they also continued the style of the Chicago school of architecture. The tinted glass

Hartford Building
(Ezra Stoller courtesy Skidmore, Owings and Merrill)

and russet beams used in the buildings give them the functional exterior framework of the old school.

Surrounded by wide plazas, these two buildings look somewhat squat and bulky, despite their 20-story height—a characteristic dictated by construction over the tracks. The wide architectural spans, similar to those used by the same architects in the Richard J. Daley Center, were made possible by the omission of any columns between the center service core and the exterior columns.

From Gateway Center Plaza along the river bank you have a distant view of two markedly different architectural neighbors just seen on the east side of the river—the Hartford Building, a contemporary expression of the still vibrant Chicago school of architecture, and its sculptured neighbor, the U.S. Gypsum Building, sitting gracefully askew on its site.

Walk west to Canal Street.

500 W. MONROE   ARCHITECT: *Skidmore, Owings and Merrill, design partner Adrian Smith (1992)*

The decorative gilded dome (note the faux windows within) and gleaming brass doors at the northwest corner of Canal and Monroe streets welcome the walker more readily than many large buildings do. Polished granite and art deco aluminum ornament also adorn the first 2 levels, while stone cladding covers the rest. The lobby features vast panels of birch and polished marble. From beneath the 44-story tower, a block-length arcade along the south side slopes gently downhill to the west, where the structure rises only 7 stories.

Follow the arcade to Clinton Street, then walk one block north and turn west on Madison Street.

PRESIDENTIAL TOWERS
555, 575, 605, and 625 W. Madison

ARCHITECTS: *Solomon, Cordwell and Buenz (1985–86)*

Presidential Towers consists of four 49-story apartment towers. Each has a 3-story base. The main entrance is through a 40-foot skylit atrium. The atrium connects the shopping mall with a winter garden and a third-level pedestrian arcade. The arcade bridges the street at two locations, linking the towers and the enclosed parking structure. The third level also contains laundry facilities, tenant storage, commercial space, a fully equipped health club with an enclosed swimming pool, basketball court, a one-seventh mile running track, and access to the outdoor recreation deck. The tower floor plans are designed for maximum efficiency, with short corridor lengths and well proportioned apartments ranging from 461 to 1,140 square feet. Chamfered corners allow eight corner units per floor. The exteriors are of painted and rusticated cast-in-place concrete and tinted glass. The ground level is extensively landscaped to provide a parklike setting.

Every effort was made to attract tenants to this previously nonresidential location in an area that had long been blighted. The complex succeeded.

Continue west.

Social Security Administration Program Service Center
(Bill Engdahl, Hedrich-Blessing courtesy Lester B. Knight)

SOCIAL SECURITY ADMINISTRATION GREAT LAKES PROGRAM SERVICE CENTER
600 W. Madison

ARCHITECTS: *Lester B. Knight & Associates (1976)*

This 10-story structure sits on a 2.3-acre site, a complete city block. It was a pioneer in the redevelopment of the Near West Side. The design is an early example of the modular systems approach to open planned office space. The utility cores are placed at the building perimeter and are expressed as solid shafts of precast concrete intercepting the silvery glass curtainwall around the office areas. The same exposed aggregate concrete is used for the plazas, sidewalks, and lobby walls of the first floor. The transparent glass used around the recessed first floor is set in mirror-finish stainless steel frames to complement the concrete finish, giving the building a distinctive, high tech image.

Three significant works of art augment the building design. On the exterior, the superscale "Bat Column" by Claes Oldenburg is positioned to interplay with the glass curtainwall. An extensive porcelain enamel mural by Ilya Bolotowsky surrounds the first floor lobby. In the employees' cafeteria, several large terra-cotta panels designed by Louis Sullivan in 1894 for the Scoville Building, formerly on the site, are used as a decorative screen.

Walk east two blocks on Madison Street.

NORTHWESTERN ATRIUM CENTER
500 W. Madison

ARCHITECTS: *Murphy/Jahn (1987)*

This 40-story combined commuter terminal and office building complex replaced the Chicago and Northwestern Commuter Station of 1911. The 1.6-million-square-foot building forms a major gateway between the Loop to the east and the urban renewal area to the west. A skywalk crosses Canal Street to 2 N. Riverside Plaza.

The steel building has a curtainwall of blue enameled aluminum and blue and silver glass in a pattern of setbacks that recalls the look of a streamlined train. A continuous arcade along Madison Street leads to a sequence of multistory atria, creating a commuter walkway full of light and spatial excitement.

The office tower above the commuter facilities is served from a sky-lobby one floor above track level. Floors vary in size from roughly 30,000 to 50,000 square feet, and the large floor areas are broken up by the shifting shapes of the building.

Continue east.

RIVERSIDE PLAZA BUILDING
2 N. Riverside Plaza

ARCHITECTS: *Holabird and Root (1928)*

With its setbacks and angles, this building is an excellent example of the Chicago skyscraper of the 1920s. A colorful remnant of the building's original occupancy by the Chicago Daily News can be seen in the excellent murals on the lobby ceiling. The work of noted Chicago muralist John Norton, the scenes depict newspaper production. Outside, carved limestone friezes facing the riverside esplanade memorialize some of journalism's pioneers. From this space you can see the building more fully, sitting sphinx-like as it was designed.

Walk north along the riverside.

MORTON INTERNATIONAL BUILDING
100 N. Riverside Plaza

ARCHITECTS: *Perkins and Will (1990)*

Morton International, for 30 years headquartered directly across the river in an Indiana limestone structure just 4 stories above grade, set a contemporary tone here. The style of this 36-story building, however, harkens back to ideas of Russian Constructivism and the Dutch de Stijl movements of the 1920s. The 12-story south end is topped off by a nonfunctional A-frame roof, and structural elements protrude from the sides and base, too. Despite the look of a work-in-progress, the tower is firmly anchored on the train tracks beneath the site—visible from the Lake Street bridge a block north. The city's riverside walkways continue here on 2 levels, the upper one a pleasingly graduated series that breaks up a long site.

Backtrack along the river to Madison Street and cross to Wacker Drive.

ONE S. WACKER ARCHITECTS: *Murphy/Jahn (1982)*

The design of this glinting edifice sets back twice to create three typical floor areas of 38,000, 32,000, and 26,000 gross square feet. This corresponds to the three elevator groups serving the building. Another setback occurs at the mechanical penthouse. The variety of possible floor arrangements is further increased by a 3-story atrium, located above and below the setbacks. This creates U-shaped floor areas that increase the perimeter and daylight exposure without an added exterior wall, resulting in an energy savings. The whole is essentially an adaptation of the typical office tower of the early 1920s to today's standards.

At the ground floor, the atrium extends into a multilevel commercial galleria that serves as a civilized public throughway between the Wacker Drive and Madison Street entrances. This arrangement puts the public space inside the building and keeps the commercial space on the exterior along the street. The facade, on a 5-foot module, reinforces the articulated shape and reduces the bulk of the tower. The facade is created by filling in the abstract grid with silver and gray reflective glass.

Cross diagonally to the Civic Opera Building.

CIVIC OPERA BUILDING
20 N. Wacker

ARCHITECTS: *Graham, Anderson, Probst and White (1929)*

Another example of the Chicago skyscraper of the 1920s is this 45-story building for a time known as the Kemper Insurance Building. The immense structure was erected at a cost of some $20 million by Samuel Insull, boss of Commonwealth Edison. It opened in the unlucky year of 1929. The subsequent ruin of Insull's financial empire, to say nothing of the dubious methods he had used in building it up, unfortunately wiped out whatever pleasant associations Chicago might have had with the name of a man who loved opera. And the fact that the construction of this building led to the closing of the Auditorium Theatre seemed to many Chicago opera lovers a cause for resentment rather than gratitude. (The Depression had a role, too; see WALK 1.) Herman Kogan has expressed this harsh but understandable judgment of Sam Insull (Kogan, Herman, and Wendt, Lloyd. *Chicago: A Pictorial History.* New York: E. P. Dutton and Company, 1958, p. 203):

> More than any one man, he was responsible for the abandonment of the glorious Auditorium as a center of music and opera, because he had built, in an illogical place and with inferior acoustics, his own Civic Opera House . . .

Civic Opera House
(Olga Stefanos)

Whatever the sentiments toward Insull, however, his building has not gone empty. The current Lyric Opera of Chicago uses its auditorium, seating 3,500 people, just as two other opera companies did before the Lyric was formed. Hundreds of offices are available in the remainder of this mammoth structure, which has never been fully occupied.

Cross diagonally again, heading north.

101 N. WACKER   ARCHITECTS: *Perkins & Will (1980)*

This 24-story office building was built with energy conservation in mind. Heat-absorbing, insulated glass is on all four sides of the building; a special reflective coating is on the inside face of the glass on the west and south sides. Horizontal bands of light and dark gray glass create a lively exterior.

Continue north.

123 N. WACKER   ARCHITECTS: *Perkins & Will (1986)*

This 30-story office tower with commercial space on the ground floor is small compared to other recent Loop high-rises. It is located on one of the broadest streets in Chicago, with this portion of Wacker Drive claiming a wide range of building styles and architectural types, everything from the world's tallest building (Sears Tower) to the art deco Civic Opera House.

The developer required a dignified and elegant building, marketable as a headquarters for an insurance company. The design challenge was to give this relatively small building a dignified prominence on the street.

Steel-frame construction and granite from top to bottom were the first step. Height is accentuated by two continuous columns, together with strong vertical stripes of alternating dark and light gray reflective glass. The uppermost three floors form a transparent pyramid, allowing an atrium and very dramatic views.

Walk east on Randolph Street to Franklin Street.

ILLINOIS BELL TELEPHONE BUILDING
225 W. Randolph

ARCHITECTS: *Holabird and Root (1967)*

This building of the Illinois Bell Telephone Company makes an effective use of vertical lines of marble and glass, dramatized at night by the interior lighting. This is a first-rate modern structure, from a period when little was built downtown.

This concludes the WALK. To return to State Street, walk east 5 blocks on Randolph Street.

1. (Old) Franklin Building
   525 S. Dearborn St.

2. Terminals Building
   537 S. Dearborn St.

3. Duplicator Building
   530 S. Dearborn St.

4. Morton Building
   538 S. Dearborn St.

5. Pontiac Building
   542 S. Dearborn St.

6. Mergenthaler Building
   531 S. Plymouth Ct.

7. Moser Building
   621 S. Plymouth Ct.

8. Pope Building
   633 S. Plymouth Ct.

9. Transportation Building
   600 S. Dearborn St.

10. Printer's Square
    600–780 S. Federal St.

11. Grace Place
    637 S. Dearborn St.

12. Donohue Building
    701–721 S. Dearborn St.

13. Rowe Building
    714 S. Dearborn St.

14. Franklin Building
    720 S. Dearborn St.

15. River City
    800 S. Wells St.

16. Dearborn Street Station
    South Dearborn St. at West Polk St.

17. Lakeside Press Building
    731 S. Plymouth Ct.

18. The Terraces

19. The High-Rises

20. The Mid-Rises

21. The Gardenhomes

22. The Townhouses

23. The Townhomes

24. The Oaks

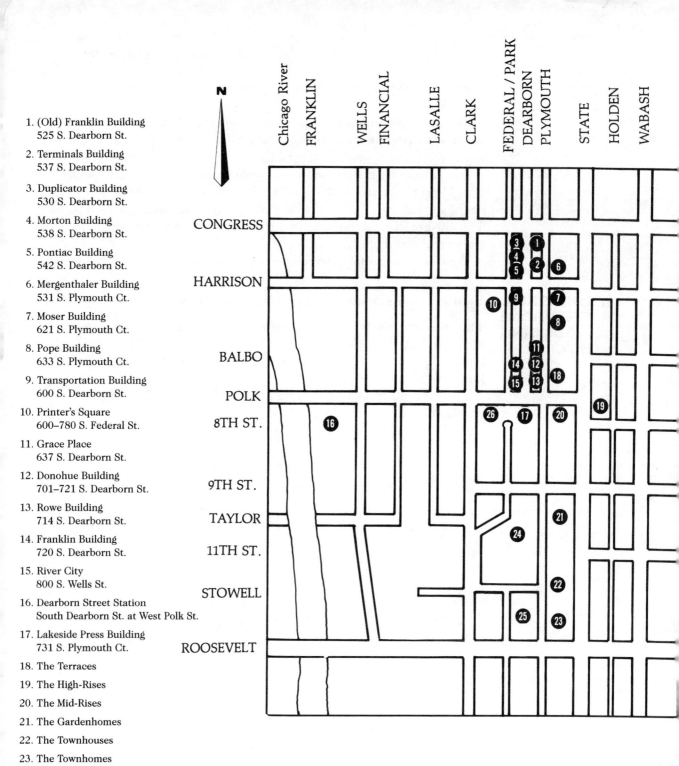

WALK 10 PRINTERS ROW AND DEARBORN PARK

WALKING TIME: About 1½ hours.
HOW TO GET THERE: Take a southbound CTA bus No. 29 on State Street and get off at Congress Street (500 S). Walk west across Plymouth Court, to Dearborn Street (36 W), which runs parallel to State Street.

Printers Row (also called Printing House Row) is a 2-block stretch of Dearborn Street, between Congress Parkway and Polk Street, consisting of historic structures once involved in the printing industry, and vacant land now used for parking. This WALK did not appear in early editions of this book because the area wasn't a neighborhood until 1977. Here are the true urban pioneers living in one of Chicago's better kept secrets.

The five general co-partners for the development were Baird and Warner, Ivan Himmell Companies, Theodore Gaines, Larry Booth, and Harry Weese. Development in the area began with the Donohue Building in 1976. The majority of projects along Dearborn Street were developed by members of the Community Resources Corporation partnership.

Harry Weese took a lead role in the revitalization of the area, including taking equity positions in individual projects and risking his own capital. He advocated the continued use and preservation of this benignly neglected section of the city after the train station had been closed. He prepared the 1976 nomination petition to place the * South Loop Printing House District on the National Register of Historic Places.

Begin the WALK on the southeast corner of Dearborn and Congress streets. Look at the clock tower on Dearborn Station at the south end of the street. It will be described later in the WALK. After the Dearborn Street Station opened in 1885, many printers and publishers built plants in this area because of the proximity of the railroads. The architects of virtually every building in Printers Row took some features from the Dearborn Station and incorporated them in the later buildings.

Old Franklin Building
(courtesy Booth/Hansen and Associates)

(OLD) FRANKLIN BUILDING
525 S. Dearborn

ARCHITECT: *Unknown (1888); for the adaptive reuse: Booth/Hansen and Associates (1983)*

Dubbed the Old Franklin Building after the newer one was built in 1912, this and the Duplicator Building across the street are the oldest on the block. The red brick, 7-story building has 54 apartments above a commercial ground floor. The exterior has been cleaned and restored and new windows have been installed. The interior has been completely renovated. The building is listed on the National Register of Historic Places.

TERMINALS
BUILDING
537 S. Dearborn

ARCHITECTS: *John Mills Van Osdel (1892); for the adaptive reuse:*
Harry Weese and Associates (1986)

Completed after his death, this was the last building of Van Osdel, who was responsible for all of Chicago's major buildings built before and shortly after the Chicago Fire. (His oldest remaining building is the McCarthy Building of 1872, at Washington and Dearborn streets.) The Terminals Building has a heavy rusticated base with a squared entrance and two very prominent oriels. Above the door, sandstone faces representing the nation's many heritages are sadly fading away.

The 14-story building has undergone exterior cleaning and the windows have been replaced. The interior was completely rehabilitated to hold 52 apartments above a commercial ground floor.

Across the street is a unique and unexpected idea: a hotel created by splicing together two buildings.

DUPLICATOR
BUILDING
530 S. Dearborn

ARCHITECT: *Unknown (1886)*

MORTON
BUILDING
538 S. Dearborn

ARCHITECTS: *Jenney and Mundie (1896); for the adaptive reuse:*
Booth/Hansen and Associates (1986–87)

Now linked as a single hotel numbered 500 S. Dearborn, these two buildings are a microcosm of the district's rebirth. The Duplicator Building was built in a style reflecting the functional requirements of the printing industry. The innovative metal frame design was the result of the latest developments by the Chicago school of architecture. Abandoned in the early 1960s, the building's interior later collapsed.

The Morton Building was erected a decade later for what is now the Morton Salt Company. Designed by the eminent architectural firm of Jenney and Mundie, the building reflects the influence of classicism, which resulted from the World's Columbian Exposition of 1893.

The hotel of 161 rooms was created by joining together the floors of two older buildings and adding a third building next door in a sympathetic style. The Duplicator, a 7-story building, uses red brick like the Old Franklin building, but is plainer. The Morton has polygonal bays like the Terminals Building across the street. Supporting the bays are remnants of the neoclassical revival—two "Atlas" figures. The building is made of a light brick and has segmental keystone lintels, an almost Georgian detail. Its up-to-date interior design features reminders of the history of Chicago.

On the northwest corner of Harrison and Dearborn streets is a reddish building with two huge, sweeping bays.

* PONTIAC BUILDING
542 S. Dearborn

ARCHITECTS: *Holabird and Roche (1891); for the adaptive reuse: Booth/Hansen and Associates (1986)*

This is Holabird and Roche's oldest surviving building in Chicago. One of the great pioneering efforts of the Chicago school, the Pontiac Building is listed on the National Register of Historic Places. Sparse in decoration, its liveliness is based on its window treatments.

The 14-story, fireproof, riveted steel frame building of dark brown masonry has a sandstone base and tile arch floor slabs. Massive projecting bays above the second floor level, trimmed with red terra-cotta, run continuously from the 3rd to the 13th floor.

Now in adaptive reuse as an office building, it has a commercial ground floor. The building has been completely renovated. The exterior was cleaned, new windows installed, new storefront detail (to match the original cast iron) was made, and a new lobby with mahogany paneling, granite flooring, and brass fittings and fixtures installed. The original brass plate cage of the elevators was also refurbished.

The short building of brick and pressed board on the northeast corner holds the offices of Booth/Hansen and Associates. This firm rehabilitated the most projects on Printers Row, including three on this block.

Turn left on Harrison Street and continue 1 block. The building on the northeast corner was originally known as the Mergenthaler Linotype Building.

MERGENTHALER BUILDING
531 S. Plymouth

ARCHITECTS: *Schmidt, Garden and Martin (1886); for the addition and remodeling: Schmidt, Garden and Martin, Samuel N. Crowen associate architect (1917); for the adaptive reuse: Ken Schroeder and Associates (1981)*

On a tour that visits many ingenious examples of adaptive reuse, this 6-story structure is one of the most clever. Into the original entrance Ken Schroeder has inserted a new post and lintel (the most basic of all architectural structures) in red, consisting of two pillars supporting a beam. As if further proof were necessary that this is no longer an old factory, there is a neon address sign above the door.

At the building's southwest corner is the remnants of Tom's Grill. The entire building is gone except for this framework. Plants grow where its floor used to be; ivy grows up the columns. This structure is also a post and lintel construction, as is the wacky parking entrance on the south side of the building. Like suburbanites returning home, the residents here use an automatic garage door opener to enter through a roll-up door supported not by a building but by a simple iron fence.

Also on the south side is one of the building's most notable additions— four wedge-shaped bays added onto the wall. These bays, with their multipaned windows, function on the outside to make people stop and observe. On the inside they create a beautiful small area with a south-facing view; mirrors inside form a "trick reveal," looking like a glass wall.

Continue ½ block south on Plymouth Court.

MOSER BUILDING
621 S. Plymouth

ARCHITECTS: *Holabird and Roche (1909); for the adaptive reuse: Lisec and Biederman (1986–87)*

This was originally the Moser Paper Company, associated with the printing businesses of the area. The 9-story building has been cleaned and all windows have been replaced with reproductions of the originals. The interior has been totally redone, only the octagonal columns with their conical octagonal capitals being retained. There are 88 apartments above a commercial ground floor. Note the original company logo preserved in the lobby floor.

POPE BUILDING
633 S. Plymouth

ARCHITECTS: *H.G. Hodgkins (1904); for the adaptive reuse: Lisec and Biederman (1986)*

This 12-story building originally housed a printing company. It is now in adaptive reuse with 91 apartments and retail space on the ground floor. The exterior, including the terra-cotta, was restored. The building boasts a lively combination of windows. Large picture windows, rising through bays containing three windows each, are followed by a story with Chicago windows, then multipaned windows whose narrow spaces create a definite vertical emphasis. All windows are replacements, conforming to the original designs. The mullions and window frames are painted an attention-getting green, also a restoration to the original, which conforms with the requirements placed on buildings listed on the National Register of Historic Places. The floors, vaulted ceilings, and elevator doors were preserved, whereas the rest of the interior was completely redone.

Walk west through the parking lot back to Dearborn Street. The huge building on the west side is called the Transportation Building.

TRANSPORTATION BUILDING
600 S. Dearborn

ARCHITECTS: *Fred V. Prather (1911); for the adaptive reuse: Harry Weese and Associates (1983)*

Originally serving as offices for many small companies involved with the railroad industry, this building of reinforced concrete with a pragmatically buff-colored brick facade almost overwhelms the street. It is very shallow, but very wide along Dearborn Street, and tall enough to sway in Chicago's winds. The 22-story building now has 294 apartments above a commercial ground floor.

During the recent work, the original integrity of the container was respected: the windows were replaced; the interior was completely remodeled, maintaining the original circulation, which was fortunately up to more modern code requirements; and the exterior was cleaned. The tall ceilings and wide windows provide wonderful views to the lake on the east and the expanse of the city to the west.

From the Pope Building's south end, cross Dearborn Street and walk west through the small park.

PRINTERS SQUARE
600-780 S. Federal

ARCHITECTS: *Frost and Granger (1909); Charles S. Frost (1912); Charles S. Frost and Charles C. Henderson (1928); for the adaptive reuse: Louis Arthur Weiss (1983)*

Printers Square is the adaptive reuse of five older buildings, known as the Borland buildings, tied to the newest one. The three northern structures were built in 1909, with additions following to the south in 1912 and 1928. Designed as manufacturing buildings, they have as high a floor load capacity as any in the city—250 pounds per square foot.

The conversion to Printers Square was one of the largest privately financed redevelopment projects in the country. Covering 600,000 square feet, the development includes 356 apartments in a total of twenty-six floor plans, a 180-car garage, 90,000 square feet of offices, and 70,000 square feet of retail space. The interiors were completely redesigned and all mechanical systems were replaced. All windows were replaced with ones in a compatible design. The addition was designed with compatible masonry and a glass curtainwall.

Walk east back through the park. On the east side of the street is a small 3-story building.

GRACE PLACE
637 S. Dearborn

ARCHITECTS: *for the adaptive reuse: Booth/Hansen and Associates (1985)*

Here in a town of lofts and rehabilitations is a church—a loft church. This small printing building, whose architect is unknown, was built about 1915. An Episcopal church and a Lutheran church, their congregants drawn from throughout the city, share the meeting hall and the chapel. There is also a newly installed dance floor.

The whole is a conglomeration of shapes and textures. The coatroom and adjoining wall have cut-out openings in the shape of gabled churches. There is also a slight nautical feel given by doors with porthole windows. The columns supporting the floors are unadorned rough-hewn timber. The newly installed ductwork is left exposed and painted gray in true high tech fashion.

The second floor is the sanctuary. At the entrance you look through more gabled church openings toward the pews, which are surrounded by a circular wall. When you enter this space your attention is focused on the pulpit, behind which a piece of sheet metal does double duty—as a bracket holding a post and beam together, and as the sanctuary's cross. Talk about melding form and function!

Walk south to midblock.

DONOHUE BUILDING
701-721 S. Dearborn

ARCHITECT: *Julius Speyer (1883)*

DONOHUE BUILDING ANNEX
727 S. Dearborn

ARCHITECTS: *Alfred S. Alschuler (1913); for the adaptive reuse of both buildings: Harry Weese and Associates (1976)*

Built for Donohue and Henneberry Company, this was one of the first printing houses in the area. This was also one of the first buildings to be converted to condominium lofts. Functional yet with Romanesque elements, the building is architecturally responsive both to Dearborn Street and to Plymouth Court (which for years was unfortunately treated as an alley), with equally nice facades on each side. The annex was designed by the same architect as the former Stone Container Building (WALK 8). It is sympathetic in style, but more subdued.

In the adaptive reuse, the buildings' exteriors were preserved in situ. The original windows were repaired (not replaced, as in many other projects), down to the glass panes. Since this was an industrial loft building, it has large expanses of clear space, which in many cases were maintained and enhanced by each tenant. Considered a democratic conversion, each owner was free to define and use his or her large open space as desired. Some are business condominiums, some are apartments. The ground floor is all condominium businesses, the first such use of that new concept. One is the Prairie Avenue Bookstore, offering the largest selection of architectural books in the country.

Directly behind you is our next stop.

ROWE BUILDING
714 S. Dearborn

ARCHITECTS: *(Possibly) William LeBaron Jenney (c. 1892); for the adaptive reuse: Ken Schroeder, George Hinds and Philip Kupritz (1980)*

This 8-story building, originally a printing loft and executed in the style of other Dearborn Street structures, was one of the first conversions in the area. The top contained a proofreading room, which was skylit. The building has a cast iron front and cast iron window mullions on the upper floors. It is of heavy timber construction with brick exterior. The window proportions vary from floor to floor. The interior was sandblasted, the floors sanded, and a new bath core was added.

Next door is one of the most interesting buildings in the district.

FRANKLIN BUILDING
720 S. Dearborn

ARCHITECT: *George C. Nimmons (1912); for the adaptive reuse: Lisec and Biederman (1987)*

This building, too, once housed printing and printing-related businesses and has undergone a major program of restoration for adaptive reuse. All masonry, lintels, terra-cotta, and the parapet were restored and cleaned. To match the windows below, some new openings were punched in the 13th story, which had none, but which boasts skylights that run from 15 to 30 feet above the level of the floor. There are now 64 condominium residences within.

An amazing array of colored tiles forming many different mosaics cover the building from top to bottom. There is an interesting illusion created with terra-cotta. You almost see tapered, two-story columns with unadorned, pentagon-shaped capitals. Near the top of each are strange images. Above the first floor are a series of small pictures of men working on the first printing press. These pictures culminate above the door in a much larger picture entitled *The First Impression*.

Continue south to Polk Street. If you stand on the northwest corner and look west, you can see River City. If you wish a closer look, walk west on Polk Street to Wells Street.

RIVER CITY
800 S. Wells

ARCHITECTS: *Bertrand Goldberg and Associates (1984)*

In the mid-1960s Bertrand Goldberg designed the twin towers of Marina City, Chicago's first "city within a city"—a combination of apartments, garages, restaurants, offices, bank, ice-skating rink, bowling alley, commercial space, and a marina—from which residents could walk to work in the Loop.

In River City, Goldberg continued this idea. The curvilinear buildings have 446 rental units and 240,000 square feet of commercial space in 10- to 17-story poured concrete towers. Inside is a winding, skylit, atrium walkway called River Road, meant to convey a sense of community. There is also a 70-slip marina. The development was planned to be expanded to the south, with three additional residential structures adding over 2,500 units to complete the "city," but construction has not begun. Rounded forms in concrete can also be seen in this architect's Prentice Women's Hospital (WALK 14).

Return to Dearborn Street.

Dearborn Station
(Olga Stefanos)

* DEARBORN STREET STATION
S. Dearborn at W. Polk

ARCHITECTS: *Cyrus L. W. Eidlitz (1885); Project architects for Dearborn Street Station Mall: Kaplan, McLauglin, Diaz of San Francisco; consulting architects for the restoration: Hasbrouck and Hunderman (1986)*

Dearborn Station, the oldest surviving railroad terminal in Chicago, is the focal point of the WALK. The station is an exuberant mass of arches, string and belt courses, and applied terra-cotta decoration. It is missing many parts, including a huge cupola (originally on the clock tower), a steeply pitched roof that was lost during a fire in 1922, and its shed, removed in the 1960s. Notice that the clock tower is not set into the middle of the building—its placement centers it on Dearborn Street. (Trains formerly running here now serve the LaSalle Street Station.)

The landmark was in danger of being demolished when the plan for a shopping mall rescued it. The Dearborn Street facade was restored with minor changes, including the glass arcade on the east. A 2-story addition of 60,000 square feet was built behind the station. The entire 120,000-square-foot project is roughly half rehabilitated space and half new addition. There are 88,000 square feet of rentable space, of which 28,000 square feet are office space and 60,000 square feet are retail. You will see the addition later in the WALK.

Walk east on Polk to Plymouth Court. On the northeast corner is the Lakeside Press Building.

* LAKESIDE PRESS BUILDING
731 S. Plymouth

ARCHITECTS: *Howard Van Doren Shaw (1897, 1901); for the adaptive reuse: Lisec and Biederman (1985–86)*

Originally the Lakeside Press Building of the R. R. Donnelley Company (note the multiple Indian chief medallions—the Donnelley seal—near the top), this 8-story brick structure was later the Racing Form building. It has undergone exterior restoration, major interior rehabilitation, and the replacement of all windows as part of its conversion into apartments. The original 12-foot ceilings and columns were retained in all apartments.

In the basement is the Printers Row Printing Museum. Open weekends: Saturday 9 A.M. to 5 P.M.; Sunday 10 A.M. to 3 P.M. Admission is free.

Next stop is the tall modern tower at Polk and State streets.

TWO EAST EIGHTH

ARCHITECT: *Seymour Goldstein (1984)*

The doorway and the rooftop mechanical sheds share a motif of telescoping faces. This 27-story apartment building has a commercial ground floor, 330 apartments, two sundecks, and an indoor pool.

Backtrack west on Polk Street.

DEARBORN PARK

In the blocks bounded by State and Clark streets and Polk Street south to Roosevelt Road is a neighborhood called Dearborn Park. When you cross over into it, you feel as if you've entered another town. Here, built over the former railway tracks serving Dearborn Station, is a variety of housing: high-rises, townhouses, "garden apartments," senior citizen housing, and even a grade school. Until 1977 none of this existed. Yet the feeling of a community grew quickly. The amazing thing about Dearborn Park, and the revitalized south loop, is that its spectacular growth was accomplished without the usual preliminary round of throwing out the less privileged people—because there were no people!

To the east of Dearborn Street Station is a building aptly called "The Terraces."

The Terraces
(Gregory Murphy courtesy Skidmore, Owings & Merrill)

THE TERRACES
801 S. Plymouth

ARCHITECTS: *Skidmore, Owings and Merrill (1983)*

These buildings with the terraced roofline, located on a 2-acre site, consist of twenty-one garden homes and an 11-story building with 198 one- and two-bedroom apartments. The 11-story building, located on top of a garage podium is an L-shaped structure adjoining the two-story garden homes. The garden homes collectively form a U-shape, creating a courtyard that provides security as well as privacy for residents. Individual entrances to the garden homes and the main entry to the mid-rise building are from the raised courtyard.

A warm red brick was used for the apartments. This color complements the other masonry buildings in Dearborn Park. Masonry was chosen because it has a residential quality and is a traditional Chicago building material.

Walk south on Plymouth Court.

THE HIGH-RISES
899 and 901
S. Plymouth

ARCHITECTS: *Ezra Gordon, Jack M. Levin and Associates (1978–79)*

These 21-story and 26-story apartment buildings with commercial ground floors are the two tallest structures in Dearborn Park. Although they are cast-in-place concrete, in keeping with the motif of the area they are faced with red brick. They also have polygonal bays reminiscent of the earlier buildings of Printers Row.

Continue south.

THE MID-RISES
1115, 1143, 1169
S. Plymouth

THE GARDENHOMES
1001, 1121, 1153
S. Plymouth

ARCHITECTS: *Booth, Nagle and Hartray (1977–81)*

On your left is a grouping of three 7-story "mid-rises." these have terraces, which the architects describe as "backyards in the sky." Each mid-rise wraps around a courtyard containing a three-story building. These are the residences known as "The Gardenhomes." There are 238 units and 144 parking spaces.

On your right across Plymouth are the Townhouses.

THE TOWNHOUSES
933-971, 1040-1080,
1122-1158 S. Plymouth;
836-888, 960-996,
1061-1097 S. Park

ARCHITECTS: *Hammond Beeby and Babka;*
Thomas H. Beeby, designer (1978)

The exteriors of these plain, grey brick buildings contain no hint of the architectural flair that has since become the trademark of Thomas Beeby. Yet a closer examination reveals a site plan that effectively shuts out the city and creates a place of public and private spaces. A tree-lined walkway runs through the center of the complex. Intersecting this "car-less" boulevard are parks and playgrounds. As you walk through you'll have to remind yourself that you are only minutes from the heart of the downtown of a major city.

Continue south on Plymouth Court.

THE TOWNHOMES
1160-1182
S. Plymouth

ARCHITECT: *Michael Realmuto (1986)*

These strikingly modern buildings are a sharp contrast to the other buildings of Dearborn Park. The first floor displays the red brick seen on Printers Row, but then a wild vernacular of colors and shapes comes into play. This includes cream-colored stuccoed walls and deep blue "streamlined" pipe rails. There are references to houses of the 19th century:

oversized quoins, keystones, and window lintels, and a hint of gabled roofs.

Backtrack on Plymouth Court until you get to the sidewalk running along the south of the Townhouses. (Just to the south of 1156 S. Plymouth Court.) Turn west and walk ½ block. Enter through the black gates on your right. This is the interior walkway of the Townhouses.

Continue walking north and exit through the gates at the end. You will now be on Park Terrace. Continue north. Here is a good angle from which to view the playful addition to the back of Dearborn Station, which faces a well landscaped little park.

The building west of the train station is called "The Oaks."

THE OAKS
820 S. Park

ARCHITECTS: *Dubin, Dubin, Black and Moutoussamy (1978)*

This 8-story, 190-unit apartment building was built as senior citizen housing with Section 8 funds from HUD. It has a reinforced-concrete frame on caissons with a masonry exterior. There are protruding bays at the ends, and a nice glass atrium entrance. It is developed in two wings with elevators in a glazed bridge connecting link.

Walk north between the Oaks and Dearborn Street Station to return to Printers Row.

1. Chicago Sun-Times Building
   401 N. Wabash Ave.

2. One IBM Plaza
   330 N. Wabash Ave.

3. 420 N. Wabash Plaza
   420 N. Wabash Ave.

4. American Medical Association Building
   515 N. State St.

5. Tree Studios Building
   4 E. Ohion St.

6. Medinah Temple
   600 N. Wabash Ave.

7. Nickerson Mansion
   40 E. Erie St.

8. American College of Surgeons
   55 E. Erie St.

9. Episcopal Cathedral of St. James
   65 E. Huron St.

10. American Library Association
    50 E. Huron St.

11. National Congress of Parents and Teachers
    700 N. Rush St.

12. Catholic Catherdal of the Holy Name
    730 N. Wabash Ave.

13. Lewis Towers
    820 N. Michigan Ave.

14. James F. Maguire S. J. Hall
    1 E. Pearson St.

15. Quigley Preparatory Seminary—North
    103 E. Chestnut St.

16. Chestnut Galleria
    1–15 E. Chestnut St.

17. The Newberry Library
    60 W. Walton St.

18. Newberry Plaza
    1000–1050 N. State St.

19. Esquire Theatre
    58 E. Oak St.

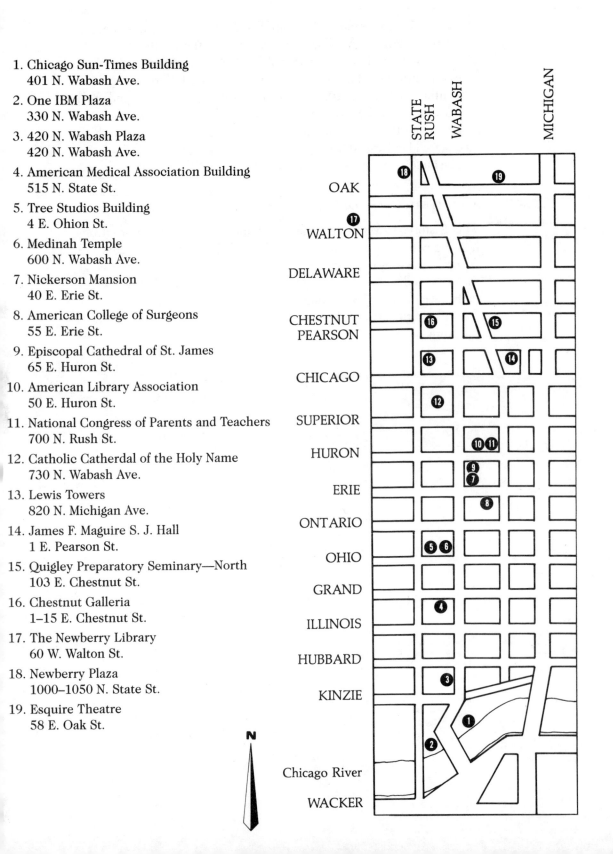

WALK 11 NORTH WABASH AVENUE

WALKING TIME: About 2 hours.
HOW TO GET THERE: Walk 1 block east of State Street at
Madison Street, then turn left on Wabash Avenue and walk 4
blocks north, crossing the river on the Wabash Avenue bridge.

If you are a lucky sightseer, you may arrive at the Chicago River just in
time to see one or more of the bridges split in two and rise, permitting
tall boats to pass by. These are bascule bridges, or—as they are sometimes
called—jackknife bridges. Don't be in a hurry; both bridges and boats
move slowly!

The WALK starts at the Chicago Sun-Times Building on the north
bank of the Chicago River at Wabash Avenue.

**CHICAGO
SUN-TIMES
BUILDING**
401 N. Wabash

ARCHITECTS: *Naess and Murphy (1957)*

This modern newspaper plant is housed in a long, low building that faces
the river the full length of its facade. The horizontal emphasis in the
building's architecture is in contrast with the many skyscrapers on all
sides. As you walk inside to the main corridor, you will see the enclosed
presses on one side of the building. Through the glass partition you can
generally watch one of the newspaper editions going to press—a fascinating process. A free 45-minute tour through this busy plant is available
at 10:30 A.M. weekdays. Call 321-3251 for reservations and information.

A pleasant open effect is achieved by the river beside the building and
the Wrigley Building Plaza, which gives easy access to Michigan Avenue.
The landscaped plaza on the east and a pedestrian walkway on the
riverside help make the building and its environs a pedestrian's delight.
Take a short side trip to the plaza and over to the pedestrian walk from
Wabash Avenue along the north bank of the river. On the way, note the
charming small landscaped terrace built by Field Enterprises.

ONE IBM PLAZA
330 N. Wabash

ARCHITECTS: *The Office of Mies van der Rohe and
C. F. Murphy Associates (1971)*

IBM's building was designed to consolidate the offices of the International
Business Machine Company's branches in downtown Chicago. The
52-story, steel-and-glass structure is sheathed in a curtainwall of bronze
aluminum and tinted glass. The granite plaza fills much of the 1.6-acre
site overlooking the Chicago River between Wabash Avenue and State Street.

At first glance the building may seem pristine or plain. A second glance
will reveal the richness of the travertine marble lobby and glass with the

119

matching gray granite of the lobby floor and plaza. This is truly a great work of architecture. More than that, it is a final statement of one of the 20th century's most distinguished architects, Ludwig Mies van der Rohe. Chicago is indeed fortunate to have been the home, for over 30 years, of this superb interpreter of the machine age. He used the precision of the machine to make clean, sculptured monuments to that particular period in time. The stunning lobby is enhanced by a bust of the architect.

There are 51 floors above the lobby. Of these, 46 are for office space. Two floors contain major computer facilities tied into a network of IBM computers across the country, available to other tenants in the building. The building's special curtainwall system and heating-cooling system were designed to meet the stringent humidity and temperature requirements of the computer areas. The building's power is all electric.

Directly north, note the striking garage structure of Cor-Ten steel designed by George Schipporeit in 1972. Across from that is an athletic club of simple ribbed-metal industrial siding.

Walk north on Wabash Avenue one block.

420 N. WABASH PLAZA
420 N. Wabash

ARCHITECTS: *J. Speyer and Son (1908); for adaptive reuse: Pappageorge Haymes (1983)*

This 7-story structure with one basement on a wood pile foundation was originally the Great Western News Company Building. It is a typical Chicago industrial building, with heavy timber interior and a brick and terra-cotta exterior, which has been restored. The main entrance of the building was moved from Hubbard Street to Wabash Avenue. To dramatize the entrance, a glass curtainwall was set back to create a 5-story entry, which leads to a symmetrical axial hallway in the center of the building and the newly located elevators. The walls are detailed with aluminum reveals and the floor is marble. The building now has 100,000 square feet of office space and a well-known restaurant on the Hubbard Street side.

Continue north to Grand Street. Turn west.

AMERICAN MEDICAL ASSOCIATION BUILDING
515 N. State

ARCHITECTS: *Kenzo Tange with Shaw and Associates (1990)*

This essentially rectangular building has two twists: The southwest corner is sliced off, allowing for a more dramatic entryway, and there is a hole punched through four floors near the top of the resulting triangular corner. As the building is 29 stories, the hole is best seen from a block or two away. Chrome and polished gray granite give the lobby a welcoming feel, all of it clearly visible through a 2-story glass wall. Part of the lobby is devoted to art displays, and the south half of the sizable lot is a grassy public plaza.

From the main door walk one block north on State Street to Ohio Street and turn east.

Tree Studios
(Olga Stefanos)

* TREE STUDIOS BUILDING
4 E. Ohio

ARCHITECTS: *for State Street side: Parfitt Brothers (1894);*
for additions on Ontario and Ohio streets:
Hill and Woltersdorf (1912, 1913)

The Tree Studios building, though rather drab in outward appearance, is nevertheless a unique structure, devoted to spacious artists' studios with high ceilings and large window areas. Note the words of wisdom carved into stone near the roof. Judge Tree, whose wife was an artist, donated the building. The Ohio Street entrance is marked rather oddly "4 Tree

Studios 6"; the Ontario Street entrance is marked "5 Tree Studios 3." Residents can reach either entrance via a delightful bit of outdoor park, complete with trees, flowers, and benches. Since the park is enclosed on all sides, this gives special privacy to a building on an otherwise very public corner.

Walk back to Wabash Avenue.

MEDINAH TEMPLE
600 N. Wabash

ARCHITECTS: *Huehl and Schmid (1912)*

The very large Medinah Temple extends from the northwest corner of Ohio Street and Wabash Avenue to Ontario Street. The building's Moorish style of architecture resembles a mosque, as of course the designer intended (it is the headquarters for the Chicago area Shriners). Inside are drill halls, offices, and an auditorium seating about 4,000 people, which is used for circus performances and other spectaculars as well as for the Medinah Shriners drill teams and bands. At one time there were plans to convert the building into a theme mall.

Continue north 2 blocks on Wabash Avenue. On the northeast corner of Wabash Avenue and Erie Street stands what was once one of the most opulent homes in Chicago.

* NICKERSON MANSION
40 E. Erie

ARCHITECTS: *Burling and Whitehouse (1883)*

Construction of this 3-story stone mansion of some 30 rooms for the Nickerson family began 10 years after their previous home on the North Side had been destroyed by the Great Fire of 1871.

Nickerson himself, an active financier and one of the founders of the first bank in Chicago to become a national bank, enjoyed the mansion for many years, selling it only in his last years, when he returned East. In his day it was referred to as Nickerson's Marble Palace, and the richness of the interior certainly merits the name.

Fortunately, those who have used the mansion since Nickerson's day have cherished its original elegance and kept it in good condition. For more than 40 years it was occupied by the American College of Surgeons. Still owned by the ACS, it was completely restored in 1991 by the art gallery that now occupies it.

Walk east.

AMERICAN COLLEGE OF SURGEONS
55 E. Erie

ARCHITECTS: *Skidmore, Owings and Merrill (1963); for addition: Graham, Anderson, Probst and White (1983)*

From 1919 until the completion of this unassuming building in 1963, the College of Surgeons occupied the Nickerson Mansion just described. At 50 E. Erie Street, across the street immediately east of the Nickerson Mansion, is the Auditorium used by the American College of Surgeons,

St. James Cathedral reflected in the windows of the office headquarters and parish house. (Allen Carr)

the John B. Murphy Memorial. The ground on which the auditorium stands was once the side yard of the Nickerson Mansion.

Backtrack west to Wabash Avenue. Turn north to Huron Street.

EPISCOPAL CATHEDRAL OF ST. JAMES
65 E. Huron

ARCHITECTS: *Edward Burling (1856); for reconstruction: Burling and Adler (possibly with Clarke and Faulkner) (1875); Civil War Memorial Tower: Calvert Vaux and Frederick Law Olmstead (1867); St. Andrew's Chapel: Bertram Goodhue and Ralph Cram (1913); Office Headquarters and Parish House: James Hammond and Peter Roesch (1968–69); for restoration: Holabird and Root (1985)*

This structure is typical of a number of churches built shortly before and after the Great Fire of 1871, for which architects followed the Gothic style in a free, somewhat inventive manner. These churches were often built of local limestone, called Joliet stone or Lemont limestone, which is seen in this building. To the east of the church is a stunning office headquarters and parish house of contemporary design.

In 1985 the church underwent extensive restoration. The roof was redone, and the stonework (especially on the east side of the tower) was restored. On the interior, the basement and main floor were remodeled; the ornamental windows and the nave floor were replaced. The spectacular 1888 interior finishes are an Arts and Crafts Movement stencil project, of twenty-six different colors, with stylized plant motifs as the central theme, the work of New York architect E. J. Neville Stemt; these were restored under the direction of project architect Walker Johnson and paint consultant Robert Furhoff.

On the north side of Huron Street are two buildings dedicated to educational purposes.

AMERICAN LIBRARY ASSOCIATION
50 E. Huron

ARCHITECTS: *Holabird and Root (1961–63)*

McCormick House—the home of Cyrus H. McCormick II until 1889 or so—was on this site. That structure was used as the headquarters of the ALA from 1945 until it was razed prior to the construction of this building. Within 20 years the ALA outgrew these quarters and began to lease space in a new building at 40 E. Huron Street.

On the northwest corner of Huron and Rush streets is the headquarters of the PTA.

NATIONAL CONGRESS OF PARENTS AND TEACHERS
700 N. Rush

ARCHITECTS: *Holabird and Root (1954)*

Funds to meet the expenses of constructing the National PTA building came largely from individual or PTA donations of anywhere from 10 cents to 10 dollars. "Quarters for Headquarters" was the slogan, and PTA members all across the country contributed whatever they could to provide a home of their own, where the national staff might work in more convenient space and better conditions than had been possible in their rented offices. PTAs may well be proud of the result, as the building was cited for excellence of design by the local architects association.

Walk west on Huron Street to Wabash Avenue. Turn north. In the next few blocks you will come to a variety of buildings representing the Roman Catholic Archdiocese in Chicago.

CATHOLIC CATHEDRAL OF THE HOLY NAME
730 N. Wabash

ARCHITECTS: *P. C. Kelly (1874); Henry J. Schlacks (1915); for renovation: C. F. Murphy and Associates (1969)*

The cathedral and the immediately related buildings occupy the entire block between Wabash Avenue and State Street, Superior Street and Chicago Avenue. School buildings, parish houses, convent, and church are all built in a similar style—the neo-Gothic used so widely for places of worship.

Along Wabash Avenue and east along Pearson Street to Michigan Avenue are buildings used by the Loyola University of Chicago graduate school.

Walk west to State and proceed north to Pearson Street. Turn east.

JAMES F. MAGUIRE S. J. HALL
1 E. Pearson

ARCHITECTS: *Graham, Anderson, Probst and White (1979)*

This 5-floor brick and steel frame building has a courtroom and lecture hall on the first floor; classrooms, seminar rooms, and a lounge on the second floor; a law library on the third and fourth floors; and administration offices on the top floor.

Walk east on Pearson Street 3 blocks on the south side of the street. The sign before Michigan Avenue also says "Michigan Avenue"—turn south here, toward the Water Tower (which is featured in WALK 12). The building on the corner is Lewis Towers.

LEWIS TOWERS
820 N. Michigan

ARCHITECTS: *Schmidt, Garden and Erikson (1925)*

Originally the Illinois Women's Athletic Club, the structure that gives this complex of buildings its name was later an office building facing Rush Street donated to Loyola University by the late Frank Lewis, Chicago philanthropist. Its dark yet exuberant Gothic design contains many amusing details. A newer building on the west side of Rush, connected with Lewis Towers by a covered walkway over the street, carries the name "Pere Marquette Campus."

Return to Rush Street and cross Pearson to the imposing Gothic seminary where youngsters start their training for the priesthood.

QUIGLEY PREPARATORY SEMINARY NORTH
103 E. Chestnut

ARCHITECT: *Gustav Steinbeck of New York City (1918)*

Archbishop James E. Quigley in 1905 had established what was then called Cathedral College. He died before his plans for an expanded school could be carried out, but his successor, Cardinal George Mundelein, fulfilled his aims. Many of the funds came as gifts from children of the archdiocese, and the school's name was changed to memorialize the man who planned it.

At Quigley Seminary you feel that you are standing before a great French Gothic municipal hall of the 12th century. Various Gothic features combine to give the effect of an authentic medieval structure: the rose window over the chapel entrance, the sculpture on either side, the high-pitched roofs, the buttresses on the Chestnut Street side, and the medieval courtyard. They almost make you expect to see knights in armor ride in on horseback—until you catch a glimpse of the cars parked inside the courtyard! Louis Sullivan thought little of the architecture, but this is a most impressive complex of buildings.

Now walk 2 blocks west on Chestnut, into a different era.

CHESTNUT GALLERIA
1-15 E. Chestnut

ARCHITECTS: *for the adaptive reuse:*
Booth/Hansen and Associates (1984–85)

Chestnut Galleria is the renovation of four turn-of-the-century apartment buildings into a new retail and business complex. The design unifies the original four buildings with a common curtainwall system, a new plaza, and a color scheme that retains a historical connection to the original buildings by treating them separately as parts of the whole project. New retail space was established at the basement, ground, and second floors throughout the project by punching through existing party walls. Upper floor tenants share a new atrium entry with elevators and stairs in what was once an exterior rear courtyard.

At this point you are at State and Chestnut streets, and it is suggested that you include in your WALK a particularly rewarding structure—the Newberry Library. Walk north on State Street to Walton Street, then west to Dearborn Street (just off the WALK map). Now you are at Washington Square Park, which the Newberry Library faces from the north.

* THE NEWBERRY LIBRARY
60 W. Walton

ARCHITECT: *Henry Ives Cobb (1892); for renovations:*
Harry Weese and Associates (1960–82)

Washington Square Park is precisely the amount of open space necessary to properly view the Newberry Library. Other institutional buildings line the east and south perimeters, and new townhouses line the west. Together, they form the classic relationship of low structural mass and open space to give the viewer the delightful experience of enjoying architecture in a way that was afforded pedestrians during the Classic and Renaissance periods in Europe.

This library of splendid Spanish Romanesque design stands on the site of the Mahlon Ogden house, a wooden mansion that miraculously escaped the Great Fire of 1871 but was later razed to make way for this building. The Newberry Library was created by a bequest from Walter Loomis Newberry, an early Chicago businessman. It houses outstanding collections of reference materials that are used by scholars working on advanced research projects in the humanities.

The Newberry Library, with its Cyclopean granite stonework, St. Giles portico, and powerful cornice, has been a landmark here since 1893. When the Board of Trustees decided to update the facility, they were faced with a difficult choice—to restore a structurally sound but mechanically obsolete 19th-century building, or to demolish it in favor of new construction. The spacious rooms, mosaic tile, oak paneling, and marble floors and wainscots would be far too difficult and costly to replace. The loss would have been great if the Board had opted for a new facility. It was discovered that restoring the original building was significantly more

Newberry Library
(courtesy Harry Weese & Associates)

economical than constructing a new library of equivalent size and grace. The renovations went on over a span of 22 years, as the institution's needs grew and changed.

In order to safeguard the library's renowned collection, air conditioning was installed to maintain 50 percent relative humidity at 70 degrees F. The existing 16- to 20-foot ceilings allowed for the addition of an air circulation system contained in trapezoidal enclosures. Thanks to their shape, these enclosures minimized the impact of the modernization efforts upon the existing architectural detail. Supply ducts and return plenums distribute air through nozzles between corridors and adjacent reading rooms. Other restorative changes include the replacement of the original wood sash with insulated aluminum windows and the addition of new elevators and mechanical rooms on either side of the existing monumental staircase. Throughout all phases of construction and renovation, utmost care was taken to protect the collections.

Before leaving, note that Washington Square, during warm weather, is a resting place for vagrants and people of the neighborhood. In the 1920s—and until as recently as the 1950s—it served as a forum for any

Esquire Theater
(Olga Stefanos)

radical or far-out speaker who chose to lend his oratory to the crowds that gathered each night in anticipation.

If you desire, return to Michigan Avenue by walking east on Oak Street. You will see a variety of chic stores, galleries, and restaurants.

To continue the WALK, go east on Walton Street to State Street and turn north. On the west side of State Street between Oak and Maple streets is a modern apartment building.

NEWBERRY PLAZA
1000-1050 N. State

ARCHITECTS: *Ezra Gordon and Jack Levin (1972–74)*

A unique feature of this concrete tower and complex is the townhouses south of the main tower. Trees growing down from the terraces enliven the streetscape. Also note the striking entrance.

Backtrack south to Oak Street and turn east.

ESQUIRE THEATRE
58 E. Oak

ARCHITECTS: *William and Hal Pereira (1937)*

This building was one of the first attempts to produce a modern theme for the motion picture theater, which up until then had been completely wallowing in "borax" (square-box) architecture. The interior also conveys the movie theme creatively.

Cathedral of the Holy Name
(Philip A. Turner)

1. Wrigley Building
   400 N. Michigan Ave.

2. Equitable Building
   401 N. Michigan Ave.

3. University of Chicago Graduate Business Center
   450 N. Cityfront Plaza

4. NBC Tower
   455 N. Cityfront Plaza

5. Tribune Tower
   435 N. Michigan Ave.

6. Realtor Building
   430 N. Michigan Ave.

7. 500 N. Michigan Avenue Building

8. The Hotel Inter-Continental
   505 N. Michigan Ave.

9. Michigan Terrace Condominium
   535 N. Michigan Ave.

10. Time & Life Building
    303 E. Ohio St.

11. McClurg Court Center
    333 E. Ontario St.

12. 625 N. Michigan Avenue Building

13. Arts Club of Chicago
    109 E. Ontario St.

14. Woman's Athletic Club
    626 N. Michigan Ave.

15. Crate & Barrel
    646 N. Michigan Ave.

16. City Place
    676 N. Michigan Ave.

17. Chicago Place
    700 N. Michigan Ave.

18. Allerton Hotel
    701 N. Michigan Ave.

19. Olympia Centre
    737 N. Michigan Ave.

20. Museum of Contemporary Art
    234 E. Chicago Ave.

21. Arby's
    115 E. Chicago Ave.

22. Water Tower
    800 N. Michigan Ave.

23. Water Tower Pumping Station
    163 E. Pearson St.

24. Water Tower Place
    845 N. Michigan Ave.

25. Plaza Escada
    840 N. Michigan Ave.

26. Fourth Presbyterian Church
    126 E. Chestnut St.

27. John Hancock Center
    875 N. Michigan Ave.

28. 110 E. Delaware Pl.

29. 900 N. Michigan Ave.

30. 919 N. Michigan Avenue Buildir

31. Knickerbocker Hotel
    163 E. Walton Pl.

32. One Magnificent Mile
    950–980 N. Michigan Ave.

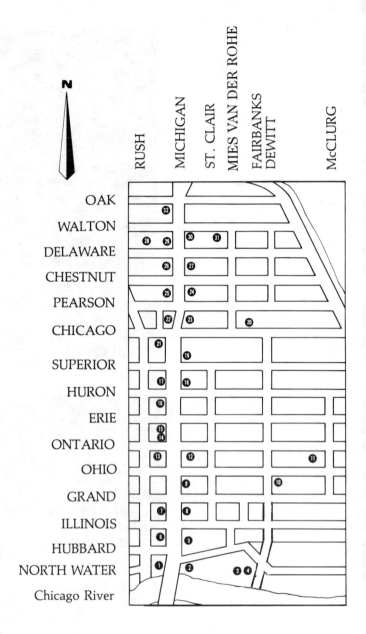

WALK 12 MICHIGAN AVENUE: THE MAGNIFICENT MILE

WALKING TIME: About 2½ hours.
HOW TO GET THERE: Take one of the following northbound CTA buses on State Street: No. 11, No. 146, No. 147, or No. 151. Get off at the Michigan Avenue bridge and East Wacker Drive (300 N).

Chicago's Magnificent Mile, beginning just north of the Chicago River, displays a catalog of architectural styles, including all manner of revival styles, Chicago school, international, and postmodern. The development of this part of Michigan Avenue (then called Pine Street) might be said to date from the 1920s, when both the street and underground levels of the Michigan Avenue bridge were completed.

During the growing season, trees, flowers, and shrubbery give the Mile color, texture, and beauty. It is a pleasure to stroll here and view these outdoor attractions as well as the enticing window displays of jewelry, books, and apparel. At Christmastime, tiny Italian bulbs strung on the branches of all the trees create an air of enchantment.

WRIGLEY BUILDING
400 N. Michigan

ARCHITECTS: *Graham, Anderson, Probst and White (1921, 1924)*

The gleaming white Wrigley Building (named for the family of chewing-gum fame) with its finger-like clock tower rises from the northern edge of the Chicago River. The white terra-cotta with which the building is covered and the powerful floodlights focused on it every night make this always a conspicuous part of the Chicago skyline. Featuring baroque ornamentation, the building is an architectural link to Chicago's earlier days. Between the main building and its annex (built in 1924) is an attractive small plaza.

EQUITABLE BUILDING
401 N. Michigan

ARCHITECTS: *Skidmore, Owings and Merrill; Alfred Shaw and Associates (1965)*

On the east side of the avenue the Equitable Building stands like another sentinel. Set far back from the street, it is approached through a spacious plaza called Pioneer Court, marked with plaques commemorating the earliest of European settlements here. A stairway leads down to an esplanade. Across the plaza a fountain and pools flow within black granite.

Wrigley Building
(Bill Engdahl, Hedrich-Blessing)

Equitable Building
(Philip A. Turner)

The building itself, a 40-story structure of metal and glass, is clearly a product of the 20th century, with a variation in the window arrangement that gives it special character. The slender external piers that separate the regular groups of 4 windows each have supportive value and are more than ornamental: They contain pipes for pumping hot or cold air into the offices as needed, from machinery located at the top and bottom of the building.

Directly to the east is one of the city's newest precincts.

UNIVERSITY OF CHICAGO GRADUATE BUSINESS CENTER
450 N. Cityfront Plaza

ARCHITECT: *Dirk Lohan Associates (1994)*

Once the site of the 1926 Mandel Building and briefly home to the Public Library, this spot again adds to the educational opportunities in the downtown area. Two basements and six stories contain the evening and weekend graduate business classes as well as the (nonbusiness) Center for Continuing Studies. The building features a 5-story entry topped by a penthouse-style conference area under an arched roof. The exterior is precast stone.

NBC TOWER
455 N. Cityfront Plaza

ARCHITECTS: *Skidmore, Owings and Merrill (1988)*

A throwback to the Art Deco style associated with broadcasting's early days, the limestone-clad NBC Tower includes several setbacks, squared buttresses, even a stone-clad needle above the 36th floor. Gleaming brass doors and 4 colors of interior marble add yet more luster. To the north is a 4-story structure housing a television studio.

Walk through the first floor to Columbus Drive and a glance at this ever-expanding annex to the old part of the city. Immediately east is the Sheraton Plaza Hotel, which addresses both the river and the street grid well. North of the hotel is Ogden Plaza, a partially sunken park featuring *Floor Clock II*, by Vito Acconci. About 70 feet in diameter, this sculpture has granite numbers on the ground and metal hands on wheels that function as a working clock.

Retrace your steps back to Michigan Avenue.

* TRIBUNE TOWER
435 N. Michigan

ARCHITECTS: *Hood and Howells (1925)*

The Tribune Tower, a Gothic revival skyscraper faced with Indiana limestone, has long been a Chicago landmark (although official designation came only in 1989). North Michigan Avenue would not be the same without the Wrigley Building, Water Tower, and the Tribune Tower. They are synonymous with the growth and strength of Chicago.

In 1922 the Tribune's publisher, Robert R. McCormick, for whom McCormick Place was named, held an international competition for the design of the building. Architects from all over the world responded, and

Tribune Tower
(Philip A. Turner)

NBC Tower
(Leslie Schwartz)

out of the many designs the winners selected were Raymond Hood and John Mead Howells, prominent New York architects.

The great Gothic arch entrance is quite impressive, as are the small pieces of stone set around the base of the building. The stones came from famous buildings around the world, such as Westminster Abbey, Cologne Cathedral, Notre Dame in Paris, the Colosseum in Rome, the Taj Mahal, even the Great Wall of China.

You must step across the street to see the crowning glory of this unusual building, the great flying buttresses, like those on the exterior of European Gothic cathedrals. To see the sunlight piercing the buttresses is a remarkable sight and most rewarding to all photographers.

Behind the Tower is a later, adjoining building, designed by Jarvis Hunt. Originally for the presses, it consists of brick that was faced with stone in 1965 to match the Tower. North of the Tower is the Annex, used for Tribune offices. This is a 15-story Gothic structure with a matching facade. A statue of Revolutionary War hero Nathan Hale stands in the courtyard.

WGN radio has its offices at street level of the Tower so passersby can watch through the windows as local radio personalities do their shows.

Cross to the west side of Michigan Avenue.

REALTOR BUILDING
430 N. Michigan

ARCHITECT: *Fred H. Prather (1963); for remodeling: Hague Richards (1972)*

This white marble structure is a fine example of a well-planned institution. As part of the original design, a plaza on the south called "Plaza of the Americas" has flags for all the nations of this hemisphere, except Cuba. The government of Mexico contributed a bust of Benito Juarez in 1977.

Walk north.

500 N. MICHIGAN AVENUE BUILDING

ARCHITECTS: *Skidmore, Owings and Merrill (1970)*

This efficiently designed, travertine marble structure expresses the steel-and-concrete construction it conceals. Deco brass lamps above the first floor help define four commercial bays.

THE HOTEL INTER-CONTINENTAL
505 N. Michigan

ARCHITECTS: *for South Tower: Walter W. Ahlschlager (1929); for North Tower: Quinn and Christensen (1961)*

Across the avenue, this hotel includes two towers of two different names. The south tower was once the Medinah Athletic Club and still carries the Egyptian-Assyrian frieze, Oriental turret, and onion-shaped dome at the top. Swimmer Johnny Weissmuller reputedly trained in the pool here.

Continue north.

MICHIGAN TERRACE CONDOMINIUM
535 N. Michigan

ARCHITECTS: *Richard A. Raggi and Guenter Malitz (1962)*

Here is a fine example of urban-center living with amenities, including an indoor swimming pool, lower-level garage, and restaurant. The building is 33 stories and contains 460 residences. The exterior is white glazed brick with olive glazed brick spandrels. The bay windows and tinted glass as well as the marble base combine to make an inviting structure.

Next, walk north to Ohio Street. Turn east and walk 2 blocks to the Time & Life Building.

TIME & LIFE BUILDING
303 E. Ohio

ARCHITECTS: *Harry Weese and Associates; Jerry Shlaes (1968)*

The Time & Life Building is superbly designed, well worth spending more time with than you may have anticipated. There are entrances on East Ohio Street and North Fairbanks Court. The 30-story structure has an extra-tall service base and rises to a height of 400 feet, with a gross floor area of 700,000 square feet. It is a rectangular tower 3 bays wide by 7 bays long. Each bay is 30 feet square.

The structure is concrete with a metal curtainwall of weathering steel, which has turned a deep rusty brown. The windows are of copper, mirrored glass; the elevator shafts, lobby walls, and raised walkways are covered with granite. The same granite is used in the sidewalk paving and the floors of the lobby. Typical floors begin 87 feet above the sidewalk and have no exposed columns.

The regular bay spacing, exposed structure, and horizontal emphasis of windows reflect the notion that an office building must be a series of equally adaptable floor plans one on top of the other. This notion bespeaks the tradition of the Chicago school, the early office buildings of Louis Sullivan, and the Carson Pirie Scott store, as well as the period inspired by Mies van der Rohe.

Originally there were 2-story elevator cabs, the first use of this system in the United States. During peak hours the 1,800 employees, all arriving at once, could reach odd-numbered floors by entering cabs at the lower level; those wishing to go to even-numbered floors entered cabs from the upper lobby. After the peak has subsided, the system was switched to normal service in which only the upper half of the 2-story cab was used, stopping at each floor. Today, with more flexible working hours, the elevators run in a more conventional manner, one set serving lower floors and another set the higher floors.

Now walk 1 block north, then 1 block east on Ontario Street to a large city within a city.

Time-Life Building
(Daniel Bartush courtesy
Harry Weese & Associates)

McCLURG COURT CENTER
333 E. Ontario

ARCHITECTS: *Solomon, Cordwell and Buenz (1971)*

McClurg Court Center covers most of the city block between Ontario and Ohio streets, Fairbanks and McClurg courts. It is a fascinating example of the trend in inner-city living towards obtaining maximum security for all tenants. In this case when a tenant enters the Center, he has at his disposal all the necessities of life.

The twin 46-story apartment towers were built with economical rectangular construction with curved columnless corners. Exposed concrete shear walls create a visual counterpoint to the exterior bronze, metal, and glass curtainwall. They also serve to restrain the buildings against the wind and offer the viewer a dramatic demonstration of power and strength. The towers were located to maximize apartment views and free the remaining site for the many facilities.

The project was conceived as a total in-city living center. Besides covered parking facilities, McClurg Court Center contains 1,028 dwelling units, three movie theaters, three tennis courts in the metal pavilion at the west end of the Center, a health club, swimming pool, medical offices, and shops.

Return to Michigan Avenue along Ontario Street.

625 N. MICHIGAN AVENUE BUILDING

ARCHITECTS: *Meister and Volpe Architects, Inc. (1971); for remodeling: Murphy/Jahn (1984–85)*

The exterior of this 27-story building is exposed, smooth, formed architectural concrete. The lower portion was sandblasted to give the concrete an even more textured appearance.

Among the building's unusual architectural features is its corner treatment. Structural corner columns were eliminated to provide open corner windows for executive offices. In 1985 the entrance was remodeled to add a glass atrium at street level, including handsome forest green marble and ivory terrazzo floors.

Cross Michigan Avenue and walk west on Ontario Street. An indispensable inside visit for this WALK is the Arts Club of Chicago.

ARTS CLUB OF CHICAGO
109 E. Ontario

ARCHITECT: *for the Club's interior: Ludwig Mies van der Rohe (1955)*

Though the 8-story exterior is very plain, the interior of the club is worth seeing, since it was designed by Mies van der Rohe. The club opens its exhibits to the public, and over the years many artists who later grew famous received their first Chicago—or even U.S.—showing here. Rodin, Picasso, Toulouse-Lautrec, Vlaminck, Utrillo, and Brancusi, for example, were given early one-man showings by the Arts Club of Chicago.

Back at the corner is the Woman's Athletic Club.

*** WOMAN'S
ATHLETIC CLUB**
626 N. Michigan

ARCHITECTS: *Philip B. Maher and Associates (1928)*

This low-key, carefully designed structure is representative of some of the best work by architects in the 1920s. It is 9 stories on pile foundations. The black granite base and sculpted Bedford limestone exterior articulate the air of quiet elegance of the interior.

Continue north.

CRATE & BARREL
646 N. Michigan

ARCHITECTS: *Solomon, Cordwell and Buenz (1990)*

A daring postmodern design opens up the store's 5 levels to outside views. The swirling ramps and railings are reminiscent of a factory, yet glass and white paint invite the browsers in.

As you walk north to the next corner, you will pass the Terra Museum of American Art at number 666. Housing an excellent collection of 19th- and early 20th-century American paintings, the museum moved here in 1987 into two older buildings innovatively reconfigured by Booth/Hansen and Associates.

CITY PLACE
676 N. Michigan

ARCHITECTS: *Loebl, Schlossman and Hackl (1991)*

The first 25 floors of this red-granite-clad structure hold the Hyatt Regency Suites, while the next 14 floors are office space. The lower portion has punched windows to distinguish it from the upper stories. Tan spandrels and a vast front of blue glass and ribbing, topped by a semicircular arch, make the building easily identifiable on the skyline.

Continue north.

CHICAGO PLACE
700 N. Michigan

ARCHITECTS: *for the base: Solomon, Cordwell and Buenz;
for the tower: Skidmore, Owings and Merrill (1991)*

Little expense was spared on this marble and granite structure. Inside the brass door are murals celebrating Chicago's history and a quotation by 1909 civic leader Daniel Burnham, who advised "Make no small plans." The 8-story base keeps Michigan Avenue's traditional retail scale and large window bays, but updates it with a deluxe shopping atrium, complete with exposed elevator works. The residential tower facing Rush street rises to 40 stories, topped off with art deco ornament.

Cross to the east side of Michigan Avenue.

ALLERTON HOTEL
701 N. Michigan

ARCHITECTS: *Murgatroyd and Ogden (1924)*

This famous 25-story hotel includes the equally famous Brooks Brothers shop. The first three floors are Byzantine revival in stone, supporting a brown brick tower.

Olympia Centre, street level
(Hedrich-Blessing courtesy Skidmore, Owings and Merrill)

As you walk north on Michigan Avenue, you will pass Tiffany's before reaching Superior Street and our next stop.

OLYMPIA CENTRE
737 N. Michigan

ARCHITECTS: *Skidmore, Owings and Merrill (1984)*

Olympia Centre combines a 63-story tower with a 4-story Neiman Marcus department store. The design was chosen to preserve the low-to-middle-rise retail character of Michigan Avenue and Superior Street, and to reinforce the open space edge already existing along Chicago Avenue. It also provides better views for the condominiums in the tower. The tower's tube structure is articulated by highlighting portions of the columns and window sills. At the top 6 floors the enclosed area is stepped inward from the corners, leaving a skeletal frame that provides a sense of enclosure for the interior terraces. The building is clad in granite of varying finishes. Note the magnificent arch, where a light fixture occupies the place usually reserved for a keystone—made unnecessary by today's structural technology. Continue north to Chicago Avenue. Walk one long block east.

MUSEUM OF CONTEMPORARY ART
234 E. Chicago

ARCHITECTS: *Josef Paul Kleihues of Berlin; Associate: A. Epstein and Sons (1996)*

Planned at this writing, the new MCA will have 5 levels as well as a sculpture garden filling half of a 2-acre site formerly occupied by a National Guard armory. The complex was planned to include an auditorium, performance space, an art library, and a barrel-vaulted ceiling on the second floor above the permanent collection. A restaurant will face the garden and Lake Michigan.

The old MCA, one-quarter the size of the Kleihues plan, occupied a 1915 building at 237 E. Ontario Street that was twice extensively remodeled. The collection includes artists' books, prints, sculpture, and drawings reflecting contemporary art trends. The Museum continues its support of avant-garde art by presenting a new show periodically. If you are one who thinks that art consists only of oil paintings on canvas or representational statuary, you may find this museum disturbing. But you can't fail to find it exciting, and you shouldn't miss it. Open Tuesday through Saturday from 10:00 A.M. to 5:00 P.M.; Sunday from noon to 5:00 P.M.; closed Monday.

Walk west on Chicago Avenue, just past Michigan.

ARBY'S
115 E. Chicago

ARCHITECTS: *for the remodeling: Stanley Tigerman, David Woodhouse, associate in charge (1979)*

This is a major remodeling and renovation of an existing 20-foot wide, 4-story structure. The facade as infill is clad in stucco and glass, with straight and curved sections of both transparent and opaque materials. The envelope is effectively detailed as a flush skin of gray brick, almost as "non-architecture."

On both sides of Michigan Avenue at Chicago Avenue stands one of Chicago's most famous—though by no means its most beautiful—landmarks, the Water Tower and Pumping Station.

* WATER TOWER
800 N. Michigan

* WATER TOWER PUMPING STATION
163 E. Pearson

ARCHITECT: *William W. Boyington (1867–69); for the interior renovations: Lloyd van Meter, Loebl, Schlossman and Hackl (1978); for restoration of park: City of Chicago (1978); for adaptive reuse: Michael Arenson and Associates (1983)*

Among the oldest structures in the city, the elaborate tower symbolizes Chicago's historic growth. When it was finished two years before the Great Fire, this fantastic, pseudo-Gothic creation, with its many turrets rising around the central tower like a section of a medieval castle, was considered a most artistically satisfactory disguise of the standpipe it concealed.

Its design is far removed from what was developed later in the century by the Chicago school of architecture—except that in a sense its form did follow function (or at least originated in function), as those later builders insisted a building should. Within the tower was an iron standpipe 3 feet in diameter and nearly 150 feet high that regulated water pressure for the Near North Side.

The park on both sides of the avenue was restored, with the railing and light fixtures obtained from the public viewing galley of the Lake

View Pumping Station, scheduled for demolition at the time. Five Kennedy hydrants from the 19th century were obtained for the Department of Water and brought to the site. The drinking fountain at the corner, a "3-level" design (for people at the top, horses in the middle, and dogs at the bottom), was obtained from the Chicago Park District. The north stairs were replaced with limestone from Valders, Wisconsin; the stone, equal in color and texture to Joliet limestone but more dense, was chosen because it should last longer.

The pumping station on the east side of the avenue—still in use!—was built of the same Joliet limestone but with less elaborate ornamentation. In 1867 it was noteworthy that the station could pump as much as 18 million gallons a day. By comparison, one hundred years later the capacity of Chicago's water system was 3 billion gallons a day. In the 1990s the station pumped about 260 million gallons a day, enough for 400,000 people.

Though in 1906 the Water Tower ceased to be of any use as a standpipe, the City cherishes its presence in the midst of Michigan Avenue traffic. For all its antiquated style, it seems strangely appropriate here among the modern structures. By its very contrast in style, it is a reminder of Chicago's triumph over the Great Fire of 1871, which destroyed practically everything else in this part of Chicago but was followed by a period of unprecedented building and architectural progress.

In 1983 the old boiler rooms in the Pumping Station were redesigned into theaters that show *Here's Chicago*. The workshops were converted into a lobby and gift shop. There is also a display by the Chicago Historical Society. The interior, which had been covered or destroyed over the years, was restored so that you can now see the Gothic terra-cotta detailing again. Both structures were designated Historic Landmarks by the City Council in 1971.

Here's Chicago is a dazzling sound and sight show, a must for any visitor to Chicago. Shows begin every half hour, starting at 9:30 A.M. Call 467-7114 for information.

Across Pearson Street is Water Tower Place.

WATER TOWER PLACE
845 N. Michigan

ARCHITECTS: *Loebl, Schlossman, Bennett and Dart; C. F. Murphy and Associates (1976)*

Covering the entire block, this all-marble structure is an astounding combination of commercial and residential uses. The 12-story base contains a shopping complex and office space.

Unique at the time, the urban mall on the first seven floors was constructed around a grand atrium and five courts. With more than 610,000 square feet of floor space, the shopping center accommodates some 100 stores, shops, and boutiques. Marshall Field and Company and Lord and Taylor are the major tenants.

The 8th and 9th floors provide more than 200,000 square feet of office space. The 10th and 11th floors include the health spa facilities of the Ritz-Carlton Hotel and the mechanical system. The 12th floor contains the hotel restaurant facilities. Rising from the southeast corner, 162 E. Pearson Street, is a 62-story tower with the Ritz-Carlton Hotel and luxury condominium residences.

Walk west on Chestnut Street.

PLAZA ESCADA
840 N. Michigan

ARCHITECTS: *Lucien LaGrange and Associates (1992)*

Little trace of indigenous Chicago architecture is seen here. The cream-colored stone is topped by a clockface and a hipped roof that speak of the French Second Empire style. Columns at the angled doorway point to classical examples, and the mere four stories of the whole structure—for a toy store and a book store—match most buildings along Chestnut Street and lend a feeling of a small-town era now gone. The project originated as a 45-story tower, scrapped in the real estate bust of the early 1990s.

* FOURTH PRESBYTERIAN CHURCH
126 E. Chestnut

ARCHITECTS: *Ralph Adams Cram (1912); for Parish House: Howard Van Doren Shaw (1925)*

Providing a diametric contrast with its newer neighbors is the Fourth Presbyterian Church, famed for its modified Gothic style. The architect designed many other Gothic revival buildings. The modifications executed here can be seen in such things as the narrowness of the side aisles and the placement of a balcony in the transept space. The building, and a connecting arcade, are of carved Bedford stone and surround a grass plot. The stained-glass windows were designed by Charles Connick.

Cross Michigan Avenue. You will be overwhelmed by the 100-story John Hancock Center, towering more than 1,000 feet in the air. It dominates the vicinity and the skyline much as the Eiffel Tower does in Paris. This characteristic, however, is all that the two structures have in common.

JOHN HANCOCK CENTER
875 N. Michigan

ARCHITECTS: *Skidmore, Owings and Merrill, partner in charge: Bruce Graham (1969); for plaza redesign: Hiltscher Shapiro Associates (1994)*

The modern steel building, surrounded by much open space at its base, is a combination office-commercial-residential project, with the residences on the uppermost 50 stories. Black anodized aluminum and tinted glass are the materials used in the exterior. To cope with Chicago's winds (It is said that the top of the building may sway anywhere from 10 to 15

Fourth Presbyterian Church
(Chicago Plan Commission)

inches—though those inside would not be aware of it!) the John Hancock has huge cross-bracing steel members, 18 stories long, that make several giant X's on each side. These produce an interesting ornamental effect as the X's become gradually smaller with the tapering of the building from foundation to top, a perfect blending of form and function.

A redesigned plaza forming half an ellipse below amphitheater steps welcomes the public more readily than the original sunken square did. Separate entrances for the observatory and the residences were also added.

The 95th Restaurant occupies the 95th and 96th floors. The observatory on the 94th floor is open every day of the year, 9 A.M. to midnight. Walk west on Delaware Place.

110 E. DELAWARE

ARCHITECTS: *Solomon, Cordwell and Buenz (1981)*

Because of the limitations of the site, an irregularly sized lot as narrow as forty-three feet, this building has windows only on its front and back facades. The exterior is of precast concrete and glass. There are sixty-seven units in the building, the maximum number allowed on the site.

Return to Michigan Avenue.

900 N. MICHIGAN

ARCHITECTS: *Perkins & Will; Kohn, Pedersen and Fox of New York associated architects (1989)*

This 66-story mixed-use development contains 2.7 million square feet; there are 200,000 square feet of retail space, plus 250,000 square feet for Bloomingdale's department store; office space takes another 500,000 square feet.

The building is of steel construction through the office floors and concrete construction above that. The cladding is a combination of French limestone (to recall and relate to the traditional use of limestone on Michigan Avenue), glass, and metal. The ornate base of the building is granite and marble.

Floors 8-27 contain office space, and above that are 19 floors for the Four Seasons Hotel. The top of the building has 125 condominium units.

The basement and 7 commercial levels rise about 150 feet, the approximate height of the old 900 N. Michigan Avenue building and the traditional cornice line of the older buildings along Michigan Avenue. After that, the tower is set back from the lot line. The setback, to the western line of the One Magnificent Mile building, allows views from both buildings.

The architecture of the tower recalls the style of Chicago buildings of the 1930s and 1940s and has a strong relationship to 333 N. Michigan Avenue, thus unifying the stretch of Michigan Avenue's Magnificent Mile from the river to Oak Street. This design uses many similar devices, including the solid corners that have windows punched into the masonry. The center sections of the tower become more vertical and more open. The top of the building is unique, giving it a special signature along the skyline.

919 N. MICHIGAN AVENUE BUILDING

ARCHITECTS: *Holabird and Root (1929); for remodeling: Ron Dirsmith and A. Epstein and Sons, Inc. (1972); for renovations: Skidmore, Owings and Merrill (1979–82); for the Mark Shale Store remodeling: Solomon, Cordwell and Buenz (1981)*

This structure was first the Palmolive Building and then, until the late 1980s, the Playboy Building. Architect Ron Dirsmith designed the former Playboy offices with splendid lighting, colors, curved wall surfaces, and dropped ceilings, making each of the several floors of offices unique and quite handsome.

The original cast iron and nickel bronze storefronts of the Palmolive Building had been replaced in the early 1970s by a black aluminum and dark glass facade. The 1979 renovations included the restoration and redevelopment of the lobby and the renovation of the facade at grade level and 2nd-story level; this style was thought to complement the original architectural vocabulary within a budget that would not permit full restoration at the time. The office lobby was refurbished with black-painted glass, patterned terrazzo, and Tennessee pink marble. The original elevator cabs, carved wooden elevator doors, and a nickel bronze mailbox cover were preserved.

The new facade is composed of large lights of glass suspended in a steel structural framework applied to the building shell. Bays of sheer glass and steel mullions, varying from 8 to 10 feet, are framed by ribbed lintels and fluted columns above a black granite base. The fluted columns of extruded aluminum replicate the remaining second-level cast-iron columns and lanterns. Pediments and medallions similar to the original Art Deco ornaments were also restored.

Walk east on Walton Place.

KNICKERBOCKER HOTEL
163 E. Walton

ARCHITECTS: *Rissman and Hirschfeld (1926); for the remodeling: Louis Arthur Weiss; for interior design: Gerald O'Hara (1980)*

Built for the Davis hotel chain and now renamed the Knickerbocker (it had been the Playboy for many years), this 14-floor hotel had 360 rooms. In the remodeling this was reduced to 254, and restoration of the grand ballroom, once the most famous in the city, included removing white spray-paint from the gold-leaf adornments. The whole building has been restored as closely as possible to its general character and original grandeur.

Return to Michigan Avenue, cross, and walk one block north. The name of the last building sums up this WALK.

ONE MAGNIFICENT MILE

950-980 N. Michigan

ARCHITECTS: *Skidmore, Owings and Merrill (1983)*

Three hexagonal concrete tubes rise 57, 49, and 21 stories and are joined together to resist wind loads as a bundled tube. A 5-story hexagonal entrance pavilion in front of the highest tower has a glazed roof sloping northeast toward the Oak Street Beach. The same motif is repeated on top of the 57-story tower. The bottom three levels contain commercial space; office space is on floors 4 through 19; and the rest of the buildings is condominiums. A 2-story mechanical floor tops the twenty-first story and is carried across the entire tower floor area, dividing the office levels and residential floors by a broad horizontal line. Fenestration is also treated in a different manner below and above this visual division. The towers are clad in granite with clear windows at the commercial level and gray reflective glass for the condominiums.

The Magnificent Mile comes to an end just beyond the Drake Hotel where Michigan Avenue loses its identity by merging with Lake Shore Drive. If the weather permits, take the underpass pedestrian walkway to the Oak Street Beach for a glorious view of Lake Michigan. The pedestrian walkway and bicycle path will take you north with Lake Michigan on your right and many handsome apartment buildings on your left. This is indeed a glamorous section of Lake Shore Drive, part of the Gold Coast of Chicago.

The Drake Hotel, on the east side of Michigan Avenue, is included in WALK 13, East Lake Shore Drive. At this point you may choose to take that or WALK 15, The Gold Coast. Each begins from where you stand now.

Water Tower
(Philip A. Turner)

1. Drake Hotel
   140 E. Walton St.
2. Drake Tower Apartments
   179 E. Lake Shore Dr.
3. Mayfair Hotel
   181 E. Lake Shore Dr.
4. 199 E. Lake Shore Dr.
5. 209 E. Lake Shore Dr.
6. 219 E. Lake Shore Dr.
7. 229 E. Lake Shore Dr.
8. 999 N. Lake Shore Dr.

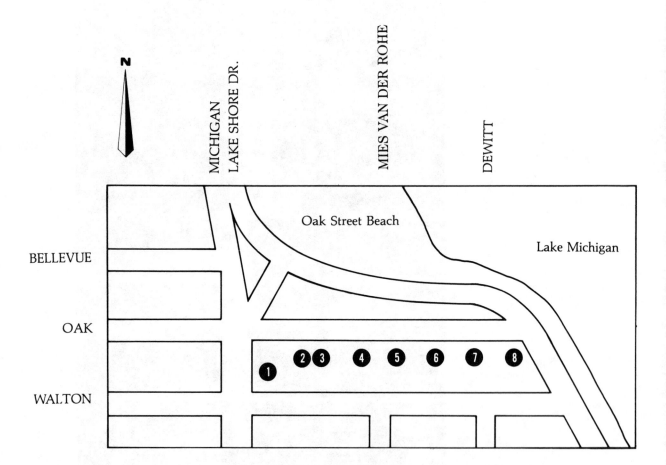

WALK 13   **EAST LAKE SHORE DRIVE**

WALKING TIME: About ½ hour.

HOW TO GET THERE: Take a northbound CTA bus No. 151 or 146 at State and Washington streets, and get off at Walton Street (900 N). (Ask the driver if the bus stops there; you may have to get off a stop earlier, at Water Tower Place, in which case you walk north 1 block on Michigan Avenue, to the Drake Hotel.)

East Lake Shore Drive belongs to both Streeterville (see WALK 14) and to the Gold Coast (see WALK 15). It is suggested, since this is a short walk, that you might want to start with WALK 14, and/or follow with WALK 15.

The street developed in the second and third decades of the 20th century, a period of significant growth in Chicago. These buildings typify the elegant urban lifestyle of their times. Architectural styles during this period fell into two categories. While the designs of Frank Lloyd Wright and Louis Sullivan did not find wide public acceptance in residential application, historical eclecticism—a return to the American Georgian, English Gothic, Italian Renaissance, or French Baroque—was deemed appropriate for the residential structures along this desirable stretch of real estate.

These buildings share a gracious appearance. East Lake Shore Drive provides an intimate streetscape in a congested area. At eye level the street appears, for a moment, to be one of grand mansions. The entrances are all grand, Beaux Arts, mostly 3- and 4-story, and most of the buildings are less elaborate above. The entrances and all the fenestration and the landscaping make this one of the finest pedestrian areas in the city. Take note of the ornate wrought-iron doors, lamps, and other hardware of the entranceways. Begin your WALK at the Drake Hotel, on the northeast corner of Walton Street and Michigan Avenue.

DRAKE HOTEL
140 E. Walton

ARCHITECTS: *Marshall and Fox (1920)*

This is truly one of the "grand hotels" of this city. It is 13 stories on pile foundations. The exterior is Bedford limestone. The fenestration is generous, affording excellent views for the fortunate guests whose rooms face Lake Shore Drive and the Oak Street Beach. The hotel has retained its air of gracious living, particularly in the Palm Court just off the lobby. At teatime the fountain, musicians, and mirrored ceiling (not original) combine to fill the large space elegantly.

Walk around to view the west and north sides of the building, then walk east on East Lake Shore Drive.

DRAKE TOWER APARTMENTS
179 E. Lake Shore

ARCHITECT: *Benjamin H. Marshall (1929)*

This is a simple brick tower above a decorated two-story limestone base. Note the top, where apartments are set back to accommodate the penthouse. The steeply pitched standing seam metal roof and the elevator equipment penthouse is formed into a pseudo-chimney in proportion with the rest of the building. Marshall was an important theater architect at the turn of the century. He also designed the ill-fated Iroquois Theater (remembered, unfortunately, because of the 1903 fire).

MAYFAIR HOTEL
181 E. Lake Shore

ARCHITECTS: *Fugard and Knapp (1924)*

This building was described in *Architectural Forum* in November 1924:

> The exterior design follows the style of the Georgian and [Robert] Adam periods. The three lower floors are of Indiana limestone, conservatively enriched with small pilasters above the first floor. The shaft of the building is of reddish face brick with light joints, while the upper portion is relieved with simple quoins and cornices of stone, and parapets which have balustrades and urns to create an interesting skyline.

The attention given to the lower few floors of the facade indicated a grand entranceway, while the simplicity of the floors above was intended to detract from the building's height. This building shares with others on the block the feature of a particularly handsome entranceway and lobby. The rooftop restaurant was added in 1979.

199 E. LAKE SHORE

ARCHITECTS: *Marshall and Fox (1915)*

This asymmetrical building is of brick with limestone trim above a 2-story limestone base. It has one tier of square bays and one of round bays. Note its similarity to 999 N. Lake Shore Drive (our last stop), designed three years earlier by the same architects.

209 E. LAKE SHORE

ARCHITECTS: *Marshall and Fox (1924)*

This limestone building shows the influence of the Renaissance style. The building is broken into three bands of design, becoming more simple as it rises above the gleaming fanlight door. A mock portcullis door stands on either side.

219 E. LAKE SHORE   ARCHITECTS: *Fugard and Knapp (1922)*

The first three floors represent a limestone Georgian mansion, topped at the third floor level with an elaborate carved stone cornice. Above that are nine floors of simple brick construction with one stone balcony and token decoration at the top.

229 E. LAKE SHORE   ARCHITECTS: *Fugard and Knapp (1919)*

This building, with a limestone facade, takes the form of a 5-story mansion at the lower levels. That is topped by 6 more floors and a cornice. The rooflines of these two buildings by Fugard and Knapp meet, though the later building contains one more floor.

999 N. LAKE SHORE   ARCHITECTS: *Marshall and Fox (1912)*

Designed in the French Second Empire style, this building is capped by a distinctive mansard roof. The wall surface curves almost 90 degrees with the streetfront and is broken by round and rectangular oriels. Red-brick spandrels interplay with white limestone trim.

1. Navy Pier
   East Grand Ave.
   and Streeter Dr., at Lake Michigan

2. Jardine Water Purification Plant
   1000 E. Ohio St.

3. Lake Point Tower
   505 N. Lake Shore Dr.

4. Onterie Center
   446 E. Ontario St.

5. 680 N. Lake Shore Dr.

6. Northwestern University
   Chicago Campus
   710 N. Lake Shore

7. Northwestern University Law School/
   American Bar Center
   375 E. Chicago Ave.

8. American Hospital Association
   840 N. Lake Shore Dr.

9. Lake Shore Center
   850 N. Lake Shore Dr.

10. The Plaza on DeWitt
    260 E. Chestnut St.

11. 860 and 880 N. Lake Shore Dr.

12. 900 and 910 N. Lake Shore Dr.

13. 990 N. Lake Shore Dr.

14. Chess Pavilion
    North end of Oak St. Beach

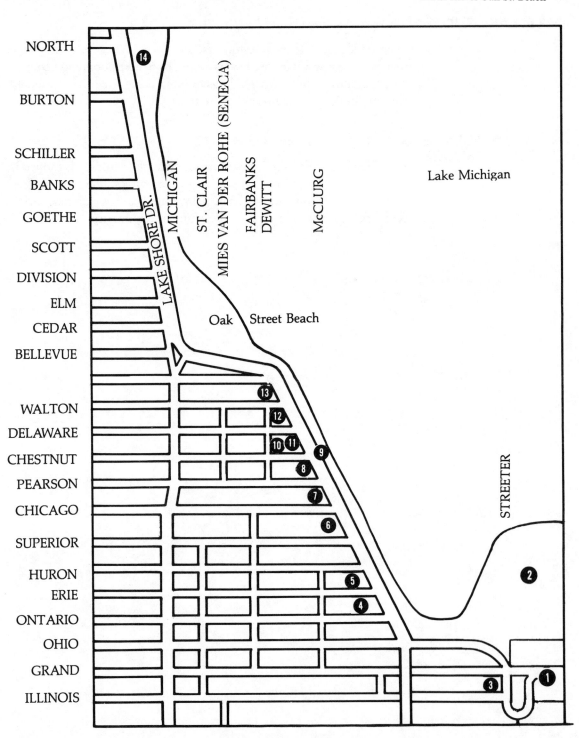

WALK 14 **LAKE SHORE DRIVE: NEAR NORTH**

WALKING TIME: 1½ hours.
HOW TO GET THERE: Take a northbound CTA bus No. 29 (State Street) (weekdays only) and get off at Navy Pier. Or take a No. 151 or 147 bus on State Street (ask for a transfer) and get off at Michigan and Illinois avenues (500 N). Walk down the steps. Transfer (at the lower level) to an eastbound bus No. 65 (Grand Avenue), which will take you to Navy Pier, the end of the line.

This WALK starts at Navy Pier, 1 long block to the east and 1 block north of the Outer Drive/Lake Shore Drive bridge.

NAVY PIER
E. Grand and Streeter
at Lake Michigan

ARCHITECT: *for west entry buildings and east end buildings: Charles S. Frost (1916); for restoration of Navy Pier: Jerome R. Butler Jr. (1976); for reconstruction: Benjamin Thompson & Associates/VOA Associates; for East Buildings rehabilitation: Bernheim and Kahn (1992–95)*

A 25-acre peninsula on which commercial, cultural, and recreational activities are provided, Navy Pier was built in 1916 as a port facility for commercial shipping and Great Lakes excursion boats. Although not always open to the public, many special events on summer weekends attract tens of thousands of visitors.

The Pier's east promenade, lying 1½ miles east of Michigan Avenue (most of it landfill), offers unparalleled views of Chicago's maritime activity and its spectacular skyline. Here is a park-like haven in which to enjoy a refreshing pause from city activity. On the promenade is the East End Recreational Facility, a complex of 3 connected structures—the opulent Auditorium, the Shelter, and the Terminal buildings—plus vintage streetlights and park benches, rooftop terraces, trees, and landscaping.

The sheds that ran from one end to the other were razed in the early 1990s as part of a complete facelift. An amusement park, a six-story atrium, an auditorium, a wooded park, and the Children's Museum were all planned.

Streeter Drive, a curving street at the foot of Navy Pier, is a reminder of the colorful, controversial shantytown that once occupied this 180-acre site stretching north from Grand to Chicago avenues and west to

St. Clair Street. Streeterville got its name from George Wellington Streeter, who for more than 30 years claimed squatter's rights to the area, insisting that neither Chicago nor Illinois laws had any jurisdiction over it. Other squatters who bought real estate from Streeter backed him in his lawsuits with the city.

This sea captain turned real estate con man seems to have been the first to redeem land from Lake Michigan and make a profit on it—a procedure that made possible the lakefront skyscrapers today! The story goes that Streeter and his wife, Maria, started this fantastic real estate project in 1886 after running their excursion boat aground on a sandbar in Lake Michigan somewhat south of Chicago Avenue. Freeing the boat proved difficult, so they decided to fill up the lake around it instead. With the help of nearby residents who contributed dirt from construction sites and whatever lay at hand, this is exactly what they did. Streeter defied all attempts by the law to oust him from his property, until someone was killed in one of the many confrontations with the police. He was then imprisoned on a charge of manslaughter. Out on parole months later, he returned to his battle with the law. Finally, in 1918, court orders were actually carried out: Streeter was removed and the shanties of Streeterville burned to make way for later development.

Out in the lake, just north of Navy Pier, spreads the James W. Jardine Water Purification Plant.

JARDINE WATER PURIFICATION PLANT
1000 E. Ohio

ARCHITECTS: *C. F. Murphy and Associates and the City Architect (1966)*

This purification plant with its 51 acres of buildings is the largest facility of its kind in the United States. It is considered one of the country's waterworks showplaces. Dozens of school groups visit this plant each year; tours are permitted by appointment only. Call 744-7007 for reservations.

Central District Filtration Plant
and Olive Park
(Orlando R. Cabanan)

A sculpture in the lobby of the main building, by Chicagoan Milton Horn, represents the history of the various uses of water.

At the west end of the plant site, over the filtered water reservoirs, is a 10½-acre public park, Milton Lee Olive Park (named for a Vietnam War hero), with fountains, beautiful landscaping, and a promenade. There is a splendid view of the Chicago skyline from this park.

Walk west on Grand Avenue toward the black high-rise.

LAKE POINT TOWER
505 N. Lake Shore

ARCHITECTS: *Schipporeit-Heinrich; Graham, Anderson, Probst and White (1968)*

The most prominent building on the shoreline to the north of the Chicago River is Lake Point Tower. This 70-story, glass-sheathed apartment building is indeed a beautiful sight. In 1921 a similar 3-lobed-cloverleaf building was designed by Ludwig Mies van der Rohe in Berlin, but it was never built. The young architects who designed Lake Point Tower, former colleagues of Mies, were obviously influenced by the master. Much of the building's sweep and fluidity, its even sensuous quality, has to do with its hidden columns, all enclosed by the bronze-tinted glass. It is almost mirror-like at times, and in the setting sun's reflection it looks like a golden shaft.

Cross the grass north to Ohio Street, taking the pedway under Lake Shore Drive, to McClurg Court. Turn north 1 block, then turn east on Ontario Street.

ONTERIE CENTER
446 E. Ontario

ARCHITECTS: *Skidmore, Owings and Merrill (1985)*

Onterie Center is composed of a 58-story multiuse tower and an adjacent 10-story office tower. A 5-story, triangular, glazed atrium connects the two structures and leads to a pedestrian galleria for easy communications with both major streets. The apartment lobby off Erie Street is independent of the two distinct office lobbies with entries from Ontario Street.

Twin elevators in each of these spacious lobbies give access to the office space on floors six through ten. A unique structural system of diagonalized framed tubes with diagonally placed concrete infill panels was developed for this building. This original and highly economical system creates a rhythmic architectural expression that lends visual strength to the building image. Dual thermal glazing and a specially prefabricated exterior panel system with incorporated insulation contribute to the buildings' exceptional energy efficiency.

Backtrack to McClurg Court and walk one block north.

680 N. LAKE SHORE ARCHITECTS: *Henry Raeder and George Nimmons (1924, 1926); for the adaptive reuse: Frank Larocca (1980–83)*

At Erie Street you stand before the 29-story tower with a bright-blue roof. The 16-story structure running east to Lake Shore Drive was designed in 1924 to provide large showrooms for the former occupant, the American Furniture Mart, one of the two major Chicago marts used by leading furniture manufacturers to display their latest creations. (The other is the Merchandise Mart. See WALK 8.) By the 1970s many of the tenants had relocated, leaving the building more than half empty despite its prime lakefront location. In a neighborhood that was experiencing revitalization, the size and configuration of the building was less than conducive to adaptive reuse. In 1979 the joint venture of Fujikawa, Conterato, and Lohan with Larocca Associates redesigned the 2,000,000-square-foot building as the largest known "adaptive reuse" project to date. Half the space was devoted to residential units; a quarter of it to office use; and the rest to retail, common areas, parking, and loading uses. An effort was made to preserve, restore, and enhance the character of the building through its classic lobbies, cast plasterwork, terra-cotta, and stone work, all as a commitment to the building's established image.

The original building had been developed in two phases. The main, 1924 facility is of reinforced concrete with round columns at 20-foot centers on wood pilings. In 1926 the 29-story section was added on the west, facing McClurg Court. It is steel framed with concrete fireproofing on concrete caissons. The steeply sloping 4-sided roof is topped by 4 stone spires and a lantern. The only structural modification in the rehabilitation work was to cut out floor sections for new concrete ramps, stairs, and shafts for the elevators.

Continue north on Lake Shore Drive.

Prentice Women's Hospital and Maternity Center
(Jim Hedrich, Hedrich-Blessing)

**NORTHWESTERN
UNIVERSITY
CHICAGO
CAMPUS**
710 N. Lake Shore

ARCHITECTS: *James Gamble Rogers (1926–32);
Holabird and Root (1929–67); Schmidt, Garden and Erikson (1968);
Bertrand Goldberg and Associates (1974)*

The Chicago campus of Northwestern University (bounded by Chicago
Avenue, Lake Shore Drive, Erie and St. Clair streets) includes the
graduate schools of medicine, dentistry, management, law, and the
evening divisions—in various buildings along the 300 block of East
Chicago Avenue, with administrative offices at 710 N. Lake Shore Drive.
It also is the main site of the McGaw Medical Center of the university,
which includes, in this location, Northwestern Memorial Hospital,
Prentice Women's Hospital and Maternity Center, the Passavant Pavilion and Wesley Pavilion, the Veterans Administration Research Hospital, and the Rehabilitation Institute of Chicago. The Institute of
Psychiatry, a part of the Northwestern Medical School, shares a building
with Prentice. Huge wrought-iron gates stand free at Superior Street and
Lake Shore Drive, left from the time of a more traditionally organized
campus.

Northwestern University Law School
(Timothy Hursley, courtesy The Arkansas Office)

NORTHWESTERN UNIVERSITY LAW SCHOOL/ AMERICAN BAR CENTER
375 E. Chicago and 750 N. Lake Shore

ARCHITECTS: *Holabird and Root (1984)*

This handsome addition to the law school was built in 1984. The architect's challenge was to design a building that served both its occupants, while still relating to the collegiate Gothic architecture on one side and the nearby 680 N. Lake Shore Drive and the Mies buildings along the Drive. The steel structure has an aluminum skin with glass and granite. The building is 13 stories tall. It has 300,000 square feet of space, almost 100,000 of it for the library. The 1st floor has classrooms, the 800-seat Thorne Hall, and a moot court. The 2nd and 3rd floors are library space with some faculty offices. Floors 6 and up are the American Bar Association's space.

Continue north on Lake Shore Drive.

AMERICAN HOSPITAL ASSOCIATION
840 N. Lake Shore

ARCHITECTS: *Schmidt, Garden and Erikson (1961–70)*

Running much of the block west on Pearson Street, these two 12-story buildings are executed in different but related styles. A three-story arcade links the two. The triangular corner site is framed interestingly by a 2-story granite colonnade that defines the space without enclosing it.

LAKE SHORE CENTER
850 N. Lake Shore

ARCHITECT: *Jarvis Hunt (1929)*

This 18-story building is a quiet and dignified reminder of the 1920s. Formerly the Lake Shore Club, it is now a Northwestern University dormitory—complete with the original swimming pool and athletic facilities.

Continue north to Chestnut Street. Turn west to the corner of DeWitt Place.

THE PLAZA ON DEWITT
260 E. Chestnut

ARCHITECTS: *Skidmore, Owings and Merrill (1966)*

Directly west of the 860-880 Lake Shore Drive buildings, at DeWitt and Chestnut streets, is another apartment building, a handsome structure of reinforced concrete covered with travertine marble. The contrast between this and "The Glass Houses" is a reminder that modern builders can use old-time building materials—as well as new—with effective results. Always present in the background of this WALK is the imposing John Hancock Building with its 100 stories, 2 blocks to the west on Michigan Avenue. (See WALK 12.)

Backtrack to Lake Shore Drive. Turn north.

860 and 880 N. LAKE SHORE

ARCHITECTS: *Ludwig Mies van der Rohe, with associate architects P A C E and Holsman, Holsman, Klekamp, and Taylor (1952)*

900 and 910 N. LAKE SHORE

ARCHITECT: *Ludwig Mies van der Rohe (1956)*

The first pair of these to be constructed have been cited by the Architectural Landmarks Commission with these words:

> In recognition of an open plan in a multistory apartment building where the steel cage becomes expressive of the potentialities of steel and glass in architectural design.

The second pair were built four years later, in 1956. These buildings reflect the skill of a great architect, engineer, and innovator. Nicknamed "The Glass Houses" because they seem to be made entirely of glass, they have been the inspiration for many buildings all over the world.

990 N. LAKE SHORE   ARCHITECTS: *Barancik and Conte (1973)*

This stunning white concrete structure with metal bay windows presents a powerful punctuation mark near the turn of the Drive.

Around the corner of Lake Shore Drive as it bends westward are several palatial apartment buildings that mark the beginning of that section of Chicago referred to as the Gold Coast. You may want to take WALK 13, East Lake Shore Drive, at this point. WALK 15, The Gold Coast, begins 1 block to the west at the corner of Oak Street and Lake Shore Drive (or the corner of Michigan Avenue and East Lake Shore Drive; it's the same corner).

If the weather permits, stroll along Oak Street Beach, which you can reach through a pedestrian tunnel on the northwest corner. Such a walk can be exhilarating, with Lake Michigan on one side and the prestigious apartment buildings of WALK 15 on the other.

CHESS PAVILION
North end of Oak Street Beach   ARCHITECT: *Morris Webster (1956)*

The Chess Pavilion at the north end of Oak Street Beach (the south end of Lincoln Park) is a fitting terminus to this WALK, well worth the stroll north along Lake Shore Drive or the lakefront. This small shelter, guarded by 2 stone chessmen, is beautiful in its unusual and simple design. The reinforced-concrete roof appears to be floating in the air.

Navy Pier
(Bill Engdahl, Hedrich-Blessing)

WALK 15 THE GOLD COAST

WALKING TIME: About 2½ hours.

HOW TO GET THERE: Take a northbound CTA bus No. 151 or 146 at State and Washington streets, and get off at Walton Street (900 N). (Ask the driver if it stops there; you may have to get off a stop earlier, at Water Tower Place.) Cross to the west side of the street and walk north to Oak Street.

---

* Portions of this WALK are in the Gold Coast Historic District, roughly bounded by North Avenue, Lake Shore Drive, and Oak Street.

In Chicago the term "Gold Coast" applies to the area bounded by Lake Michigan on the east, LaSalle Street (150 W) on the west, Oak Street (1000 N) on the south, and North Avenue (1600 N) on the north. The name was given many years ago, indicating that this section of the city was peopled by those with most of the city's gold. (Suburbs and country houses were still a thing of the future.)

This WALK starts with the lakefront high-rises, then focuses on another part of the Gold Coast, starting at State and Division streets and moving through Scott Street, Astor Street, and Burton Place. (It seems especially appropriate that the Gold Coast should include a street that carries the glittering name of John Jacob Astor!)

You will be struck by the beauty and tranquility of this residential area. What is unseen is the struggle to preserve these qualities in the face of change. At one time the section was zoned for single-family residences only, but as land values increased, zoning laws changed to accommodate the economic forces. As in Kenwood (WALK 19), most people could no longer afford to maintain such establishments—with rising taxes, increased cost of operation, and the dearth of household help. The choice for many was selling the property to high-rise developers or converting the interior into apartments. Wherever feasible, the latter was attempted. Fortunately, some of the homeowners have been able to keep their property as single-family dwellings.

ONE THOUSAND PLAZA
1000 N. Michigan

ARCHITECTS: *Sidney Morris and Associates (1964)*

This 55-story steel and concrete condominium building faces the city in commanding fashion.

As you walk north, look at the sculpture by Bernard Rosenthal on the face of the next building. It depicts the other, less fortunate Gold Coast, that in Africa.

1000 N. LAKE SHORE

ARCHITECTS: *Sidney Morris and Associates (1954)*

This 24-story condominium building has a concrete frame and a brick and glass exterior. The unique balconies of punched concrete add movement to the north face.

Cross Bellevue Place.

THE CARLYLE
1040 N. Lake Shore

ARCHITECTS: *Hirschfeld, Pawlan and Reinheimer (1966)*

This condominium building has a concrete and steel frame with a masonry and limestone exterior wall. The aluminum framed windows are bayed at each end of the building. Note that the entrance is not on the front, but from the driveway to the west. The Borden-Stevenson mansion formerly stood on this site.

As you walk west on Bellevue Place, note the rainbow of colors and styles—particularly the innovative doorways—on this block of elegant townhouses.

* THE FORTNIGHTLY OF CHICAGO
120 E. Bellevue

ARCHITECTS: *McKim, Mead and White (1892); for the remodeling: Perkins & Will (1972)*

This imposing 3-story mansion, designed by Charles F. McKim, was originally the Bryan Lathrop house. It is 3 windows wide at the center with wide bays on each side. The symmetry of the facade, in keeping with its 18th-century Georgian style, is pleasantly relieved by having the entrance set in the left, not the center, of the three central arches. It can be compared to some of the fine 19th-century mansions in Boston and New York City designed by this leading architectural firm of that period. It is one of only three remaining examples in Chicago of the work of McKim, Mead and White.

The mansion has been restored and modernized to function as a gathering place for members of the club and their friends. Continue west.

50 E. BELLEVUE

ARCHITECTS: *Solomon, Cordwell and Buenz (1980)*

Since the site does not back on an alley, this 27-story building was designed to provide all service activities through the front. It was set behind a paved courtyard, creating a pleasant entrance area. The street facade is designed to be elegant yet totally functional (except for the pyramids atop the canopy). The base is limestone, the upper floors concrete and glass.

Backtrack to Lake Shore Drive and walk 1 block north.

1100 N. LAKE SHORE

ARCHITECT: *Harry Weese (1980)*

This 40-story luxury condominium tower was constructed of reinforced concrete with punched window openings. Windows are solar bronze-tinted glass and the exterior an off-white concrete. The 38 apartment floors contain 76 three-bedroom condominium units, half of which are duplexes. The units are stacked in such a way that each two-floor layer contains two duplex units and two single-level units.

Walk 2 blocks north.

1212 N. LAKE SHORE

ARCHITECTS: *Barancik and Conte (1969)*

This condominium is easily the most handsome and rugged of the newer structures on this portion of Lake Shore Drive. It is a 36-story, concrete and steel building with a glass curtainwall facing the lake. Black marble forms the entryway and canopy.

* 1244 and 1254 N. LAKE SHORE

ARCHITECTS: *for 1244, Gustav Hallberg (1890); for 1254, Frank Abbott (1891); for the restoration: Artgo Development (1991)*

Two heavy, rusticated stone mansions have been linked at the middle to create 4 apartment units within. Their quality and their Romanesque style make them stand out on this strip.

Cross to the next block.

* 1258 N. LAKE SHORE

ARCHITECTS: *Holabird and Roche (1898)*

This charming 3-story Venetian Gothic townhouse was originally the Arthur Aldis house. Compare its window treatments to those just seen!

1260 N. LAKE SHORE

ARCHITECTS: *Holabird and Roche (1910)*

There is a charming Georgian house at the corner, its stone-canopied door facing Goethe Street. Note the unusual brick quoins at the corner and the simple keystone over each window.

Continue north 2 blocks. You'll cross Goethe Street, which in Chicago is pronounced "GO-thee," with a hard "th" as in "thick."

1418 N. LAKE SHORE

ARCHITECTS: *Solomon, Cordwell and Buenz (1984)*

The configuration of this 29-story building was dictated by the narrow site and the requirements of the City's Lake Front ordinance, which required the approval of adjoining property owners and the necessity of not blocking views of the extant buildings. There is one large luxury unit on each floor. The unusual configuration of the front facade allows views of the lake and Lake Shore Drive to the north and south.

Backtrack to Schiller Street. Walk west.

* 36-48 E. SCHILLER

ARCHITECT: *Possibly C. M. Palmer (c. 1889–91)*

These seven 3-story, vine-covered townhouses, some with bay windows and each with a distinctive subtle design of its own, were built by Potter Palmer. It is likely they were designed by C. M. Palmer, who often worked on the other Mr. Palmer's projects.

Cross Astor Street (which we visit later) to State Parkway. Turn north.

1410 N. STATE

ARCHITECTS: *Solomon, Cordwell and Buenz (1981)*

This 27-story luxury high-rise was designed to give exposures in three directions to each of the two apartments on each floor. The exterior is finished in an attractive brick and with bronze-tinted windows.

Return to Schiller Street. Walk west to Dearborn Parkway, then turn north.

ST. CHRYSOSTOM'S CHURCH
1424 N. Dearborn

ARCHITECTS: *Clinton J. Warren (1894); Clark and Walcott; Bennett and Parsons, consulting architects (1923)*

This fine English Gothic church was built in 1894. In the early 1920s one adjoining building was removed and the others were incorporated into the complex you see today. The original facade was changed, and interior changes made. Work was completed in 1925. The design of the church received a gold medal from the American Institute of Architects in 1926. Walk inside to see a mosaic replica of St. John, copied from a 10th-century mosaic in the Church of St. Sophia in Constantinople. The design of the altar and sanctuary was the last commission of architect David Adler.

Return to Schiller Street. Walk west to Clark Street (the western border of the old Gold Coast) and turn south for a view of Carl Sandburg Village.

CARL SANDBURG VILLAGE
1255-1560
N. Sandburg

ARCHITECTS: *L. R. Solomon and J. D. Cordwell and Associates (1960–72)*

This "village," named for Chicago's famous and well-loved poet Carl Sandburg, consists of high-rise apartment buildings (all named for noted American writers), townhouses, studios, gardens, fountains, and shops. A landscaped central pedestrian mall covers the parking areas, an early use of this approach to land use.

The complex runs between Clark and LaSalle streets, Division Street and North Avenue. An urban renewal plan referred to as the Clark-LaSalle Redevelopment Project cleared the slums to which the area had deteriorated.

St. Chrysostom's Church
(Olga Stefanos)

1211 N. LaSalle
(Paul Zakoian,
courtesy Weese Hickey Weese)

Continue south to Division Street and turn west. Across the parking is an apartment building painted with murals.

LaSALLE TOWERS
1211 N. LaSalle

ARCHITECTS: *for the renovation: Weese Seegers Hickey and Weese (1980–81)*

This renovation changed a 1920s, 187-unit apartment hotel into a 68-unit apartment building. The original arched openings and concrete coffered ceilings were retained to unify the new space. Under the architects' direction, artist Richard Haas painted three murals to complete the three raw elevations. Entitled "Homage to the Chicago School of Architecture," the trompe l'oeil murals incorporate memories of Chicago's heritage—Sullivan's Transportation Building arch, Adolf Loos's 1922 Chicago Tribune competition entry, and three tiers of Chicago bay windows—all to astounding effect.

Walk east on Division Street to Dearborn. Walk north 1 block to Goethe Street and turn right.

BEEKMAN PLACE
55 W. Goethe

ARCHITECT: *Michael Gelick (1986)*

This was the last parcel of land developed in Sandburg Village. Forty-three townhouses are arranged in nine buildings to maximize the number of end units. A four-level office structure comfortably bridges the transition from commercial space on the south to the townhouses of Sutton Place to the north. The exterior of the commercial building, brick and limestone with granite trim and an atrium entry, emphasizes its location and blends well with the brick and limestone trim on the townhouses. The private wing in the center of the development adds a sense of neighborhood and security.

Proceed east on Goethe Street to State Parkway.

AMBASSADOR EAST HOTEL
1301 N. State

ARCHITECT: *Robert S. De Golyer (1926)*

AMBASSADOR WEST HOTEL
1300 N. State

ARCHITECT: *Schmidt, Garden and Martin (1919)*

At the corner are the Ambassador hotels, home of the noted Pump Room (in the East), where so many famous people have dined and danced—or entertained those dining and dancing there. Gregory Peck as Arthur Thornhill paid a visit here in Hitchcock's film *North by Northwest.*

Walk south on State Street. On the east side you will come to a brick apartment building painted white with glass block windows and small terra-cotta figures in the brickwork.

FRANK FISHER APARTMENTS
1209 N. State

ARCHITECT: *Andrew Rebori (1936–37)*

Built just after the 1933–34 Century of Progress in the style of the time, Art Moderne, this structure has high ceilings, balconies, and terraces. Architect Andrew Rebori and artist Edgar Miller closely collaborated to create this unique building, planned to take maximum advantage of a narrow city lot. Skillful detailing of its painted white brick, glass block, and sculptured elements recall an era of faith in the industrial crafts.

Backtrack north to Scott Street.

1 E. SCOTT

ARCHITECTS: *Dubin, Dubin, Black and Moutoussamy (1970)*

The building's tower is a 24-story, reinforced- concrete structure that employs a poured-in-place, reinforced- concrete strut, exterior wall system. This exterior is infilled with glass-and-aluminum fenestration. The typical floors and rooftop pool are serviced by 3 high-speed elevators. Each floor contains 12 dwelling units.

Walk east on Scott Street.

* 17-19-21 E. SCOTT Note these delightful limestone-and-brick facades. The bay windows and individual entrances give each house a bit of Old World charm. The houses at numbers 28 and 32 across the street may have been the work of the same architect.

* 23 E. SCOTT This old townhouse has been handsomely remodeled. The below-grade entrance with the white limestone wall and black columns behind a black iron picket fence give it a modernized look. The mustard-yellow facade of the upper three stories is quite striking.

Continue east to the southeast corner of Scott and Astor streets.

* 1223 N. ASTOR ARCHITECT: *Unknown (c. 1893); for the restoration: Ralph Youngren (1980–81)*

This house of red brick and molded limestone has 2 distinct wood cornices framing the third story. For conversion to condominiums, the interior was gutted and split into three apartments. The exterior was restored.

Walk north on Astor Street.

* 1240-42-44 N. ASTOR Here are three charming townhouses built around 1890. The delightful 3-story structures have bay windows. The below-grade entrance and curved facade on the northern one give an 18th-century character to the house.

* 1250 N. ASTOR ARCHITECT: *Unknown (1890)*

This 3-story townhouse, with limestone facade, imitates an Italian Renaissance design.

* 1260 N. ASTOR ARCHITECT: *Philip B. Maher (1930)*

This is a 10-story, limestone-faced apartment building in the Art Moderne style of about 1930. Kitty-corner is a similar structure. These are two of the elegant cooperative apartment buildings that have replaced some of the earlier one-family residences, and they were designed for very much the same kind of homeowner.

* 1301 N. ASTOR ARCHITECT: *Philip B. Maher (1929)*

See listing above. The Potter Palmers once occupied the top 3 floors here as their Chicago home.

ASTOR TOWER
1300 N. Astor

ARCHITECTS: *Bertrand Goldberg and Associates (1963)*

The building was originally a hotel, designed by the architects of Marina City (see WALK 4).

Continue north on Astor Street.

* 1308-10-12 N. ASTOR

ARCHITECTS: *Burnham and Root (1887)*

Burnham and Root designed these three delightful rowhouses in 1887, and John W. Root chose the center house for his personal residence. After his death in 1891, the house continued to be occupied by his widow, and at times by his sister-in-law, Harriet Monroe, founder of the magazine *Poetry*. The houses are of sandstone and red brick, with beautiful bay windows at the 2nd and 3rd floors.

Backtrack south to Goethe Street. Turn west to State Parkway. Turn north.

PLAYBOY MANSION (HEFNER HALL)
1340 N. State

ARCHITECT: *James Gamble Rogers (1899)*

This large Georgian mansion was originally built for surgeon George Isham. The famous multimillionaire owner of the Playboy empire, Hugh Hefner, owned the building for years, though he lived around the corner. Later owned by the Art Institute of Chicago as a dormitory, the mansion was sold in the mid-1990s.

Walk south to Banks Street. Turn east to Astor Street, then turn north. On the east side of the street is the Court of the Golden Hands, a charming apartment complex with a delightful courtyard.

* COURT OF THE GOLDEN HANDS
1349-53 N. Astor

ARCHITECT: *Howard Van Doren Shaw (1914–15)*

Originally the residence of lumberman William O. Goodman, donor of the Goodman Theatre, this was designed by the architect of that theater as well as of the family mausoleum at Graceland Cemetery (see WALK 30). Each of the golden hands at the entrance seems to be holding an apple. The Georgian facade and marble figure set in a niche make this a memorable sight.

* 1355 N. ASTOR

ARCHITECT: *Howard Van Doren Shaw (1910s)*

Formerly the Goodman Mansion, this is a well-designed, large-scale English Georgian mansion (despite the Italian letterbox), copied from 18th-century originals.

* CHARNLEY HOUSE
1365 N. Astor

ARCHITECTS: *Adler and Sullivan (1892); for renovations: John Vinci (1980); for restoration: Skidmore Foundation (1986)*

This 11-room, 3-story house, a single-family residence until the 1970s, is now occupied by the Chicago Institute for Architecture and Urbanism. Although the official architects were Adler and Sullivan, this is understood to be a design by Frank Lloyd Wright, drawn up for the famous partnership of architects, for whom he was then working as a young draftsman. The building's compactness contrasts with Wright's later rambling Prairie House style but is similar to other earlier works. Some see Sullivan's touch in the wooden balcony and copper cornice.

One owner built an extension to the south to hold a kitchen, which obviously detracted from the original symmetry of the design. The house underwent some renovations in 1980, and in 1986 the Skidmore Foundation removed the addition and restored the house to its original condition. Tours are available by calling 951-8006.

Continue north.

amley House
slie Schwartz)

* 1406 N. ASTOR

ARCHITECT: *David Adler (1921)*

On the west side of the street is a house built for Joseph T. Ryerson from plans by society architect David Adler. The house has a limestone facade and a mansard roof.

* 1412 N. ASTOR

Next door you come to a combination limestone and yellow-brick house. A pediment at the roof line, leaded-glass window, and ornament on the facade give it a Dutch quality.

* 1416 N. ASTOR

ARCHITECT: *Arthur Heun (c. 1917)*

Of Georgian design, this house was built for William McCormick Blair, who with his wife lived on this street longer than all others, it was said—until the 1970s. It is the only house on Astor Street with a side yard and formal gardens.

* 1427 N. ASTOR

ARCHITECT: *William LeBaron Jenney (1889)*

Across the street is a 4-story rusticated red brick house with a handsome, pristine look. Boldly fronted with red rough-faced brick and bandings of limestone, the facade of this significant work by skyscraper pioneer William LeBaron Jenney has been cleaned and restored by its owners.

* 1431 N. ASTOR A curved facade embraces the brick of this building, with white Ionic columns supporting a pediment over the porch. Edward Ryerson, chairman of Inland Steel, lived here.

1435 N. ASTOR This house was built in two stages. It is another facsimile of a great Georgian mansion, a style so popular here at the turn of the century. The pilasters at the corners with their Ionic caps give the facade a somewhat heavy appearance. The pleasant ornamentation below the cornice somehow lends an air of authenticity. Black iron picket fences enclose the grounds.

1432 N. ASTOR ARCHITECT: *James Eppenstein (1936)*

Back on the west side of the street is a remodeling of a townhouse, converting it into 3 apartments. Limestone and large horizontal glass areas give this daring design a contemporary look.

* 1443 N. ASTOR ARCHITECT: *Joseph Lyman Silsbee (1891)*

This is a fine Romanesque Revival composition, built in 1891 for the H. M. May family. Although usually credited to architect Joseph Lyman Silsbee, it may well have been designed by George W. Maher, whose best work is seen in WALK 31.

* 1444 N. ASTOR ARCHITECTS: *Holabird and Root (1936)*

This interesting 4-story house with a limestone facade and bay windows was built for Edward P. Russell. Designed by a firm famous for their Art Deco skyscrapers, it has some of the appearance of Art Moderne.
Continue north. Turn west on Burton Place across State Parkway.

* MADLENER HOUSE
4 W. Burton

ARCHITECTS: *Richard E. Schmidt, Hugh M. G. Garden, designer (1902); for interior remodeling: Brenner, Danforth, and Rockwell (1963)*

This is an architectural landmark. The noted Madlener House, built for a prominent brewer, has been successfully restored by the Graham Foundation for Advanced Studies in the Fine Arts and is the home of the foundation. Note the Sullivan-like ornamentation around the door, relieving somewhat the severity of the design as a whole. In the courtyard to your left is an "architectural fragment" sculpture garden. Open Monday through Thursday 9 A.M. to 4:30 P.M. Call 787-4071 for an appointment.

Backtrack east to the northwest corner of Astor Street and Burton Place.

Madlener House
(Olga Stefanos)

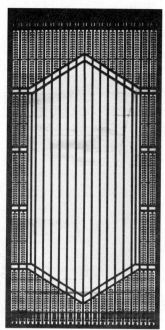

Madlener House detail
(Philip A. Turner)

* THE PATTERSON-McCORMICK MANSION
1500 Astor

ARCHITECTS: *McKim, Mead and White, Stanford White, designer (1891); David Adler (1927); for rehabilitation and conversion: Nagle Hartray and Associates (1978–79); for restoration: Wilbert R. Hasbrouck (1978–79)*

Here stands another landmark residence, now converted to condominiums. The building's historical associations are with Chicago's society life. It was built in an Italian palazzo style for Mrs. Robert W. Patterson, daughter of Joseph Medill (once mayor of Chicago and editor of the Chicago Tribune) by the ill-fated Stanford White. A later owner, Cyrus McCormick, had extensive alterations made in 1927. There is a Chicago flavor to the front windows. A private school occupied it for many years.

This orange brick and terra-cotta building with marble columns— once a mansion of some 40 to 90 rooms (the count depends on one's definition of a room)—was the scene of some of Chicago's most sumptuous social functions. Here, it is said, slept visiting kings and queens as guests. The interior of the house had a graceful winding staircase, 3-inch-thick doors, and marble bathrooms. A step into 20 E. Burton Place (as it was then numbered) was a step into the glittering past.

* Astor Street was designated a historic and architectural Landmark District in 1976 by the Commission of Chicago Historical and Architectural Landmarks and the Chicago City Council. This building is part of the Astor Street Landmark District.

Patterson-McCormick Mansion
(Philip A. Turner)

Cross to the northeast corner of Astor Street and Burton Place.

* GREEK ORTHODOX DIOCESE OFFICE
40 E. Burton

This red-brick house was built for W. Beale in the 1910s, featuring two gently rounded bays and three dormer windows. It is now the office of the Greek Orthodox Diocese of Chicago.

Walk north on Astor Street.

* 1505 N. ASTOR

ARCHITECTS: *Jenney, Mundie and Jensen (1911)*

This Georgian mansion has been converted to condominiums. The ornamental treatments in brick around the second-floor windows and the bracketed cornice are noteworthy.

* 1511 N. ASTOR

ARCHITECT: *Arthur Heun (1917)*

This fine Georgian house was designed by Arthur Heun (see also number 1416). Note the alternating rows of common and Roman brick.

* 1518 N. ASTOR

ARCHITECTS: *Jenney, Mundie and Jensen (1911); for the renovations: Grunfeld and Associates (1986)*

Built for Francis Dickenson, the building is a red-brick Georgian design with bay windows and a well-proportioned entrance. It has been carefully renovated.

Continue to the north end of Astor Street.

1555 N. ASTOR

ARCHITECTS: *Solomon, Cordwell and Buenz (1975)*

This stunning 47-story condominium building overlooks Lincoln Park on one of the most desirable pieces of land in the Gold Coast neighborhood. The base of the building repeats the faceting of the tower in brick and contains the garage and service functions. On top of the base is a landscaped deck with tennis court and enclosed pool. Bronze-tinted glass bays highlight the tower's exterior and frame the spectacular views from each unit.

Walk west on North Boulevard.

* RESIDENCE OF ROMAN CATHOLIC ARCHBISHOP
1555 N. State

ARCHITECT: *Alfred F. Pashley (1880)*

Facing Lincoln Park is a large 19th-century mansion. Many chimneys (you will count 19 if you see them all!), several roof peaks, and impressive facades make this building a distinctive landmark. This has been the home of Chicago's Roman Catholic Archbishop since the 1880s.

Cross to the southwest corner.

1550 N. STATE

ARCHITECTS: *Marshall and Fox (1912)*

This magnificent building was designed by Marshall and Fox. It originally had a single, 15-room apartment on each floor. The enormous apartments and the dignified Beaux Arts facade made this a most desirable address.

Continue west.

THE LATIN SCHOOL OF CHICAGO
59 W. North

ARCHITECTS: *Harry Weese and Associates (1969)*

The Latin School of Chicago is one of the city's finest progressive private schools. This structure houses the upper grades; one block east is the lower-grade school building, at 1531 N. Dearborn Parkway.

The 5-story concrete frame and brick structure serves an enrollment of 450 pupils. Among the features of the building are an Olympic-size swimming pool at the lowest level and a theater-auditorium seating 450 on the ground level. The ground level also includes a large, fully covered loggia at the entry and a two-level spacious gallery. A full-service cafeteria with an outdoor terrace for autumn and spring use is on the 4th level. There are, of course, classrooms, laboratories, and recreation areas.

The urban renewal site and subsequent land use prompted the inclusion of a rooftop recreation area. The music and art studios and the chemistry and physics laboratories are on the top floor, receiving generous amounts of natural light from the top glazed projections visible on the north and west sides. A rooftop botanical laboratory is connected by a spiral stair to the labs. Before urban renewal, this site was occupied by the Plaza Hotel, constructed in 1892 and designed by architect Clinton J. Warren.

Cross Clark Street. Just south of North Avenue is Germania Place.

* THE GERMANIA CLUB
108 W. Germania

ARCHITECTS: *August Fiedler (1889); for the renovation: Harold D. Rider and Nidata Inc. (1992–93)*

The Germania was long the center of activity for many families of German ancestry. The membership dwindled as, in so many other instances, the present generation either moved to the suburbs or no longer felt tied to its roots, and the building stood mostly empty for years. It is now renovated to hold a bank, a restaurant, and its original grand ballroom.

Backtrack north to North Avenue. Turn west to LaSalle Street. Turn south to Burton Place.

BURTON PLACE

Between LaSalle and Wells streets, West Burton Place has a 1-block stretch of some of the most unusual do-it-yourself architecture in all of Chicago. Unique and imaginative remodeling and rehabilitation by the owners themselves make Burton Place fascinating. Tile mosaic, glass block, marble, terra-cotta, and old brick, garnered from nearby demolished structures, are some of the materials used in what is obviously self-help work without benefit of an architect.

Behind the brick walls you will see patios with marble walks, fountains, sculptured figures, flowers, and trees. A plaque on the wall at 155 Burton Place states that this building was restored in 1927 by Edgar Miller and Sol Kogen. Kogen was the first owner on Burton Place to attempt rehabilitation by himself. Working in close association with artist Miller (who also had a hand in the Frank Fisher Apartments), they produced a fascinating and delightful environment for living in the 1920s and 1930s. They were responsible for much of the Burton Place rehabilitation.

Walk through Burton Place, and through the small park to Wells Street.

Germania Club and Sandburg Village
(James Cornelius)

OLD TOWN You are now in the center of a 1½-mile strip known as Old Town. Besides the many restaurants, taverns, bookstores, and boutiques, there is Piper's Alley, an early shopping and entertainment mall. Nearby is the famous Second City, nationally known for its high-quality satirical performances.

   This concludes the WALK. You will find a southbound CTA bus 2 blocks east, on Clark Street, to take you back to the Loop. Or you can start WALK 24 (Old Town Triangle) or WALK 25 (Lincoln Park: Museums, Zoos, and Conservatory) from this point.

1. The Great Court
2. University Hall
3. Jane Addams' Hull-House Museum
   800 S. Halsted St.
4. Chicago Fire Academy
   558 W. DeKoven St.

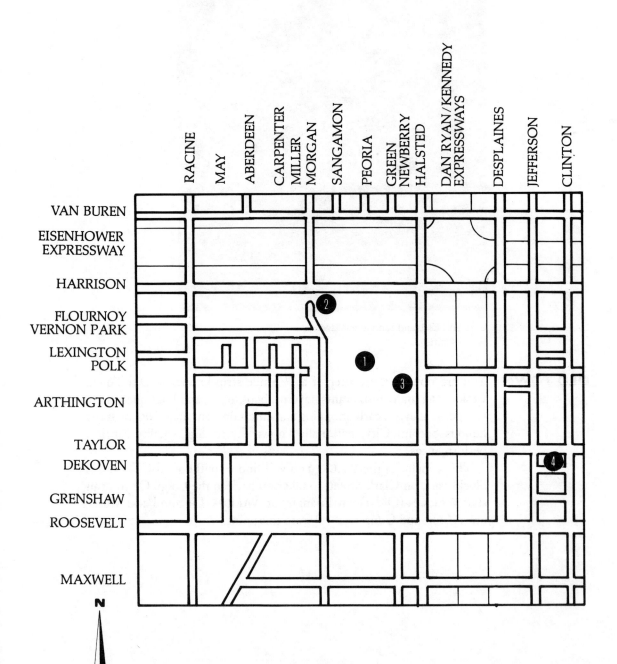

WALK 16 UNIVERSITY OF ILLINOIS AT CHICAGO

WALKING TIME: 1 to 2 hours, depending on how much you "browse" among the buildings.

HOW TO GET THERE: Walk south to Jackson Boulevard. Take a CTA bus No. 7 (Harrison) west and get off at Halsted Street (800 W). Or walk to Dearborn and take the Congress-Douglas "El" to U of I/Halsted.

UNIVERSITY OF ILLINOIS AT CHICAGO

ARCHITECTS: *Skidmore, Owings and Merrill, Walter A. Netsch Jr., partner in charge (1965, 1968, 1971); for the Chicago Circle Center (Student Union Building): C. F. Murphy Associates; for the Great Court renovation: Daniel J. Coffey Associates (1994)*

The modern, urban university has emerged to serve students who live with speed, movement, and change. One of these is the campus of the University of Illinois at Chicago (called UIC), less than a mile southwest of Chicago's Loop. Prior to the building of this campus the University's Chicago undergraduate division operated for nearly 20 years (1946–65) at Navy Pier.

This new location is accessible to students from every part of the Chicago area. Intended originally as a "commuter college," with no resident students, UIC is easily reached by every kind of transportation—commuter railroads bringing passengers to different stations in Chicago, subway and buses, and, of course, private cars. (The college provides extensive parking space.) There is a kiosk with a campus map at Halsted and Harrison streets.

THE GREAT COURT

When built, the campus was referred to as the University of Illinois Circle campus—from the Circle Interchange, where the Eisenhower, Kennedy, and Dan Ryan expressways exchange an unending flow of moving horsepower. But the name alone was not the only contribution of the freeways to the campus. In this constant stream of vehicles the architect, Walter A. Netsch Jr. (who had already designed the Air Force Academy in Colorado) must have seen the elements of his campus design—power, dash, energy, freedom of movement, and strength.

Much of the plan, however, proved unpopular with the people who have used the campus, and the centerpiece of Netsch's design, a vast rooftop Amphitheatre surrounded by 3 smaller concrete lecture pits, was torn down in 1993. Planned as an open forum to be used for drama, debate, "outside classrooms," political rallies, or just socializing, the

179

Great Court with Science and Engineering Offices in background
(Allen Carr)

Amphitheatre was the center of the Great Court, which constitutes the common roof of six lecture buildings. Open elevated concrete walkways led from all major buildings. Defenders of the design said insufficient maintenance, both on top and underneath, caused much cracking and leakage, devaluing the work. Critics said that the many dark corners beneath were a hazard and that so much concrete was antihuman.

With conventional rooftops installed, the Great Court at ground level was redesigned to retain the site's social focus. Greenery was planted and wooden benches and other seating were installed.

UNIVERSITY HALL Presiding over the Great Court with its forum and the surrounding group of buildings, garden courts, and lecture centers is University Hall, a 28-story administration and faculty office building. This high-rise structure spreads in width as it stretches skyward—it is 20 feet wider at the top than at the base—so that the upper floors provide more space. Narrow, almost Gothic windows squeeze between concrete channels.

The campus, developed on a former slum that was Chicago's "Port of Entry" for thousands of immigrants, retains an important link to the past—the two buildings of the original Hull-House, now a National Historic Landmark, resting quietly and with dignity near the main campus entrance on Halsted Street at Polk Street.

Jane Addams' Hull House
(Philip A. Turner)

JANE ADDAMS' HULL-HOUSE MUSEUM
800 S. Halsted

ARCHITECTS: *for Hull-House: Unknown (1856); for the Dining Hall: Alvin and Irving K. Pond (1905)*

These buildings, named for their first owner, perpetuate the saga of Jane Addams and her dedicated aides in helping the forefathers of many of today's students adjust to their new urban environment. Although UIC now occupies the site, Jane Addams's work goes on at more than two dozen sites in metropolitan Chicago.

The University of Illinois has rehabilitated and restored the original two structures. Jane Addams's furniture and fixtures are in their proper places, so that here you have a delightful example of the architecture and furnishings of a late 19th-century Chicago residence in the Italianate style, reflecting the individual qualities of the extraordinary, indomitable woman who once lived and worked there.

The Dining Hall contains an extensive exhibit of historical materials on the history of the near West Side. On the second floor are orientation slide shows on the history of Hull-House and the surrounding neighborhood, shown on request. As a museum, these buildings now make a fitting memorial to Jane Addams.

The Museum is open Monday to Friday, 10 A.M. to 4 P.M., and Sunday noon to 5 P.M. Admission is free. Call 413-5353 for information.

In some ways it is unfortunate that this beautiful restoration stands on its original site, for it is now dwarfed by the massive contemporary structures around it. But in the controversy about the siting of the University's campus (which necessitated taking over a whole block of the Hull-House complex), sentiment for keeping the original Hull-House at its original location was so great that respecting this wish of the area's residents became a necessary compromise.

THE UIC CAMPUS Not only the architectural student will be fascinated with Chicago Campus. Anyone will be thrilled by the scale of this vast complex, reminiscent of the Mayas, yet definitely modern in design and function.

In 1970 the campus was extended south of Roosevelt Road and north of Harrison Street. The total acreage continues to climb and is now more than 180 acres. The current enrollment is about 25,000 students, making it the largest commuter campus in the nation, though some students now live on campus. Students choose among 99 fields for undergraduate credit, master's degrees in 87 areas, and doctoral degrees in 54 specializations. Just 1½ miles west are the University's Medical, Dental, and Pharmaceutical Colleges located on the West Side Medical Center Campus.

The southernmost building on campus is the Physical Education Building located on Roosevelt Road between Morgan Street and Newberry Avenue. Its primary feature is an Olympic-size swimming pool, complete with diving facilities and underwater windows for viewing swimming and diving. It is the largest indoor swimming pool in the Midwest. The Pavilion, on the northeast corner of Harrison and Racine streets, hosts commencement ceremonies as well as basketball and hockey games, for which it has one of the largest seating capacities among U.S. colleges.

The Education and Communication Building is located on Harrison Street between Morgan and Congress Parkway. This structure houses the College of Education, departments of speech, theater, and music. The Jane Addams Graduate School of Social Work is also housed here. One feature is a small theater that can be converted for any type of show use—proscenium, theater-in-the-round, or motion picture.

In contrast with these contemporary buildings is the Maxwell Street Market, only 1 block south of the campus. There is an Old World atmosphere about this, the only outdoor marketplace in Chicago, where almost anything can be purchased, especially on Sunday. UIC's expansion has gradually diminished the market's area.

Another contrast is at the north end of the campus, just across the Eisenhower Expressway. Known as "Greek Town," the neighborhood features a church, homes, and especially shops and restaurants that preserve some of the immigrant and post- immigrant experience.

Walk east on Polk Street, over the expressway, to Des Plaines Street. Turn south to Taylor Street, then east again 1 block. From this vantage, you have an excellent view of River City (featured in WALK 10) across the Chicago River to the east. On the southeast corner of Taylor and Jefferson streets is the Chicago Fire Academy.

CHICAGO FIRE ACADEMY
558 W. DeKoven

ARCHITECTS: *Loebl, Schlossman, and Bennett (1960)*

Several blocks to the east of the University of Illinois at Chicago campus is the Chicago Fire Academy. In front of the orange brick Academy stands a large bronze sculptured flame, by Chicagoan Egon Weiner, expressing the fury of the Fire of 1871, which may have started on this very spot. The Fire Academy was built on the site of the old house and barn of the O'Leary family, whose famous cow is alleged to have kicked over a lantern and thus set off the whole catastrophe, though all admit that the story could not be verified.

A 30-minute introduction to how our present-day firefighters are trained for service in the Chicago Fire Department is available in a tour of the Academy—an experience that always has a fascination for everyone, especially young people, whether fire buffs or not. They also teach fire prevention and fire safety. Tours by appointment: 9 A.M. to 3 P.M.; call 747-6692 for reservations.

While you are at the Academy, don't miss the exhibit of photographs in the main lobby or the restored 1835 horse-drawn hand-pumper fire engine.

Walk west to Halsted Street and turn north to return to your starting point. Or, to get to the Loop, walk north on Clinton Street to Van Buren Street and turn east.

1. Field Museum of Natural History
   Lake Shore Dr. at Roosevelt Rd.

2. John G. Shedd Aquarium
   1200 S. Lake Shore Dr.

3. Adler Planetarium
   1300 S. Lake Shore Dr.

4. Merrill C. Meigs Field
   15th St. at the Lakefront

5. Soldier Field
   425 E. McFetridge Dr.

6. McCormick Place-On-The-Lake
   2301 S. Lake Shore Dr.

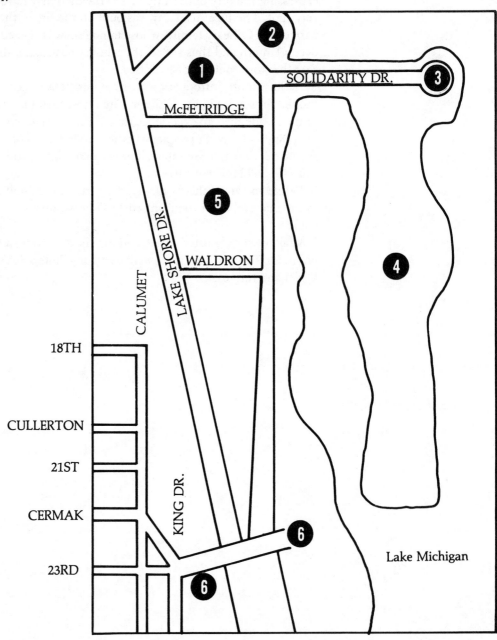

WALK 17   BURNHAM PARK: MUSEUMS

WALKING TIME: About 1 hour for outside viewing. (For inside visits: each museum rates a separate trip. You may want to spend two hours, say, at the Shedd Aquarium and whole days at the Field Museum. Hours vary somewhat; it is wise to call just before making your visit.)

HOW TO GET THERE: You can reach the Burnham Park area over the footbridges from Michigan Avenue at 11th Street or through Grant Park along Columbus Drive and the adjacent formal gardens. Or you can take a southbound No. 146 bus (Marine-Michigan) on Michigan Avenue directly to the Field Museum at the north end of Burnham Park; on summer weekends the No. 130 bus runs from the two main commuter train stations to the museums. (Call the CTA at 836-7000.) If you drive, you will find the best parking near the Adler Planetarium or Soldier Field.

On Chicago's lakefront just south of Grant Park is a great concentration of museums and other public facilities. Still just a portion of Lake Michigan in 1910, it was filled with land and developed in accordance with the Burnham Plan of 1909. Construction of the Field Museum was started in 1911, Soldier Field in 1924, the Shedd Aquarium in 1929, and the Adler Planetarium in 1931. In 1933–34 this stretch of land reclaimed from the lake was the site of Chicago's Century of Progress exposition and a few years later of the city's Railroad Fair. Here, too, are the airstrip of Meigs Field as well as McCormick Place-on-the-Lake, the nation's largest convention center.

Start at the Field Museum, pausing on the long flight of steps for a glorious view of Chicago's downtown skyline.

* FIELD MUSEUM
Lake Shore at
Roosevelt

ARCHITECTS: *D. H. Burnham and Company;*
Graham, Anderson, Probst and White (1911–20); for the interior of
Stanley Field Hall: Harry Weese and Associates (1968);
for the renovation: Harry Weese and Associates (1975);
for the restoration: Harry Weese and Associates (1986–87)

The Field Museum is regarded as the largest Georgia marble building in the world. It was built—and is partly maintained —with funds donated by Marshall Field I, the founder of Marshall Field and Company, then by other members of this and other Chicago families interested in its

Field Museum
(Philip A. Turner)

program. The huge structure is a variation of the Fine Arts Building in Jackson Park (now the Museum of Science and Industry—see WALK 21), which was built in 1893 for the Columbian Exposition and used as the Field Museum from then until 1920, when the Field collections were moved to their present quarters.

Part of the celebration of the Field Museum's 75th anniversary, in 1968, was a redesigning of Stanley Field Hall. This tremendous entrance space on the first floor was named for the founder's nephew, who was closely identified with the museum's development.

The effects of acid rain on the marble and terra-cotta exterior of the museum were studied at length in the 1980s, and possible solutions were identified. A plan evolved to clean and restore the marble walls and base (on which the building sits), the terra-cotta cornice, and the caryatids. On the interior, the staircase network was restored. The principle of the restoration was to remain true to the designs of Daniel H. Burnham, and none of his elements were altered.

The Field Museum is a distinguished showcase for prehistoric and recent cultures, with a staff of scholars behind the scenes who are constantly extending knowledge as the result of their investigations in the fields of anthropology, botany, geology, and zoology. Though the exhibits are classified according to these four areas of knowledge, they seem endless in variety—from the enormous stuffed African elephants and dinosaur skeletons in Stanley Field Hall, and corridor after corridor of dioramas showing hundreds of stuffed animals in their native habitats, to the life-sized figures of prehistoric man in his environment; from one

of the world's finest collections of Oceanic art and of Native American art and artifacts, to displays of meteorites, rare gems, and flowers. The museum is in fact filled with priceless specimens.

The museum is open daily 9 A.M. to 5 P.M. except major holidays. Call 922-9410 for information.

Just northeast of the Field Museum, via a pedestrian tunnel under the Outer Drive, is the Shedd Aquarium.

JOHN G. SHEDD AQUARIUM
1200 S. Lake Shore

ARCHITECTS: *Graham, Anderson, Probst and White (1929); for Coral Reef: Donal A. Olsen (1970); for remodeling: Donal A. Olsen (1975, 1980); for remodeling: FCL (1985, 1986); for Oceanarium: Lohan Associates (1987–89)*

The aquarium was built with funds donated by John G. Shedd, former chairman of the board of Marshall Field and Company. Far smaller than the Field Museum, this is nevertheless one of the world's largest buildings devoted exclusively to living specimens of aquatic life. A white marble structure with bronze doors, it has a simple Doric design, another example of the neoclassical tendency that inspired the style of so many public buildings of that day.

In more than 130 tanks of water the Shedd Aquarium displays some 7,500 living specimens, representing 350 different species of marine and freshwater creatures.

Improvements have been made steadily. In 1970 a Caribbean-ecosystem Coral Reef was added. In 1975 the education center was added. For

Shedd Aquarium
(Chicago Association of Commerce)

the 50th anniversary, in 1979, there was major refurbishing of the Balanced Aquarium room and the main foyer, as well as other upgrading. The Oceanarium, on landfill east of the original building, includes a submerged 3-million-gallon tank for dolphins and whales that appears to merge with Lake Michigan.

The new displays have proved so popular that the Shedd recommends advance ticket purchases. The aquarium portion is open daily except Christmas and New Year's Day from 9 A.M. to 6 P.M. To visit the Oceanarium, an additional few dollars are required. Call 939-2438 for information.

Walk east of the aquarium along Solidarity Drive for the equivalent of 5 city blocks to reach the Adler Planetarium.

* ADLER PLANETARIUM AND ASTRONOMICAL MUSEUM
1300 S. Lake Shore

Adler Planetarium detail
(Allen Carr)

ARCHITECT: *Ernest A. Grunsfeld Jr. (1931); for underground addition: C. F. Murphy Associates (1975)*

The planetarium is named for its donor, Max Adler, a former vice-president of Sears Roebuck and Company. It is located at the lakefront. The small granite structure with its planetarium dome is handsome and strong, devoid of most architectural ornament.

The Astronomical Museum section contains one of the finest collections in the world of antique astronomical and mathematical instruments (second only to the collection in Oxford, England) as well as some of the most modern. Frequent demonstrations are given of how some of these instruments work.

For anyone interested in stars and planets—and who of any age isn't?—the chief attraction of the Planetarium lies in its daily sky show inside the domed chamber. There, the Zeiss projection instrument, also called a "planetarium," reproduces the natural night sky at any time or any place selected. The fascinating lectures that accompany these projections of the sky make faraway scientific information simple and clear for anyone. The sky show varies from month to month.

Admission to the planetarium itself and the other exhibits is free. The building is open daily, except Thanksgiving Day and Christmas Day, from 9:00 A.M. to 5:00 P.M.; Friday to 9 P.M. Call 322-0300 for information.

South of the planetarium on the lakefront is Chicago's "downtown airport."

MERRILL C. MEIGS FIELD
15th at the lakefront

ARCHITECTS: *Consoer and Townsend (1961)*

The architects produced a delicate, well-planned building to serve as the passenger terminal for Meigs Field (which is not readily approachable by walkers). This lakefront airstrip for light planes and helicopters is one of the largest downtown facilities of its kind in the country.

South of the Field Museum, in the area between the southbound and northbound lanes of Lake Shore Drive, is Soldier Field.

* SOLDIER FIELD
425 E. McFetridge

ARCHITECTS: *Holabird and Roche (1922–26); for remodeling: Chicago Park District (1939, 1971); for sky boxes: Chicago Park District (1980–81)*

The stadium, Soldier Field, with a seating capacity of about 106,000, was constructed as a memorial to the troops of World War I. It has been the site of an annual All-Star football game, political rallies, rock concerts, and various other activities. The 100-foot Doric columns that surround Soldier Field bring its architecture into harmony with that of the Field Museum, just to the north. In 1939 the north end of the stadium was

McCormick Place-on-the-Lake
(Hube Henry, Hedrich-Blessing)

closed by the addition of the Administration Building for the Chicago Park District.

In 1971 the stadium was remodeled to accommodate the Chicago Bears professional football team. The remodeling consisted primarily in improving the seating and in adding seating at the north end of the field, replacing temporary stands. Synthetic turf was also placed on the field.

Walk south along the yacht basin for about 1 mile to reach Chicago's premier convention center.

McCORMICK PLACE-ON-THE-LAKE
2301 S. Lake Shore

ARCHITECTS: *C. F. Murphy Associates (1971); for the addition: Lester B. Knight and Associates; Skidmore, Owings and Merrill (1987)*

McCormick Place was built on the site of the previous, 1960 building, which was destroyed by fire in 1967. This structure has outstripped its predecessor as the nation's largest convention center. Gene Summers was the architect in charge for C. F. Murphy Associates. He had previously been an associate of Mies van der Rohe, and the design clearly shows Mies's influence.

The basic requirements submitted to the architects were 1) to reconstruct the severely fire-damaged building with expediency; 2) to enlarge the prime exhibition area to 600,000 square feet; and 3) to maximize the residual value of the existing structure. The increase in building area had to be accomplished without unduly removing valuable lakefront area. Special considerations consisted of a complete fire-protection system. The design concept was to contain the two dominant functions of exhibit and theater under a single unifying roof resting on a platform sheathed

in masonry. A 75-foot cantilever of the roof affords protection to the pedestrian and vehicular passageways around the theater unit and to the truck dock area around the exhibit area.

Overall, the section of the convention center along the lakefront contains approximately 600,000 square feet of exhibition area, a 4,300-seat theater, 100,000 square feet of meeting rooms, a dignitary suite, and 42,000 square feet of restaurant and cafeteria facilities. A below-grade parking facility is located immediately south of the building for 2,000 cars.

Building materials consist chiefly of exposed face brick, painted concrete block, painted structural steel, terrazzo, and exposed concrete floors, plaster, and metal pan ceilings. The exterior curtainwall is made of painted steel framing with 7- by 8-foot polished gray plate glass. The building, or rather project, is a stunning and powerful statement that does credit to the distinguished firm of architects as well as the many city officials involved.

The 1987 addition, designed by Skidmore, Owings and Merrill, provides another 1,150,000 square feet of space. If you walk far enough for a view of the roof, you will see the support system of the "hung roof," which allows for the creation of the largest column-free space in the world. It has an aluminum and glass window wall to blend with the extant structure. A covered pedestrian mall connects the two structures.

The South Building, scheduled for opening in 1997, will add 2 million square feet of space, more than doubling capacity. To make way for it on the west side of Lake Shore Drive, the McCormick Hotel of 1973 was torn down, as was a former Donnelley printing plant of 1947 that had later served as exhibition space. The South Building was to be financed by the largest bond sale in the state's history, the $1 billion to cover renovations on existing buildings as well. A glass-enclosed concourse will span the viaduct over Lake Shore Drive to link the two halves of this massive convention center.

Adler Planetarium
(Olga Stefanos)

1. Widow Clarke House
   1836 S. Prairie Ave.

2. Glessner House
   1800 S. Prairie Ave.

3. Kimball House
   1801 S. Prairie Ave.

4. Coleman-Ames House
   1811 S. Prairie Ave.

5. Elbridge Keith House
   1900 S. Prairie Ave.

6. Marshall Field II (or Schwartz) House
   1919 S. Prairie Ave.

7. William H. Reid House
   2013 S. Prairie Ave.

8. Edson Keith, Jr. House
   2110 S. Prairie Ave.

9. Charles D. Hamill House
   2126 S. Prairie Ave.

10. Second Presbyterian Church
    1936 S. Michigan Ave.

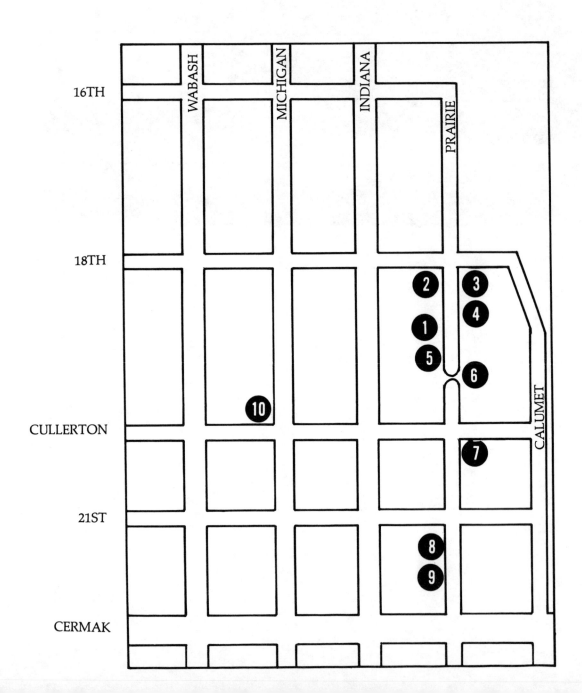

WALK 18 * PRAIRIE AVENUE HISTORIC DISTRICT

WALKING TIME: About 1½ hours.
HOW TO GET THERE: Take a CTA southbound No. 1, No. 3, or No. 4 bus on Michigan Avenue. Get off at East 18th Street. Walk 1½ blocks east to the gates leading into the yard.

This historic district has been restored with 19th-century gas lamps and cobblestones along with the renovation of 5 celebrated houses—Glessner, Kimball, Keith, Coleman-Ames, and the Widow Clarke House—around an architectural park that can be considered an outdoor museum. The Widow Clarke House, which was not part of the original Prairie Avenue district, has been relocated here.

The Chicago Architecture Foundation gives several tours of the Clarke and Glessner houses on Wednesday, Friday, Saturday, and Sunday afternoons. Call the Foundation at 922-3432 for further information. The Foundation also holds lectures and offers tours of several other Chicago-area sites. Call 782-1776.

* WIDOW CLARKE HOUSE
1836 S. Prairie

ARCHITECT: *Unknown (1836); for restoration: Wilbert R. Hasbrouck and Joseph Casserley (1978–82)*

The Widow Clarke House, believed to be the oldest in the city, was built in 1836 for Henry B. Clarke, a hardware merchant and banker, on Michigan Avenue near 16th Street. In 1872, shortly after the Great Fire, the house was moved to 4526 S. Wabash Avenue. In 1977 the City of Chicago moved it and had it restored on the east side of South Indiana Avenue, south of 18th Street.

This handsome Greek revival house is operated as a museum to interpret life in Chicago between 1836 and 1860 when the Clarkes occupied it, at a time when it was one of the two grandest homes in the city. The basement (new space on the new foundation) holds a museum of the history of the house itself from 1836 to 1977.

In the yard toward Prairie Avenue, along with masonry fragments, is the statue George M. Pullman commissioned to honor the 53 settlers killed nearby in the Fort Dearborn Massacre of 1812. Pullman lived at the northeast corner of 18th Street and Prairie Avenue.

Walk out the gates and turn right to the corner.

Widow Clarke House
(Olga Stefanos)

* GLESSNER HOUSE
1800 S. Prairie

ARCHITECTS: *Henry Hobson Richardson (1887);*
for the exterior cleaning: John Vinci (1984)

This is the only remaining example in Chicago of a design by one of the earliest and greatest of American architects, Henry Hobson Richardson. The masterwork is owned by the Chicago Architecture Foundation, which was formed to rescue the house. Since 1967 they have continued their commitment to its restoration. The Historic House museum, a National Historic Landmark, has the appearance and furnishings of the 1890s.

J. J. Glessner, a founder of the International Harvester Company, in 1885 commissioned the great architect to design a house for him on Prairie Avenue, referring to the street as the finest residential street in Chicago. The result is fortress-like, whereas neighboring houses recall the more genteel styles of Europe. With a little imagination you can see an abstract HHR in the two pedimented windows and front-door-with-tympanum-and-arch.

Although this massive 35-room, rough-hewn granite house seems a far cry from the delicate atrium houses of architect Y. C. Wong in Kenwood (see WALK 19), they have one feature in common: window placement in both is designed for privacy and quiet. All main rooms of the Glessner house face a private courtyard, rather than the street. English Arts and Crafts designs predominate in the furnishings.

Glessner House
(Olga Stefanos)

The citation from the Architectural Landmarks Commission reads:

In recognition of the fine planning for an urban site, which opens the family rooms to the quiet serenity of an inner yard; the effective ornament and decoration; and the impressive Romanesque masonry, expressing dignity and power.

Cross the street.

* KIMBALL HOUSE
1801 S. Prairie

ARCHITECT: *Solon S. Beman (1890)*

A "French chateau," which cost an estimated $1,000,000 when it was built in 1890 for W. W. Kimball (head of the piano company), the Kimball House was designed by Solon S. Beman, architect of the town of Pullman. This and the Coleman- Ames house next door are owned by R. R. Donnelley and Sons Company, the country's largest printers, under a protective agreement negotiated by the Historic District Committee. The two were linked in the 1940s by a dual coach house.

* COLEMAN-AMES HOUSE
1811 S. Prairie

ARCHITECTS: *Cobb and Frost (1886)*

Joseph A. Coleman, a hardware manufacturer, built this stone-faced Romanesque-inspired house. The arched entrance porch and turret nicely echo the 2-story bay and gabled dormer.

* ELBRIDGE KEITH HOUSE
1900 S. Prairie

ARCHITECT: *Unknown (c. 1872)*

Elbridge Keith, a hat wholesaler and banker, had this 3-story gray sandstone and brick house built to include huge paneled rooms and parquet floors, anticipating the needs of his Prairie Avenue lifestyle. It is a fine Italiante mansion, with mansard roof and Corinthian columns at the porch. Colonettes frame every window.

MARSHALL FIELD II (or SCHWARTZ) HOUSE
1919 S. Prairie

ARCHITECT: *Solon S. Beman (1887)*

Although added to and reworked many times over the years, this sandstone and brick home clearly bears evidence that Beman was responsible for early work in the 1880s. The enormous house, last used as a nursing home, stood abandoned in the 1980s and 1990s.

WILLIAM H. REID HOUSE
2013 S. Prairie

ARCHITECT: *Unknown (c. 1905)*

This 3-story Classical Revival house has a facade of brick with stone trim. Note the Palladian motif at the 3rd-floor window and the Ionic columns at the porch level. Built as one of a row, the home now stands out among the nearby factories.

EDSON KEITH Jr. HOUSE
2110 S. Prairie

ARCHITECT: *Unknown (c. 1889)*

This is a 3-story house with a limestone facade in Romanesque style, and a large gable at the top. The design may have been influenced by Richardson. Edson Keith Jr., the original occupant, worked in the family millinery business.

CHARLES D. HAMILL HOUSE
2126 S. Prairie

ARCHITECT: *Unknown (c. 1907)*

Charles D. Hamill was president of the Board of Trade, a supporter of the Chicago Symphony Orchestra, and a founding trustee of the Art Institute of Chicago. The red brick house is Classical Revival with a center entrance. It is 5 bays wide.

This is all that remains of the once great wealth-laden avenue of fine houses and mansions. In 1890 one of the grandest mansions on this same Prairie Avenue was that of Marshall Field, built for the multimillionaire merchant by Richard Morris Hunt, the famous architect who had also designed the luxurious dwellings of such New York millionaires as William H. Vanderbilt and John Jacob Astor. Now gone forever are houses torn down in most decades since the 1930s. At number 1808 the great architect Louis Sullivan had rented an office room in 1920.

Nearly all the property in the area has been acquired by the Lakeside Press of R. R. Donnelley and Sons Company, who have constructed an enormous complex of buildings to print—among other things—magazines and telephone directories.

Backtrack north to Cullerton Street. Walk west 2 blocks to South Michigan Avenue.

* SECOND PRESBYTERIAN CHURCH
1936 S. Michigan

ARCHITECT: *James Renwick (1871–74); for remodeling: Howard Van Doren Shaw (1900)*

This fine old semi-Gothic South Side landmark church is a vestige of 19th-century Chicago, standing in what was then the city's finest neighborhood. Renwick also designed Grace Church in New York and the Smithsonian castle in Washington, D.C.

The congregation here was a wealthy and powerful one. Robert Todd Lincoln was on the Board of Trustees. Many of the wealthy packinghouse millionaires, such as the Swifts and Armours, and undoubtedly some of the nearby residents such as the Glessners, Pullmans and Marshall Fields attended here. Howard Van Doren Shaw was responsible for the remodeling after a fire in 1900. After hitting a low point in membership in the 1960s, membership rebounded. The Church now has city, state, and National Register of Historic Places landmark status.

Note the stained glass windows of green pastoral scenes, lavender irises or fields of thick glass lilies. Eight of the windows were designed by the Tiffany Studios and two were done by British artist-designer Sir Edward Burne-Jones.

Tours are available by advance reservation; a donation is requested. Call 922-4533 for information.

To return to the Loop, board any northbound bus on Michigan Avenue.

1. Heller House
   5132 S. Woodlawn Ave.
2. Madison Park
3. 1239–41–43 E. Madison Pk.
4. 1302 E. Madison Pk.
5. 1366–80 E. Madison Pk.
6. Farmer's Field
7. 1351–1309 E. 50th St.
8. 1243 E. 50th St.
9. 1229 E. 50th St.
10. 1220 E. 50th St.

11. 1207 and 1203 E. 50th St.
12. 4940 S. Greenwood Ave.
13. Magerstadt House
    4930 S. Greenwood Ave.
14. 4935 S. Greenwood Ave.
15. 4929 S. Greenwood Ave.
16. 4920 S. Greenwood Ave.
17. 4906 S. Greenwood Ave.
18. 4900 S. Greenwood Ave.
19. 1044 and 1050 E. 49th St.
    and 4858 S. Greenwood Ave.

20. 4901 S. Ellis Ave.
21. 4819 S. Greenwood Ave.
22. 1126 E. 48th St.
23. 1125 E. 48th St.
24. 1144–1158 E. 48th St.
25. 1222 E. 49th St.
26. 1322 E. 49th St.
27. 4858 S. Kenwood Ave.
28. 4852 S. Kenwood Ave.
29. 4915 S. Woodlawn Ave.
30. 4912 S. Woodlawn Ave.

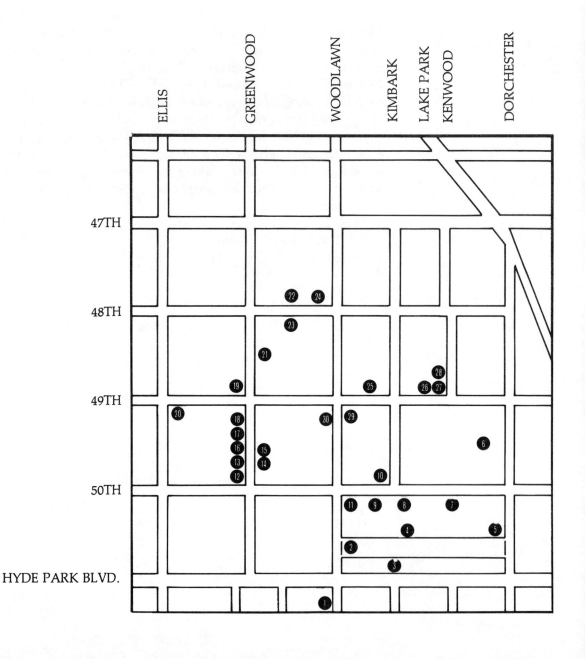

WALK 19 KENWOOD—MADISON PARK

WALKING TIME: At least 2 hours.
HOW TO GET THERE: Take a southbound CTA bus No. 1 (Indiana–Hyde Park) on Michigan Avenue. Get off at Hyde Park Boulevard (5100 S) and Woodlawn Avenue (1200 E).

* Portions of this WALK are included in the Hyde Park-Kenwood Historic District, roughly bounded by 47th and 59th streets and Cottage Grove and Lake Park avenues.

You are now at the south end of Kenwood, which lies just north of the Hyde Park area. Here are some of the finest old mansions, wooded gardens, and boulevards in the city. Among the houses called to your attention here are a number that are famous because of the architects who designed them; these of course will be identified. On the whole, however, houses have been selected for their individual architectural quality, whether or not a well-known architect designed them.

At the turn of the century, Kenwood was actually a suburb of Chicago, where many of the wealthiest families built their estates. Residents have carried some of Chicago's most noted—and notorious—names: Julius Rosenwald, Max Adler, Ben Heineman, Harold Swift, and the tragically doomed families of Leopold and Loeb. As the Depression of the 1930s struck some of the owners and later, when the return of prosperity only increased the costs of domestic help, as well as the difficulty of securing it, the expenses of maintaining such mansions often became too exorbitant to meet. Between much absentee ownership and neglect of property by some who still lived there, Kenwood was rapidly deteriorating. Houses were being sold indiscriminately, and the usual flight of white residents at the appearance of a few black families was threatening.

Citizens of Kenwood are to be thanked—and congratulated—for saving the neighborhood. Beginning in the 1960s, an interracial committee of homeowners took the situation in hand, working with real estate dealers to establish a stable, well-integrated community. Naturally, because of the kind of houses available, most Kenwood homeowners have upper-middle or high incomes.

In Kenwood, too, as in Hyde Park, urban renewal has been responsible for some effective rehabilitation and redevelopment. Two citizens' organizations that cooperated actively with the city government in recent changes are the Hyde Park-Kenwood Community Conference and the South East Chicago Commission.

201

Heller House
(Allen Carr)

* HELLER HOUSE
5132 S. Woodlawn

ARCHITECT: *Frank Lloyd Wright (1897)*

This 3-story blond-brick house is an early example of Wright's work. At first it seems quite unlike the "Prairie House" that he designed 12 years later, for the compact upright lines of the first 2 stories contrast markedly with the widespreading horizontal lines of the Robie House (see WALK 20). Yet the widely projecting eaves and the openness of the 3rd story suggest some of the later design.

The molded plaster frieze at the top of the building is the work of sculptor Richard Bock.

Cross Woodlawn Avenue at Hyde Park Boulevard (51st Street), and walk north about half a block to the entrance of Madison Park.

MADISON PARK   Between Hyde Park Boulevard and East 50th Street, running from Woodlawn to Dorchester avenues, Madison Park is not a park in the usual sense of the word. It is, instead, a small residential section that seems to belong completely to itself; indeed, it has a degree of small village atmosphere about it. As you pass through the large brick and iron gate that tells you the name and the fact that it is private, you see a long stretch of green, with trees and mounds, bordered on each side by a street. Inside the gate, you are overwhelmed by the almost rural quiet of the place. Madison Park stretches from east to west 3 blocks with no north-south streets coming through, and east-west traffic from outside is minimal. The strip of park down the center is used only by the residents—usually a few children playing happily and perhaps an adult lounging on the grass reading. On the west end are apartment buildings, on the east end mostly houses, all dating mainly from the early 1900s. They are home to people of many races and ethnic origins, who have cooperated to maintain the beauty and serenity of this delightful area.

About 150 yards from the west end of Madison Park, stop on the south side of the street.

1239-41-43 E.   ARCHITECT: *Y. C. Wong (1967)*
MADISON PARK

Here are three handsome townhouses, and although they are newer than most buildings in the Park, they seem to blend very well with their neighbors. A yellow brick wall shields lovely private gardens from the view of passersby. The horizontal lines of the stucco upper wall and glass windows give the north facade an appearance of strength. The south facade, which faces Hyde Park Boulevard, has garages tucked just below the livingroom terraces.

Across the yard is a charmingly unconventional yellow brick apartment building.

1302 E.   The pitched roof and garage below the main entrance suggest the style
MADISON PARK   of many buildings in San Francisco. Other features that give this building individuality are the curving bay, the stairs to the first-floor apartments on each side of the garage, and attractive metal grillwork across the balcony of the main entrance.

At the end of the same side you come to eight stunning townhouses well known in the Chicago area—architect Y. C. Wong's "Atrium Houses."

1302 E. Madison Park
(Allen Carr)

**1366-80 E.
MADISON PARK**

ARCHITECT: *Y. C. Wong (1961)*

The exterior walls of these 8 1-story units have no windows whatever, the outside light for all the rooms coming instead from an interior open court, or atrium, not visible from outside. The complete privacy and quiet provided by this arrangement may be considered a decided advantage in urban living. (Compare Glessner House, in WALK 18.)

Walk out to Dorchester Avenue and turn north to East 50th Street. At the northeast corner stands the Church of St. Paul and the Redeemer, two merged Episcopal churches, in a relatively new building constructed after the old St. Paul's was damaged by fire. At the northwest corner is Kenwood Community Park. This stretch of plain green "pasture," covering an entire block, has long been known to Chicagoans as "Farmer's Field."

FARMER'S FIELD
50th to 49th and
Dorchester to
Kenwood

Although the history of Farmer's Field seems somewhat hazy, a house-owner on 50th Street said that a resident of days gone by told him that a cow used to graze there every day as recently as the 1920s. A downtown bank is credited with having bought the property with the commendable intent of keeping it unchanged.

Now walk west on 50th Street and note the row of townhouses extending down the block.

1351-1309 E. 50th

Running almost corner to corner are these well-maintained 3-story homes of the early 1900s. The middle set of stone are all attached, while others stand free.

1243 E. 50th

This is an older house, built about 1875, a charming wooden structure with pergolas flanking the porch, all set in a garden.

1229 E. 50th

Two doors to the west is a gray frame house with very high ceilings. Its setting on the lot lends an appearance of great dignity and serenity.

1220 E. 50th

Across the street is an enormous red brick Georgian house with white door, shutters, and trim. The windows and entrance are in good scale. Note the companion carriage house and gate.

Cross back, and proceed to the corner.

1207 and 1203 E. 50th

ARCHITECTS: *Grunsfeld and Associates (1965)*

Look at these two red brick, 2-story townhouses. Set back from the street, they blend very well with their older neighbors.

Continue west a block to Greenwood Avenue and enjoy the beauty of the many old trees, fine shrubbery, and delightful front yards there and along the way. These provide much of the charm of the area, and Kenwood homeowners are determined to keep it that way. Walk north on Greenwood Avenue to the second house on the west side of the street.

4940 S. GREENWOOD

The majority of the houses along Greenwood Avenue were built between 1910 and 1925. This 3-story red brick mansion is of collegiate Gothic design. Unusual Gothic ornamentation surrounds the front windows and doors. At the rear are a tremendously large yard and garden, and a garage with living quarters above.

Be sure to note the mansion across the street at 4939 S. Greenwood Avenue—an enormous red brick house with quoins at the corners and high-pitched roof. Doric pilasters adorn the entrance porch. This was the home built by Max Adler, of Adler Planetarium fame (see WALK 17).

Back on the west side of the street is a renowned home.

MAGERSTADT HOUSE
4930 S. Greenwood

ARCHITECTS: *George W. Maher (1906); for the remodeling: Arthur Myhrum (1968)*

The Magerstadt House was designed by a contemporary of Frank Lloyd Wright and quite naturally reflects to some extent Wright's style—the long plan and side entrance, for instance, and the wide overhang. On the other hand, Wright would surely not have used the two unnecessary pillars that pretend to support the porch roof. And the building as a whole is more massive than most of Wright's. Occupants of the house completed its rehabilitation in 1968. The interior lighting, bathrooms, and kitchen were completely remodeled; the woodwork was restored and repainted. In general, the interior was given a new glow, making this a truly delightful home.

4935 S. GREENWOOD

This is a heavy 3-story building with semicircular facade extending the entire height. Note the stone columns at the entrance porch and the ornament on the pediment at the roof line.

At 4935½ Greenwood, to the rear, is a 2-story coach house of similar design and material, remodeled in 1963. It is typical of many of the old coach houses in the area.

4929 S. GREENWOOD

This is a well-proportioned red brick house of Georgian design. The white wood trim is in good scale with the rest of the facade.

On the west side of the street is a house of a different school of design.

4920 S. GREENWOOD

This 3-story limestone English Tudor house is worth particular viewing. Also take note of the enormous grounds and gardens, and of the iron picket fence.

4906 S. GREENWOOD

Here you will see a red brick symmetrical facade with a design similar to early Louis Sullivan houses. Projecting bays seem to bracket the roof, thereby drawing the eye upward.

4900 S. GREENWOOD

Walk around to the north side of this enormous, light gray limestone house. Doric columns give an appearance of a large apartment building rather than a private residence. Constructed about 1900, it still dominates its corner. Note the ironwork before the garage to the west.

1044 and 1050 E. 49th and 4858 S. GREENWOOD

ARCHITECTS: *George F. and William Keck (1967)*

Here is a cluster of 3-story, red brick, freestanding townhouses, all with pitched roofs (one of them a mansard roof). They make a handsome addition to this section of Kenwood.

Walk west on 49th Street to Ellis Avenue and turn south.

4901 S. ELLIS   ARCHITECT: *George C. Nimmons (1901)*

This was the home of businessman and philanthropist Julius Rosenwald. The style bears some early ideas of the Prairie school.

Backtrack to Greenwood Avenue and walk halfway north on the east side.

4819 S. GREENWOOD   This stately Georgian mansion has red brick walls with quoins of the same material at the corners. The grand scale of the windows and the ceiling heights give the house an appearance of enormous dignity. The immense, well-landscaped grounds, with matching low wall, include a tennis court at the rear.

Walk north on Greenwood Avenue and then east on 48th Street until you come to a gray brick house on the north side.

1126 E. 48th   ARCHITECTS: *Unknown (1888); for the remodeling: James Eppenstein (1941); Arthur Myhrum (1963)*

Constructed in 1888, this house has been remodeled twice, the major part taking place in 1963. By removing the original front staircase, the architect was free to design a stunning 3-story entrance hall on the east side, which faces a landscaped patio. He set a library adjacent to the entrance hall, with a wall of grillwork between, and placed a large livingroom at the front of the building, facing 48th Street. Other alterations have provided this house with modernized kitchen, a splendid master bedroom with separate "His" and "Her" dressing rooms, studies, and guest rooms on both the 2nd and 3rd floors.

Across the street is a gray wooden frame house behind a hedge.

1125 E. 48th   ARCHITECTS: *Unknown (1895); for the remodeling: Ernest A. Grunsfeld (1938)*

The main house, with the late-Victorian upper story, has an elegant entrance hall, diningroom, and kitchen on the first floor, four bedrooms and two baths on the second. The livingroom is in a 1-story east wing, with windows to the south, facing a large landscaped garden and play area.

Farther east on 48th Street you come to a row of 8 townhouses that have been cited for architectural excellence.

1144-1158 E. 48th   ARCHITECT: *Y. C. Wong (1965)*

These 8 townhouses were designed by the same architect who planned the famous atrium houses in Madison Park. The 7-foot wall that encompasses the gardens around these homes are characteristic of this architect's emphasis on privacy for the homeowner.

Walk south on Woodlawn and turn east on 49th Street.

1222 E. 49th   ARCHITECTS: *Unknown (1906); for the remodeling: Crombie Taylor and Edward Noonan (1946)*

Mostly hidden by foliage in summer, this charming former coach house merits a peek. The all-glass west wall of the livingroom was formerly the coach entrance.

Continue 1 block east to see a very different coach house.

1322 E. 49th   ARCHITECT: *Frank Lloyd Wright (1907)*

Here you see a 2-story coach house, larger than it first appears. The yellow Roman brick and the wide eaves clearly mark this small structure as the work of Frank Lloyd Wright, who designed it for the house below.

Continue east to the corner of Kenwood Avenue.

4858 S. KENWOOD   ARCHITECT: *Frank Lloyd Wright (1892)*

This yellow frame, Colonial revival house was built for insurance broker George Blossom in 1892. While "moonlighting" from his job as chief draftsman for Adler and Sullivan, Wright designed this and several other (now known as the "bootleg") homes in his off hours to help support his growing family. To avoid raising Louis Sullivan's ire, Wright designed these houses under the name of an architect friend, Cecil Corwin, but Sullivan found out in 1893, and abruptly launched Wright on his illustrious independent architectural career. Blossom later had Wright add the coach house (see above).

Now look next door.

4852 S. KENWOOD   ARCHITECT: *Frank Lloyd Wright (1891, 1902)*

Like the Blossom House next door, this brick and stucco residence was clandestinely designed by Frank Lloyd Wright while he was working for Adler and Sullivan. The client, Warren McArthur, also had Wright execute major alterations to the interior in 1902. The Palladian arches on the front porch echo the great 3rd-floor window but do not blend well with an otherwise traditional design.

Backtrack west to Woodlawn Avenue, then turn south to view the last two houses.

4915 S.
WOODLAWN

This is another red brick Georgian house, with an excellent formal facade. The two rounded bays extend from grade to roof. The limestone hoods, white wood trim, and slender white Ionic pilasters at the entrance are all in good scale.

Across the street is a modern house in the heart of this middle-aged group of homes—well set back from the sidewalk and shielded by trees and shrubbery.

4912 S.
WOODLAWN

ARCHITECT: *John Johansen of New York City (1950)*

Although now two generations old, the house looks surprisingly contemporary. The base is of random-cut limestone and the overhanging balcony is of wood. Painted sections of the base—large rectangles in yellow, blue, and green—give a splendid, light feeling to the house. The all-glass stairwell contributes a special quality to this excellent design.

There are many more homes in Kenwood that are beautiful and noteworthy, as those who continue exploring will discover.

1. University Apartments
   1400 and 1450 E. 55th St.

2. St. Thomas the Apostle Church
   5472 S. Kimbark Ave.

3. Lutheran School of Theology
   1100 E. 55th St.

4. Augustana Lutheran Church
   5500 S. Woodlawn Ave.

5. Stanley R. Pierce Hall
   5514 University Ave.

6. 5551 S. University Avenue Building

7. Cochrane-Woods Art Center
   5540–5550 S. Greenwood Ave.

8. Court Theater
   5535 S. Ellis Ave.

9. Quadrangle Club
   1155 E. 57th St.

10. Mitchell Tower
    1131 E. 57th St.

11. Mandel Hall
    1131 E. 57th St.

12. Cobb Gate and Hull Court

13. Joseph Regenstein Library
    1100 E. 57th St.

14. Hitchcock/Snell Hall
    5709 S. Ellis Ave.

15. Nuclear Energy

16. Laboratory for Astrophysics and Space Research
    933 E. 56th St.

17. High-Energy Physics Building
    935 E. 56th St.

18. Biosciences Learning Center
    930 E. 57th St.

19. Kersten Physics Teaching Center
    5720 S. Ellis Ave.

20. John Crerar Library
    5730 S. Ellis Ave.

21. Henry Hinds Laboratory
    5734 S. Ellis Ave.

22. Searle Chemistry Building
    5735 S. Ellis Ave.

23. Cummings Life Science Center
    920 E. 58th St.

24. Cobb Hall
    5811 Ellis Ave.

25. University of Chicago Quadrangle

26. Julius Rosenwald Hall
    1101 E. 58th St.

27. The Walker Museum

28. Albert Pick Hall for International Studies
    5828 S. University Ave.

29. Oriental Institute
    1155 E. 58th St.

30. Chicago Theological Seminary
    5757 S. University Ave.

31. Woodward Court
    5825 S. Woodlawn Ave.

32. Robie House
    5757 S. Woodlawn Ave.

33. Chicago Theological Seminary—Faculty Q
    E. 58th St. and S. Dorchester Ave.

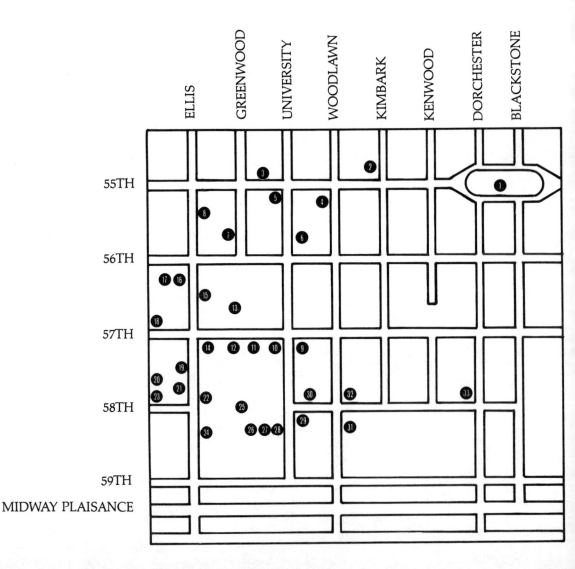

WALK 20 HYDE PARK: NORTH OF THE MIDWAY

WALKING TIME: 2 hours.

HOW TO GET THERE: Take an Illinois Central (IC) suburban train at its Randolph Street and Michigan Avenue underground station, and get off at 55th Street. (Ask before buying your ticket which train makes that stop.) Walk west on 55th Street. If you go by car, take the Lake Shore Outer Drive south to 47th Street, turn west under the IC railroad's viaduct, and then south on Lake Park Avenue (1400 E) to 55th Street. Turn west.

---

* This WALK is within the Hyde Park-Kenwood Historic District, roughly bounded by 47th and 59th streets and Cottage Grove and Lake Park avenues.

HYDE PARK and UNIVERSITY OF CHICAGO

Hyde Park and the University of Chicago are practically inseparable. Faculty, university staff, married students, graduate and undergraduate students, alumni, and friends of the University are clustered about the campus in new and old houses, townhouses, and apartments. And a large percentage of the nonuniversity residents of this multiracial community are business and professional people.

Hyde Park residents are civic-minded to a high degree and guard with real concern their parks, lakefront, and trees. They have sometimes been very much concerned about individual houses that were razed by urban renewal projects. At the same time, they recognize that urban renewal has made many desirable changes in the neighborhood—removing some badly deteriorated apartment buildings, restoring many fine old homes, and constructing new buildings where land was cleared.

Because of the close relation between Hyde Park and the University of Chicago, no attempt has been made in this WALK to separate University buildings from others in the area (though of course each University building is identified as such). For anyone interested in making a more thorough tour of the university campus itself, free tours are available Monday through Friday at 12:30 P.M., leaving from the Admissions Office (room 186) in Harper Memorial Library (seen in WALK 21). Call 702-8650 for information.

It has seemed desirable, however, to divide this area into two WALKS, 20 and 21. These WALKS must not be interpreted as a division between "town and gown." They are suggested only as a geographical division of a large area, in the hope that each WALK will be more pleasurable and less tiring than both together would be. Since an arbitrary separation was necessary, it has been made at the most obvious geographical dividing line—the Midway Plaisance. WALK 20 will take you north of the Midway; WALK 21 will take you to the Midway and to buildings along both the north and south sides of it.

UNIVERSITY APARTMENTS
1400 and 1450 E. 55th

ARCHITECTS: *I. M. Pei; Harry Weese and Associates; Loewenberg and Loewenberg (1959–62)*

A part of the Hyde Park renewal is evident in these two first-rate apartment buildings in the middle of 55th Street. The street has been widely extended on each side to allow a continuing flow of east and west traffic. Known as the University Apartments, these 10-story buildings constituted one of the first large-scale urban renewal projects of its kind. Citizen and government cooperated to bring them about.

Built in an extremely simple form, the twin apartment towers have a forceful horizontal rhythm, resulting largely from the long stretches of closely positioned windows. Although the buildings are set in the midst of city traffic, the landscaping—trees, flowers, pool, and fountain—softens the effect. The many townhouses that surround University Apartments, to the north and the south of 55th Street, were designed by the same architects.

Walk west on 55th Street to Kimbark Avenue.

ST. THOMAS THE APOSTLE CHURCH
5472 S. Kimbark

ARCHITECT: *Barry Byrne (1922)*

The influence of Frank Lloyd Wright on his former apprentice can be noted in the design of St. Thomas the Apostle Church. The warmth of color in the building material, the sculpture around the entrance, and the human scale on which all seems to have been constructed give this church an especially appealing effect. Inside, the fourteen Stations of the Cross, carved in bas-relief by Italian sculptor A. Faggi, are justifiably famous for the sweep and rhythm of their design.

Two blocks west of St. Thomas, on the north side of a boulevard-like 55th Street, is the Lutheran School of Theology.

LUTHERAN SCHOOL OF THEOLOGY
1100 E. 55th

ARCHITECTS: *Perkins and Will Partnership (1968)*

The school consists of 3 stunning sections. Each has transparent enclosures of lightly tinted glass between sweeping curved steel columns that rest on sturdy pins, much like those in bridge construction.

Diagonally to the east across 55th Street is a Lutheran church.

AUGUSTANA LUTHERAN CHURCH
5500 S. Woodlawn

ARCHITECTS: *Loebl, Schlossman, Bennett, and Dart (1968)*

The low, spacious design of this brick church was planned by Edward D. Dart. Generous landscaping adds to the sense of repose. Within the main entrance stands an impressively unconventional bronze statue of Christ, the work of Egon Weiner. The statue was cast in Norway.

One half block west is a University of Chicago residence hall.

STANLEY R. PIERCE HALL
5514 University

ARCHITECTS: *Harry Weese and Associates (1959–60)*

This is a residence for undergraduate students. A high-rise tower, with an effective 2-story extension that echoes Robie House, it has become a distinguished addition to the University of Chicago campus. Tiers of bay windows—a feature restored by this architect to local building after years of disuse—accentuate the vertical lines of the structure.

Now walk south on University Avenue on the east side of the street almost to 56th Street.

5551 S. UNIVERSITY AVENUE BUILDING

ARCHITECTS: *George F. and William Keck (1937)*

This building was one of the earliest modern buildings in the area. Each of the three apartments extends over an entire floor. Across the front of the building at ground level are 3 garages, and the entrance is placed inconspicuously at the side, far back from the street. Contrast in the brick facade on the University Avenue side is provided by dark metal louvres, two at each floor level—for the two wide windows—with a stretch of contrasting wood between them. At the time this building was erected its design was considered quite extreme, though today it blends well with other architecture in the area and seems to meet naturally the needs of the city dweller. The two architects lived here for a time.

Walk west on 56th Street to Greenwood Avenue.

COCHRANE-WOODS ART CENTER
5540-5550 S. Greenwood

ARCHITECT: *Edward Larrabee Barnes (1974)*

The Center's 2-story limestone-faced contemporary structures face each other across a court. The Art Department, at the north, houses classrooms and offices. The David and Alfred Smart Gallery, at the south, was designed to contain sculpture. (The university has an extensive collection of modern art pieces on display around the campus.) The interior exhibition space was designed for the permanent collection and temporary exhibits. On the mezzanine of the dramatic entrance hall are the Gallery offices, a conservation workshop, and a prints and drawings study room. The permanent collection includes representative works of art—paintings as well as sculpture—from Classical Greece through modern times, including Oriental art.

Admission to the Gallery is free. Hours: Tuesdays to Saturdays 10 A.M. to 4 P.M.; Sundays noon to 4 P.M.; closed Mondays.

The Court Theater can be reached two ways: on weekdays you can walk straight through the courtyard, which contains a figure by Henry Moore and a bronze by Arnaldo Pomodoro. (Take note of these forms because you will see another sculpture by each artist later in the WALK.) There is also a sculpture by Richard Hunt that used to sit in the main quadrangle. If the entrance gates are locked, walk back to 56th Street, then continue west ½ block. Court Theater is visible up a pathway on your right.

COURT THEATER
5535 S. Ellis

ARCHITECTS: *Harry Weese and Associates (1981)*

The new home of Court Theater is a technically sophisticated 250-seat theater. The audience sits in three banks of upholstered seats wrapped around the front of the thrust stage. The thrust area of the stage can be shortened, altered, or eliminated altogether for conventional proscenium staging. The building's lobby has approximately the same dimensions as the stage so that rehearsals can be conducted there when necessary. State-of-the-art technology was used so that lighting equipment could be hung anywhere in the auditorium and lighting and sound cues for an entire production can be prerecorded. Note that the coursing of the stone blocks is a scaled-down version of the neighboring Cochrane-Woods building.

Backtrack to University Avenue, turn right, and continue to 57th Street.

QUADRANGLE CLUB
1155 E. 57th

ARCHITECT: *Howard Van Doren Shaw (1914)*

On the southeast corner you will see the faculty club known as the Quadrangle Club. Designed in a University Gothic style, it contains a second-floor, cathedral-type dining hall with great wood trusses that span the room, as well as smaller dining and meeting rooms. There are tennis courts south of the club.

On the southwest corner is Mitchell Tower.

MITCHELL TOWER
1131 E. 57th

ARCHITECTS: *Shepley, Rutan and Coolidge (1903)*

Mitchell Tower is the entrance to Mandel Hall and Hutchinson Commons, part of a complex of buildings that form the northeast portion of the original quad. The exteriors of the English Gothic structures are Indiana limestone. The tower, copied from the tower of Magdalen College, Oxford University, houses the Alice Freeman Palmer Bells and campus radio station (WHPK-FM). It has no ground floor, instead sitting atop Reynolds Student Clubhouse, north of Mandel Hall. Hutchinson Commons is a vaulted dining hall, with massive stone fireplaces and wood wainscoting, modeled on that of Christ Church College, Oxford.

* MANDEL HALL
1131 E. 57th

ARCHITECTS: *Shepley, Rutan and Coolidge (1903); for the remodeling: Skidmore, Owings and Merrill (1978)*

The exterior was modeled after the great hall of Crosby Place in England, built about 1450 as the home of Sir John Crosby. The entire building has been carried out in English Gothic and harmonizes with the other early member structures of the Quadrangle. The donor was Leon Mandel, a prominent Chicago retailer.

The auditorium, seating about 1,000, has been for years a show place for drama, dance, ballet, musicals, and symphony concerts. The building is not only a University landmark but one for the entire Chicago area as well. The great hall, lounges, and theater are well worth a visit. A bronze tablet in the lobby by sculptor Lorado Taft is a portrait of Senator Stephen A. Douglas.

In 1978 the University began a program to upgrade the capabilities for continued viable use of Mandel Hall. Ongoing University arts activities over the years have required a level of technology not available to the original architects. For decades, makeshift additions of lighting and sound equipment and control and projection facilities had been made. The renovation program developed a new, enlarged, and more appropriately shaped music platform at the audience side of the proscenium arch. This platform, which comfortably seats 100 musicians, is separated from the stage house at the back of the proscenium arch by a system of hard movable panels. This isolation of the absorbent stage house from the music environment allows music and theater activities to go on simultaneously without striking or resetting sets. A system of acoustical reflectors is suspended over the music platform. Sight lines and sound have been improved on the main floor by moving the side aisles to the outside wall and relocating the side seats closer to center.

Projection, sound, and light equipment in the balcony were moved into new facilities constructed behind the hall, which allowed the reinstallation of 60 center seats with excellent sight lines. New provisions for contemporary theater lighting and appropriate musicians' lighting were provided at the sides of the proscenium and in the ceiling. Between the backstage area and the neighboring Eckhart Hall to the south, a small building was inserted to provide loading and unloading capability, general backstage work space, and storage for musical instruments, risers, theater props, rigging, and costumes. Dressing room space for performers was created by redeveloping facilities below the stage, including three private dressing rooms and a small performers' lounge.

The interior of the hall was returned to much of its original rich, Victorian-era palette. R. Lawrence Kirkegaard was the acoustical consultant, Lustig and Associates was the consultant on stage lifts and theatrical lighting, and John Vinci assisted in the determination of the original palette and techniques.

Walk west on 57th Street.

COBB GATE and HULL COURT
Opposite the Regenstein Library

ARCHITECT: *Henry Ives Cobb (1897)*

The great Gothic gate, in the spirit of those at Oxford and Cambridge universities, was constructed as a part of Hull Court of the Quadrangle. The court consists of the Anatomy, Botany (named the Ida B. and Walter Erman Biology Center), and Zoology buildings, and Culver Hall. Notice how effectively this Gothic courtyard shuts out the outside world. We will return to this beautiful space later.

Across 57th Street is the Regenstein Library.

JOSEPH REGENSTEIN LIBRARY
1100 E. 57th

ARCHITECTS: *Skidmore, Owings and Merrill, Walter Netsch, partner in charge (1970)*

The University's Graduate Research Library is an exceptionally popular addition to the intellectual life and to the architecture of the campus. Of the same gray limestone as its Gothic neighbors, it has a modern design that is impressive in scale and its door aligns with Cobb Gate.

The university's collections in the social sciences and the humanities, excluding law, art, and theology, are held here. There are 7 service floors and some 577,000 square feet. The original capacity was 3.5 million books; this was increased by about one quarter in the early 1990s with more shelving squeezed in. Costing $21 million, it was built principally through the generosity of Chicago industrialist Joseph Regenstein.

The interior is highly functional. Each of the major service floors is divided into four areas; book stacks, offices, faculty studies, and reading areas. The architecture harmonizes well with the adjoining buildings. The vertical wall elements and narrow recessed bay windows relieve the structure's mass. Exterior walls are formed by deeply grooved, cut limestone slabs, which add nice texture to the surface.

Continue west. Wrapping around the southeast corner of Ellis Avenue and 57th Street is a residence hall.

HITCHCOCK/ SNELL HALL
5709 S. Ellis

ARCHITECTS: *for Snell: Henry Ives Cobb (1893); for Hitchcock: D. H. Perkins (1902)*

The older building, originally a women's residence and an integral part of the early Quadrangle, has an Indiana limestone facade styled in the English Gothic period. Its later neighbor, originally for men, was designed by Dwight Perkins, an early advocate of shedding old architectural trappings, and the simplified Gothic style is representative of his approach. It contains an infirmary and a library, and a "preacher's room" was furnished at one time. With its low pitched roof, shed dormers, and horizontal emphasis it really could be described as "Prairie Gothic." The two residences are now linked internally as one.

Now walk north ½ block on Ellis Avenue.

* NUCLEAR ENERGY
Ellis between 56th and 57th

SCULPTOR: *Henry Moore (1967)*

To the west of Regenstein Library, on Ellis Avenue between the tennis courts, is a great bronze sculpture—12 feet high, weighing 3 tons, standing on a round base of black polished granite. Entitled "Nuclear Energy," this extremely simple but impressive work of art by the distinguished British sculptor Henry Moore commemorates man's achievement in bringing off the first controlled atomic chain reaction—as explained in one of the 4 plaques mounted on a slab of marble near the curb. Under a Stagg Field bleacher near this same spot, on December 2, 1942, Enrico Fermi and 41 other leading scientists accomplished the great breakthrough that introduced the Atomic Age. Speaking of the sculpture, Moore explained that it relates both to the mushroom cloud of a nuclear explosion and to the shape of a human skull, with reminiscences of church architecture in the lower part. Walk all around it to appreciate all its facets.

Continue north to 56th Street, then turn left.

LABORATORY FOR ASTROPHYSICS AND SPACE RESEARCH
933 E. 56th

ARCHITECTS: *Skidmore, Owings and Merrill (1964)*

This and the next building, its smaller neighbor, are part of the Enrico Fermi Institute. In this particular building scientists carry out research in the space sciences. It is a 2-story cast-concrete structure atop a small berm; the siting and the recessed walls of glass windows cause it to loom out of proportion to its size.

HIGH-ENERGY PHYSICS BUILDING
935 E. 56th

ARCHITECTS: *Hausner and Macsai (1967)*

Appearing like a loading dock, the 3-story and penthouse building is actually a reinforced concrete research laboratory for the physical sciences. The simple, sturdy design serves the purpose well. Its entrance is around on the south.

Overleaf:
"Nuclear Energy" sculpture by Henry Moore
(Philip A. Turner)

BIOSCIENCES LEARNING CENTER
930 E. 57th

ARCHITECTS: *Loebl, Schlossman and Hackl with Stubbins Associates (1993)*

In yet another modification of the Gothic style, this long narrow limestone structure of 4 stories includes a tower above one corner and six 3-story windows across the front, divided by limestone piers. In both features it is reminiscent of the Rockefeller Chapel (see WALK 21). Here the depth of the rectangle is broken up by an interesting pattern of short-tall-short windows on each long side, as well as by two angled bays announcing the doorway on the east side. The building also contains the Jules F. Knapp Medical Research facility.

Return to Ellis Avenue south of 57th Street. The buildings on the east side of the street are part of the main University Quadrangle. They are a mix of original structures and some more recent construction. Before we enter the main quad, this WALK will take you to see a newer quadrangle for the sciences.

On the west side of the street walk through the gate.

KERSTEN PHYSICS TEACHING CENTER
5720 S. Ellis

ARCHITECTS: *Holabird and Root (1985)*

With the completion of this building, the Science Quadrangle became the ninth of the university's quadrangles. It is instructive to compare this to the original Cobb-designed quadrangle across the street. The corner site demanded a formal limestone facade to complement the surrounding buildings. The side of the building facing the quadrangle is less formal. The building is organized around a central circulation spine that forms a pedestrian bridge at the second level and links the Research Institute north across the street. This spine supports all vertical circulation and provides space for displays and meeting areas for students and faculty. If you look up into the postmodern gabled entrance, you will see steel bristles attached to the upper supports as an antipigeon device.

Cross the quad to the low white building.

JOHN CRERAR LIBRARY
5730 S. Ellis

ARCHITECTS: *Stubbins Associates of Cambridge, Mass.; Loebl, Schlossman and Hackl (1984)*

John Crerar established an independent science library in 1894 in the Loop. Three homes later (at Field's upper floors; 150 N. Michigan Avenue; and the IIT campus), the collection was merged with the university's in 1984, at last fulfilling its patron's wish that the South Side have a permanent counterpart to the Newberry Library on the North Side. The public may use this 4-story, million-volume repository of medical and scientific knowledge.

The building, situated at the hub of the physical and medical science block, was planned as the fulcrum of a new quadrangle, the first to be built in two decades. The limestone facade is in keeping with the character and tradition of the existing campus buildings. The focal point of the project is a 3-story skylighted atrium space containing a large suspended sculpture of aluminum and crystal entitled *Crystara* by artist John David Mooney.

The inspiration for the impressive, free-standing arch outside is the Gothic arch on the old Abbott Memorial Hall. The tall building just south of the library is the Cummings Life Science Building (which we will see later), and Abbott is south of that.

To account for the anticipated water table beneath the library, its lower level and pedestrian connections were located 7 feet below grade, while the main floor was raised 7 feet above grade.

On the quad's east side is the Henry Hinds Laboratory. To get a better view, walk back through the gate and cross Ellis Avenue.

HENRY HINDS LABORATORY
5734 E. Ellis

ARCHITECTS: *I. W. Colburn and Associates; J. Lee Jones, associate architect (1969)*

The University's Geophysical Sciences Building was the first in the science center that now occupies the entire block. Much of the design was determined by the new demands of research and teaching in the geophysical sciences. It seems at first to have no relation to the neo-Gothic buildings of the original Quadrangle directly across from it, but its design includes many concessions to the earlier style. The brick walls (for instance), which carry the load, are covered with a thin layer of Indiana limestone, the material used in the older buildings; the brick is allowed to show only here and there; the numerous towers, though of highly individual form, attempt to bring the entire building into greater harmony with the Gothic-towered structures of the old campus. Note the metal bay windows that are not only colorful, but highly practical.

If you can, enter the foyer to see Ruth Duckworth's wonderful ceramic mural-as-environment entitled *Earth, Water and Sky* (1969). (Another of her works can be seen in the Exchange Center, WALK 6.)

Cross to the east side of Ellis Avenue.

SEARLE CHEMISTRY BUILDING
5735 S. Ellis

ARCHITECTS: *Smith, Smith, Haines, Lundberg and Waehler of New York (1967)*

This 5-story structure is mainly a series of scientific laboratories and offices. It is sheathed in Indiana limestone to harmonize with its neighbors. However, the Gothic design has been simplified to create no visual "cacophony" whatever.

Cross the street and walk past the red brick bookstore of 1901. At the mall, turn right about 100 yards.

Henry Hinds Laboratory
(Philip A. Turner)

**CUMMINGS LIFE
SCIENCE CENTER
920 E. 58th**

ARCHITECTS: *I. W. Colburn and Associates; Schmidt, Garden and
Erickson; Harold H. Hellman, University Architect (1973)*

The stunning high-rise research center is designed with vertical piers of
red brick in relief against a background of the Indiana limestone facade.
The small windows clearly indicate the necessarily confined interior
research laboratories.

At 10 stories with 2 penthouses, this is the tallest building on campus.
The construction is reinforced concrete. The 40 narrow brick towers
around the perimeter contain exhaust ducts from laboratories. The
varying pattern of the bases of these piers is delightful.

Colburn has reversed the use of brick and limestone and has varied the
tower heights from his treatment in the Hinds Laboratory just around
the corner. Nevertheless, there is a strong similarity in style, as both
buildings appear to be part of a great medieval fortress through which
one enters across a symbolic moat. Both rely on the updated flying

buttresses for their vertical lines; and both achieve a rightful place on campus.

Walk back east, but stop at the plaza to your right. This is the Surgery-Brain Research Pavilion, seen in WALK 21. The 12- foot bronze disc by Arnaldo Pomodoro, whose work we saw earlier, used to be easily rotated.

Cross back to the east side of the street.

COBB HALL
5811 Ellis

ARCHITECTS: *Henry Ives Cobb (1892); for the remodeling: Burnham and Hammond (1967)*

This structure, at the central west edge of the Quadrangle, is one of the original members. It is 4 stories with an Indiana limestone exterior that is rich with bay windows. The undergraduate classrooms and facilities include an auditorium, biology laboratory, art gallery, and office of the Renaissance Society.

The building was named for a patron, Silas B. Cobb, not for the architect.

Walk east on the footpath along the north side of Cobb Hall.

UNIVERSITY OF CHICAGO QUADRANGLE
57th and 59th, between Ellis and University

ARCHITECTS: *Henry Ives Cobb; Shepley, Rutan and Coolidge; Charles Z. Klauder; and others (1891 to the present)*

This is the original campus of the University of Chicago, called "the Quadrangle." Occupying 4 city blocks, the Quadrangle as a whole follows the original plan prepared by Henry Ives Cobb in 1890—a large central quadrangle flanked by 3 small quadrangles to the south and 3 more to the north, all surrounded by buildings of Indiana limestone in the late English Gothic style. Cobb himself designed all the buildings that were constructed before 1900, and later architects used the neo-Gothic style exclusively through the 1940s. This mass of Gothic structures comprises the architectural heritage to which subsequent architects generally deferred.

The University Administration Building sits on the main east-west axis at the western side of the Quadrangle. A 6-story structure with a highly simplified Gothic exterior, it also contains the University of Chicago Press. As you step into the Quadrangle, you are struck by the planned arrangements of structures, walks, roads, landscaping into a large, intricate, but orderly web of convenience for students and faculty. Buildings are laid out on the various axes and subaxes, and many do not meet the eye at first glance. It is a joyful experience to wander onto a small Gothic chapel that is partly hidden behind a large academic building and surrounded by trees. Yet each building has been designed or renovated to form a complex of similar disciplines.

Cobb Hall
(Leslie Schwartz)

The student newspaper, the *Maroon*, quoted Eero Saarinen ("Campus Planning: The Unique World of the University," *Architectural Record*, November 1960), during the time he served as consulting architect to the university:

Wandering in the University of Chicago today, one is amazed at the beauty achieved by spaces surrounded by buildings all in one discipline and made out of a uniform material; where each building is being considerate of the next, and each building—through its common material—is aging in the same way. . . . All are in the Gothic style, [giving] us today a beautiful, harmonious visual picture.

The cohesiveness of the old quadrangles does not rest entirely on the use of the Gothic style. Some of the buildings defy major elements of the tradition, conforming only in the material used.

If you are standing in the center of the Quadrangle, the buildings to the southeast are the business school.

JULIUS ROSENWALD HALL
1101 E. 58th

ARCHITECTS: *Holabird and Roche (1915); for the renovation: Samuel A. Lichtmann (1972)*

This Indiana limestone, English Gothic structure is a part of the complex of business school buildings. The modernized group of classrooms, offices, and library replaced the former geography disciplines. Rosenwald, along with several other of the original Gothic structures in the Quadrangle, has been successfully renovated inside while retaining the original qualities of the exteriors.

Directly to the east of Rosenwald Hall is The Walker Museum.

THE WALKER MUSEUM

ARCHITECTS: *Henry Ives Cobb (1893); for adaptive reuse: Nagle Hartray and Associates (1980)*

Designed by Cobb as a geological museum, this is now in adaptive reuse as a part of the business school. Go through the carved oak doors to see how the designers totally changed the inside to make it serve its new function.

Immediately to the east is Albert Pick Hall.

ALBERT PICK HALL FOR INTERNATIONAL STUDIES
5828 S. University

ARCHITECTS: *Ralph Rapson and Associates; Burnham and Hammond (1971)*

Albert Pick Hall is at the eastern edge of the Quadrangle. As you approach it, your eye catches the remarkable combination of planes and surfaces—all in gray limestone to match the color of its neighbors. It is like emerging from the 12th to the 20th century in one short WALK. The Gothic spiral is there, not only in the limestone, but in the great flying buttresses, and some of these are corbeled while others are supported on columns. The entire effect of the great verticality—the reaching for the sky—is indeed a strong architectural statement. The University Avenue entrance has an interesting use of glass and metal for a portion of the facade. Their horizontal lines seem to balance the verticality.

The Adlai Stevenson Institute of International Affairs, formerly housed in the Robie House, moved here in 1976.

Walk across the street. On the southeast corner of 58th Street and University Avenue is the internationally famous Oriental Institute.

ORIENTAL INSTITUTE
1155 E. 58th

ARCHITECTS: *Mayer, Murray and Phillip (1931)*

The Oriental Institute contains one of the world's major collections of art, religious, and daily life objects from the Ancient Near East: the Nile Valley, Palestine, Syria, Anatolia, Mesopotamia, Persia, and parts of the Ottoman Empire. The timeline covered is from approximately 5000 B.C. to about 100 A.D. Hours are Tuesdays to Saturdays 10 A.M. to 4 P.M.; Sundays noon to 4 P.M.; closed Mondays. Admission is free.

Across the street is the Chicago Theological Seminary.

CHICAGO THEOLOGICAL SEMINARY
5757 S. University

ARCHITECT: *Herbert H. Riddle (1926)*

This striking red brick structure with stone trim is a unique combination of English Georgian and Gothic design. The soaring 162-foot tower can be seen from the Quadrangle or from the Quadrangle Club 1 block away.

A driveway bisects the building on the ground floor by the tower. In the west wing are two chapels (one seating 200), a library, and the classrooms. The stained-glass windows of the larger chapel were executed by the Willett Stained Glass Studios of Philadelphia. The residential floors are located in the east wing.

Walk east on 58th Street and turn south on Woodlawn Avenue.

WOODWARD COURT
5825 S. Woodlawn

ARCHITECT: *Eero Saarinen (1958)*

This residence hall for 300 students, the door set well beyond the steps, is interesting for the positioning of its components. But the design is not up to the very high standards established by Saarinen in the Laird Bell Law Quadrangle. (See WALK 21.)

At the northeast corner of Woodlawn Avenue and 58th Street is Frank Lloyd Wright's famous Robie House.

* ROBIE HOUSE
5757 S. Woodlawn

ARCHITECTS: *Frank Lloyd Wright (1909); for the restoration: Frank Lloyd Wright Office, Wesley Peter in charge (1964); Skidmore, Owings and Merrill (1967); consulting architect for restoration: John Vinci (1983)*

This house was designated a National Historic Landmark in 1963. It was renovated in 1964—the funds coming from public subscriptions—after the house was donated to the University by William Zeckendorf. Built as a private home, this is probably the best-known example of Wright's Prairie House.

The Citation by Chicago's 1957 Architectural Landmarks Commission reads:

> In recognition of the creation of the Prairie House—a home organized around a great hearth where interior space, under wide sweeping roofs,

Robie House
(Olga Stefanos)

opens to the outdoors. The bold interplay of horizontal planes about the chimney mass, and the structurally expressive piers and windows, established a new form of domestic design.

The Citation on a second plaque, presented by the 1968 Commission, which includes preservation of historical as well as architectural landmarks, reads:

> Robie House combines all the elements of Wright's mature style. It is his boldest example of a Prairie House design and one of the most significant buildings in the history of architecture.

In 1967 the Robie House was restored and refurnished in its original style. It now houses the Alumni Association offices. Subsequent restoration of the south balcony was done in 1983 under the direction of John Vinci. There are free tours seven days a week at noon. Call 702-2150 for information.

Walk east on 58th Street 3 blocks to Dorchester Avenue to see a surprisingly unconventional group of homes.

CHICAGO THEOLOGICAL SEMINARY FACULTY QUADRANGLE
Northwest corner of E. 58th and Dorchester

ARCHITECTS: *Loebl, Schlossman, Bennett and Dart, Edward D. Dart, partner in charge (1963)*

No attempt was made here to harmonize the architecture of these houses with that of the older buildings nearby. On the contrary, they defy previously accepted patterns with refreshing individuality. Instead of following the lines of the street, for instance, as do the endless rows of houses in Chicago—and most other cities—their sides face the street on a diagonal, deliberately set askew. The roofs, instead of being flat or gabled, slope steeply from one side to the other with wide overhang. All eight houses, harmonizing well with each other, are clustered around a central green that is elevated, rolling and sloping gently toward the sidewalk. The houses won an award for excellence in architecture.

This is the end of WALK 20. To return to the Loop, walk north to 57th Street and then east 3 blocks to the elevated station of the Illinois Central suburban line that brought you to Hyde Park.

1. Sonia Shankman Orthogenic School
   1365 E. 60th St.

2. Public Administration Center
   1313 E. 60th St.

3. New Graduate Residence Hall
   1307 E. 60th St.

4. Laird Bell Law Quadrangle
   1111 E. 60th St.

5. School of Social Service Administration Building
   969 E. 60th St.

6. Social Services Center
   950 E. 61st St.

7. Midway Studios
   6016 S. Ingleside Ave.

8. Fountain of Time

9. The University of Chicago Medical Center
   5841 S. Maryland Ave.

10. William Rainey Harper Memorial Library
    1116 E. 59th St.

11. Social Science Research Building
    1126 E. 59th St.

12. The University President's House
    5855 S. University Ave.

13. Rockefeller Memorial Chapel
    5850 S. Woodlawn Ave.

14. Ida Noyes Hall
    1212 E. 59th St.

15. Emmons Blaine Hall
    1362 E. 59th St.

16. Henry Holmes Belfield Hall
    5815 S. Kimbark Ave.

17. University High School
    5834 S. Kenwood Ave.

18. Bernard E. Sunny Gymnasium
    5831 S. Kenwood Ave.

19. International House
    1414 E. 59th St.

20. Museum of Science and Industry
    E. 57th St. at South Lake Shore Dr.

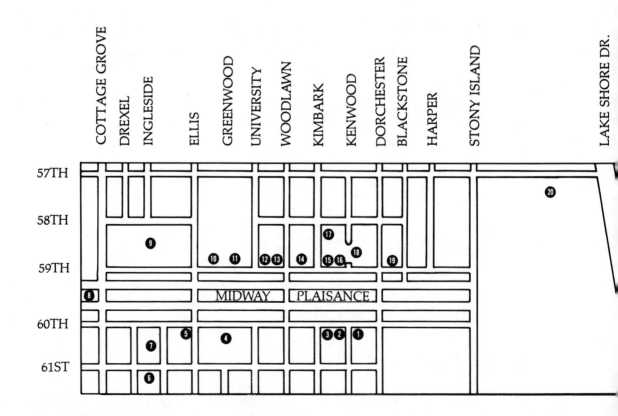

WALK 21 MIDWAY PLAISANCE: ITS SOUTH AND NORTH SIDES

WALKING TIME: 1½ hours.

HOW TO GET THERE: Take an Illinois Central (IC) suburban train at its Randolph Street and Michigan Avenue underground station, and get off at 59th Street. (All express trains and many of those marked "Special" stop at 59th. Check before boarding the train.) If you go by car, take the South Lake Shore Outer Drive south to 47th Street, turn west under the IC railroad's viaduct, and then south on Lake Park Avenue (1400 E). Continue on Lake Park to 59th Street, where this WALK begins.

---

* Portions of this WALK are within the Hyde Park-Kenwood Historic District, roughly bounded by 47th and 59th streets and Cottage Grove and Lake Park avenues.

Midway Plaisance stretches from Jackson Park on the east to Washington Park on the west, between 59th and 60th streets. Before coming down from the IC elevated platform, look west for a view of the Midway Plaisance, a block wide and some dozen blocks long, all green lawns, trees, and sidewalks, with two one-way drives and two local drives for east-west traffic.

This great green mall was constructed as part of Frederick Law Olmstead's original South Park Plan of the 1860s. Later, in 1893, it served as the amusement and ethnographic section of the World's Columbian Exposition. The term "midway" for a carnival amusement area originated here.

Other reminders of that famous world's fair are the enormous gilded statue of the Republic, by Daniel Chester French, now placed near the lake in Jackson Park, where it is passed daily by thousands of commuters on their way to and from the Loop, and the Museum of Science and Industry, which will be the last stop on this WALK. (Though it stands 2 blocks north of the Midway, it seems an appropriate end for a Midway WALK.)

Called merely "The Midway" by neighborhood residents, this parkway is especially popular with University of Chicago students, who use its long stretch of sunken lawns for sunning and studying in summer and for exercise in winter, when it is flooded for ice skating.

Statuary marks each end of the Midway. On the east stands a huge statue on red granite base of Thomas Garrigue Masaryk (d. 1937), first president of Czechoslovakia; he is portrayed as a sturdy, mail-clad warrior

229

on horseback, a descendant of the Blanik knights who according to legend slept in the Blanik mountains in Czechoslovakia until the time should come to arise and rescue their country. On the west is Lorado Taft's *Fountain of Time*, which will be included in this WALK. On the north side of the Midway near Ellis Avenue is a statue of the Swedish botanist Carl von Linné, relocated from Lincoln Park in 1976.

The Midway is part of the South Campus of the University of Chicago. A considerable portion of this campus was developed through Chicago's urban renewal program, enabling the University to expand and achieve greater service to the community and its students and faculty. For tours of the campus, call 702-8650.

SONIA SHANKMAN ORTHOGENIC SCHOOL
1365 E. 60th

ARCHITECTS: *for renovation and addition:*
I. W. Colburn and Associates (1966)

This rather strange combination of a renovated Georgian church and a 3-story residential wing houses this famous school for emotionally disturbed children; it was founded by the equally famous Dr. Bruno Bettelheim. The school is part of the University. The untitled ceramic sculpture (1965) under the arcade is by Jordi Bonet. (The university has an extensive collection of modern art pieces on display around the campus.)
Walk west.

PUBLIC ADMINISTRATION CENTER
1313 E. 60th

ARCHITECTS: *Zantzinger and Borie (1937)*

The center houses the offices of several city, state and national organizations interested in government and public administration, as well as an extensive library also used by university scholars. The 4-story Gothic design of Indiana limestone and brick reveals a bit of Art Moderne influence in the piers and spandrels. The donor for the construction was the Spelman Fund of New York. The main floor lounge contains portraits of Louis Brownlow and Charles Merriam, two of the center's founders.
Continue west.

NEW GRADUATE RESIDENCE HALL
1307 E. 60th

ARCHITECT: *Edward Durell Stone (1963)*

This building was originally the Center for Continuing Education, the University's conference and hotel center, made possible by funds from the W. K. Kellogg Foundation. It is now used as a dormitory and for technical offices. Especially noteworthy are the patterns in the concrete, which are continued onto the underside of the cantilevered roof.
Continue west.

LAIRD BELL LAW QUADRANGLE
1111 E. 60th

ARCHITECTS: *Eero Saarinen; for addition: Cooper-Lecky (1985–87)*

This elegant low quadrangle is far and away the most successful modern building on the campus. It also blends well with its neighbors.

At the east end of the complex is a completely closed auditorium, which contrasts markedly with the enormous library west of it, for the library uses all-glass walls set at angles to each other. Inside the building, the auditorium is connected by wide corridors with lecture rooms and lounges that extend to the west. Actually, there are 2 auditoriums—one, used as a courtroom for demonstration, is set atop the other, used for lectures. The sculpture in the pool outside, called *Construction in Space in Third and Fourth Dimensions,* is the work of Antoine Pevsner, who created it for the site.

An addition extending the back of the library matches the original. In addition, all windows were replaced with a thicker glass to make the building more energy efficient.

Continue west.

SCHOOL OF SOCIAL SERVICE ADMIN'STRATION BUILDING
969 E. 60th

ARCHITECT: *Mies van der Rohe (1965)*

The Social Service Administration Building of the university, the last building to be noted on the south side of the Midway, is a creation of Mies van der Rohe. Though it is but 1 story over a partly exposed basement, black steel and glass and an open plan give the structure an imposing appearance. It seems not at all out of place or off tempo here. The policy of inviting distinguished 20th-century architects to design new buildings has been most rewarding to the campuses of Harvard, Yale, and the University of Chicago.

Walk south on Ingleside Avenue to the northeast corner of 61st Street.

SOCIAL SERVICES CENTER
950 E. 61st

ARCHITECTS: *Hausner and Macsai (1971)*

The University of Chicago has assumed an active role in serving the adjacent community here by training students and helping local children and mothers. Through child care training, the mothers are made to feel confident and better able to meet their responsibilities.

The structure is plain, presenting a facade of efficiency and strength. Window variation relieves the exterior Indiana limestone.

The cost of construction was shared by the U.S. Department of Housing and Urban Development and the U.S. Department of Health, Education and Welfare's Children's Bureau.

Backtrack north on Ingleside Avenue.

* MIDWAY STUDIOS
6016 S. Ingleside

ARCHITECTS: *Otis F. Johnson (1929); for the renovation: Edward Dart (1965); for the addition: Loebl, Schlossman, Bennett and Dart (1973)*

The university donated this shed-like building and land to Lorado Taft, and this is where he successfully executed many sculptural commissions throughout his career. Now a National Historic Landmark, it is an art center for the university and contains major studio workshops. Painting is taught in Taft's stone-cutting studio; sculpture is taught in the former plaster-casting workshop. Painting is also taught in a former studio and lithography in still another. One former studio now serves as a student center, and Taft's private studio is used by students for independent work. All in all, it represents a fine tribute to a great sculptor of the late 19th and early 20th centuries.

Return to 60th Street and walk west. Here you can see a later addition and, in front of it, what appears to be a concrete automobile. Actually it is a 1957 Cadillac Sedan imbedded in 16 tons of concrete by artist Wolf Vostell in 1970, titled *Concrete Traffic.*

Continue west to Cottage Grove Avenue. At the east entrance to Washington Park is one of the most monumental fountains in Chicago.

FOUNTAIN OF TIME
West end of Midway Plaisance, at entrance to Washington Park

SCULPTOR: *Lorado Taft (1922)*

After an interval of neglect, Lorado Taft's haunting sculpture of pebbled concrete, called *The Fountain of Time,* was restored. A hooded, "crag-like" figure of Time (to use Taft's own adjective in describing his mental image), with his back to the Midway, gazes across a pool at a long procession of human beings as they move through life. The Chicago sculptor said that his inspiration came from these lines in a poem by Austin Dobson:

> Time goes, you say? Ah no!
> Alas, time stays; we go.

Both the immobility of Time and the onward sweep of human life are well expressed in this unusual sculpture. Be sure to walk around it in a clockwise direction, to view it from every angle. On what seems to be the back is another procession of people, including a figure of the sculptor himself and his Italian assistant. A triangular marker on the ground points to them.

Now return east, but this time go to the north side of the Midway.

THE UNIVERSITY OF CHICAGO MEDICAL CENTER
5841 S. Maryland

The University of Chicago Medical Center fills the blocks between the Midway and 58th Street, Cottage Grove Avenue and Ellis Avenue, covering about 25 acres at the southwest corner of the campus. It consists of almost a score of interconnected hospitals and clinics with a total licensed bed capacity of 654. The hospitals provide clinical teaching and research facilities for the Pritzker School of Medicine, the prototype of the medical school in the total academic setting.

The continuing practice of adding so many buildings and wings all interconnected has resulted in a great limestone, metal, and glass monolith. There is no evidence of an original plan. The result is an appearance of constant improvisation, which it undoubtedly is. The multitude of buildings here makes it difficult to identify each one without a map (ask for one at the reception desk). In general, the early facades run along 59th Street; some of the newer buildings can be seen along Maryland Avenue. To credit the architects in roughly chronological order, here are the main buildings.

ARCHITECTS: *Coolidge and Hodgson*
Albert Merritt Billings Hospital (1927)
Bobs Roberts Memorial Hospital for Children (1930)
Nancy Adele McElwee Memorial Hospital (1930)
Gertrude Dunn Hicks Memorial Hospital (1930)

ARCHITECTS: *Schmidt, Garden and Erickson*
Chicago Lying-In Hospital (1929)
Nathan Goldblatt Memorial Hospital (1950)
Franklin McLean Memorial Research Institute (1953)
Charles Gilman Smith Hospital (1953)
Goldblatt Outpatient Pavilion (1961)
Clarissa C. Peck Pavilion (1961)
Philip D. Armour Clinical Research Building (1963)
Silvain and Arma Wyler Children's Hospital (1966)
A. J. Carlson Animal Reseach Facility (1968)
Surgery-Brain Research Pavilion (1977)

ARCHITECTS: *Perkins and Will*
Arthur Rubloff Intensive Care Wing (1983)
Bernard Mitchell Hospital (1983)
Magnetic Resonance Facility (1986)

Continuing east on 59th Street, you will pass the 1926 Wieboldt Hall for modern languages at number 1050. Its cloister contains a stone from Douglas Hall of the first, pre-Rockefeller, University of Chicago (1856–86).

WILLIAM RAINEY HARPER MEMORIAL LIBRARY
1116 E. 59th

ARCHITECTS: *Shepley, Rutan and Coolidge (1912); for the renovation: Metz, Train, Olson and Youngren (1972)*

This impressive English Gothic structure was for many years the main library of the University of Chicago. Since the completion of the Regenstein Graduate Library, Harper now serves the undergraduate student body. As can be seen, it is part of the original Quadrangle group. It has 3 stories and a high, handsome, commanding tower. On the 3rd floor, the south reading room is reminiscent of a 12th-century collegium with its oak wainscoting, 2-story Gothic windows, and stone-and-brick vaulted ceiling; note the gargoyle-laden stone entry. The modernized north reading room retains its high wooden trusses.

SOCIAL SCIENCE RESEARCH BUILDING
1126 E. 59th

ARCHITECTS: *Shepley, Rutan and Coolidge (1912)*

This solid greystone Gothic structure, with its door along the side, serves as part of a great 12th-century facade along the north side of the Midway.
　　Continue east.

THE UNIVERSITY PRESIDENT'S HOUSE
5855 S. University

ARCHITECTS: *Henry Ives Cobb (1895); for the renovation: Arthur Myhrum (1969)*

A fairly large house, 3 stories of limestone and Roman brick in English Tudor Gothic style, this sits commandingly at the corner of University Avenue and the Midway Plaisance. Directly to the east is the mammoth Gothic Rockefeller Chapel. Strangely, the house is not overpowered by the chapel, principally because of the equally strong, open green spaces that separate the two.
　　The house has been remodeled several times. The original entrance was on the Midway and is now on University Avenue. The delightful garden to the east is a part of the grounds that is used for receptions when weather permits. One must confess that although the house appears gloomy from the exterior, the garden and the Midway Plaisance Park upon which it faces more than compensate for any of its shortcomings.
　　Next, walk east to Rockefeller Chapel.

ROCKEFELLER MEMORIAL CHAPEL
5850 S. Woodlawn

ARCHITECTS: *Bertram G. Goodhue and Associates (1928)*

At East 59th Street and South Woodlawn Avenue stands Rockefeller Memorial Chapel, one of the most imposing buildings in the entire city, donated by and named in honor of the founder of the University of Chicago. This is an excellent example of the late Gothic style by a prominent architect interested in the Gothic revival. The Carillon Tower bells (72 of them) are noteworthy for the excellence of their tones and the quality of their sound. They were given, a few years after the chapel

Rockefeller Memorial Chapel
(Philip A. Turner)

was completed, by the same donor in memory of his mother, Laura Spelman Rockefeller.

The chapel is the scene of many university functions, such as concerts, pageantry, graduation ceremonies, and other convocations. The colorful banners hanging inside come from a collection of 44 liturgical banners created by Norman Laliberte for the Vatican Pavilion at the 1964–65 World's Fair held in New York. The banners are known officially as the Mary MacDonald Ludgin Collection.

As you stand outside Rockefeller Chapel on the corner, look north for a glimpse of 2 other places of worship—the beautifully executed carved-stone tower of the Chicago Theological Seminary's chapel 1 block north and 1 block west, and the exquisite pure spire of the First Unitarian Church, 2 blocks due north.

Continue east.

IDA NOYES HALL
1212 E. 59th

ARCHITECTS: *Shepley, Rutan and Coolidge (1916); for the renovation: Vickrey/Oversat/Awsumb (1983–86)*

This student activities center has meeting rooms, lounges, a cinema, and a recreational pool. Inside, note the plaster ceiling and the double stairway with elaborately molded bannisters of iron and wood.

Continue east to the next block.

EMMONS BLAINE HALL
1362 E. 59th

ARCHITECT: *James Gamble Rogers (1903)*

This sedate-looking building holds the rambunctious lower-school students of the University of Chicago Laboratory Schools. The Lab Schools, an independent K–12 school long known for its high calibre of education, is housed in 3 buildings here (plus a gymnasium), which form their own quad.

Walk north on Kimbark Avenue.

HENRY HOLMES BELFIELD HALL
5815 S. Kimbark

ARCHITECT: *James Gamble Rogers (1904)*

Here is the Middle School, also in French Gothic style in Indiana limestone. A building for teacher training at the university separates Belfield from Blaine Hall, though the two are linked internally.

If it is open, walk east across the yard on the north to Kenwood Avenue.

UNIVERSITY HIGH SCHOOL
5834 S. Kenwood

ARCHITECTS: *Perkins and Will (1960); for the addition: James G. Gimpel, university architect; Nagle, Hartray and Associates (1993)*

The original exterior was modern in every sense—limestone, aluminum, and tinted glass that tried to fit with the Gothic surroundings. However, in an effort to create a quadrangle entirely in keeping with the rest of the university campus, the Kimbark Avenue entry was razed in 1991 and replaced with a limestone front nearly identical to the other Lab School buildings—including the playful stone finials arrayed along the gabled rooftop. Corridors link it to the lower and middle schools.

BERNARD E. SUNNY GYMNASIUM
5831 S. Kenwood

ARCHITECTS: *Armstrong, Furst and Tilton (1930)*

The street was closed to allow students easier access here. The Gothic structure of Indiana limestone contains a 2-story gymnasium and swimming pool. There are also exercise rooms, locker rooms, and offices. The athletic field to the east is more than ample for the various athletic events and daily exercise routines.

Walk east on 59th Street.

INTERNATIONAL HOUSE
1414 E. 59th

ARCHITECTS: *Holabird and Root (1932)*

The stately modified Gothic structure, built of limestone, is one of 4 such centers founded by John D. Rockefeller Jr. The other 3 centers are located in New York City; Berkeley, California; and Paris, France. Although these different houses share common origins and goals, each is a separate institution with no formal or legal ties to each other.

International House of Chicago was established in 1932 as a department of the University of Chicago. It serves as a social and cultural center for approximately one thousand foreign students, staff, and visitors associated with the University each year. The building has the capacity for approximately 500 residents. The director of International House also serves as adviser to foreign visitors for the university. It is financially self-supporting and has its own Board of Governors, who establish general policy for the House and are responsible for its overall operation, subject to final review by the university's Board of Trustees.

Now return to Dorchester Avenue and walk north to East 57th Street. On the way note the elegant old Cloisters Apartments—home to many faculty families. At East 57th Street turn east into Jackson Park.

MUSEUM OF SCIENCE AND INDUSTRY
E. 57th at S. Lake Shore

ARCHITECTS: *D. H. Burnham and Company, Charles B. Atwood, designer (1981–82); for the restoration: Graham, Anderson, Probst and White for the exterior; Shaw, Naess and Murphy for the interior (1929–40); for the addition: Hammel, Green and Abrahamson (1986)*

A visit inside, as with the museums around Burnham Park (see WALK 17), rates a separate trip. You could spend days here trying to see all the exhibits.

Just a view of this enormous building is an experience. Erected as the Palace of Fine Arts for the 1893 Columbian Exposition, it follows an elaborate Greek revival style—precisely duplicating various parts of temples on the Acropolis at Athens. Ionic columns, doorways, and the

Museum of Science and Industry
(Robert J. Frett courtesy Illinois Bell)

giant-sized carytids (13 feet tall, weighing about 6 tons each) are copied from the Erectheum; the carving on the metope panels and frieze is reproduced from the Parthenon. Materials used, however, were not those of the Acropolis temples. For the original "temporary" building heavy brick walls were merely covered with plaster, and the Ionic columns were constructed of wood lattice frame, then covered with a plaster composition called staff.

Though widely admired as the showpiece of the Columbian Exposition, this building and others in the neoclassical style brought forth the bitter and oft-quoted statement from Chicago architect Louis Sullivan: "The damage wrought by the World's Fair will last for half a century from its date." Whatever its influence on architecture, however, the "Palace of Fine Arts" has become a decidedly modern museum with chief emphasis on technology, a popular place visited by millions of people each year. Ponder the incongruity between the beautiful, Greek-temple exterior and the 20th-century science and technology it houses!

The transformation was by no means simple or painless. The Palace of Fine Arts building was abandoned in 1920, when the Field Museum, which had been using space here, moved to its own building nearer the Loop. Not until several years later was this building rescued from neglect. The extraordinary amount of money needed to restore both exterior and interior as a permanent building and to establish it as an industrial museum came largely from Julius Rosenwald of Sears, though his initial contribution of $3 million was apparently inspired by a bond issue of $5 million for this purpose—a bond issue passed by the voters of the South

Park District. (Rosenwald's later contributions brought his total gift up to about $7.5 million.)

The exhibits in the museum are varied. Some are permanent, such as the simulated coal mine; a small-scale model of a fantasy-land castle, with lights that light and willow tree that weeps; and the U505 submarine. Some are seasonal, such as the Christmas trees of all nations. And some are visiting exhibits or on loan.

In 1986 the Henry Crown Space Center was added, designed by Hammel, Green and Abrahamson of Minneapolis. The 36,000-square-foot building contains 12,000 square feet of space exhibits, including actual spacecraft, satellites, and space probes. The addition also houses the Omnimax Theater, a 76-foot-diameter dome screen surrounding a 334-seat auditorium. Two or three new presentations are given each year.

The museum is open Monday through Friday, 9:30 A.M. to 4 P.M.; Saturday and Sunday, 9:30 A.M. to 5:30 P.M. Summer hours: 9 A.M. to 5:30 P.M. every day. Omnimax Theater shows: from 10 A.M., hourly; most evenings. Call 684-1414 for information. Thursdays are free.

To return to the Loop, climb the stairs at 57th Street and Lake Park, where you can get an IC suburban train as frequently as at 59th Street.

WALK 22

1. Administration Building and Clock Tower
2. Hotel Florence
   11111 S. Forrestville Ave.
3. Pullman Stables
   11201 S. Cottage Grove Ave.
4. Greenstone Church
   11211 S. St. Lawrence Ave.
5. Market Hall
6. Pullman Housing

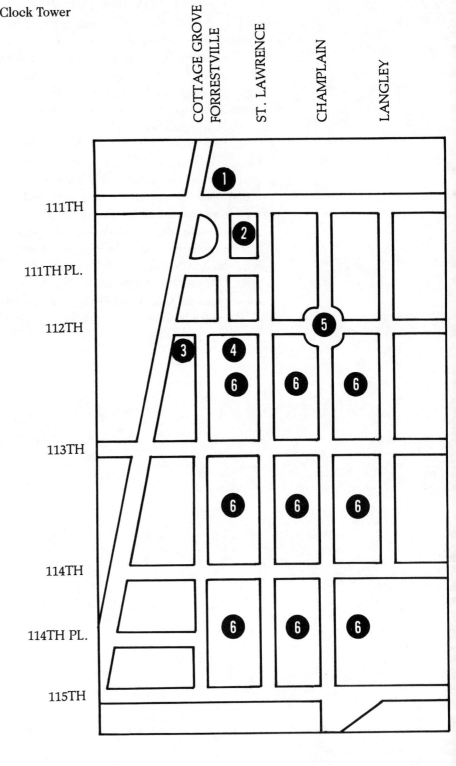

WALK 22 **PULLMAN**

WALKING TIME: 1 hour.

HOW TO GET THERE: Take an Illinois Central (IC) suburban train at East Randolph Street and North Michigan Avenue (underground station) to Pullman. (Inquire about which train you should take.) Time—about 30 minutes. If you drive, take the Dan Ryan Expressway (Route 94) to 111th Street, Pullman Exit. Drive west to the second stoplight.

* This entire WALK is within the Pullman Historic District. Note that all the buildings were designed by the same architect, Solon Spencer Beman.

The community of Pullman, near Lake Calumet on metro Chicago's Far South Side, was built as a model industrial town by George M. Pullman, an early Chicago industrialist. The town and all its buildings, one of the first developments in this part of the Chicago area, were designed by architect Solon S. Beman and landscape engineer Nathan F. Barrett. In the late 1870s Pullman selected this site for his Pullman Palace Car Company, which manufactured his recently devised Pullman railroad cars. (The first sleeping car was built in 1858, and the Pullman Palace Car Company was formed in 1867. He later developed a dining car and a vestibule car.)

For his model company town Pullman bought a huge tract of land covering 4,500 acres of what was then undeveloped prairie in the Village of Hyde Park (not yet a part of the City of Chicago). Most of this land was owned by the Pullman Land Association, with only the factory belonging to the Pullman Palace Car Company.

Pullman built on land bordered by 104th Street on the north, 116th Street on the south, the Pullman Railroad on the east, and the Illinois Central Railroad on the west. The town, which would be served by the Illinois Central Railroad, was designed with most of the community facilities near the IC depot at 111th Street—a hotel, a church, a school, and an arcade building with stores, offices, library, theater, and bank—everything owned, of course, by the Pullman company.

Work began on the Pullman plants and the first of the 1,750 housing units in 1880. Early the next year the first residents moved into the row houses and the cheaper apartment buildings planned for lower-income workers. The factories of the car company were located north of 111th Street. Other related enterprises, such as the Union Foundry and the Spanish Curled Hair Company (later Sherwin Williams Paint Company), were located between 104th and 106th streets and 115th and 116th streets respectively.

A walk through Pullman today gives you the sense of visiting a small town of the past, with the houses, hotel, and village square much the same as they first looked—an excellent showcase of town planning principles of the late 19th century. In this "model town" project Pullman was doubtless motivated partly by philanthropy as understood in his day and partly by enlightened self-interest. He believed that his employees would be happier if they could live near their work, in houses or apartments more attractive than the usual workers' homes, surrounded by all the facilities needed for daily living.

But Pullman's model town failed to bring happiness to his workers. Unrest hit the community—in those days made up mostly of workers of Scandinavian, Dutch, British or Irish descent—because they couldn't own their homes and they felt that rents were too high. (Contrary to what some sources say, there was never a company-owned store. The company leased stores but did not operate them.) By 1889, when petitions were filed for the annexation of Hyde Park to Chicago, feeling was so strong among the Pullman workers that they voted for annexation over Mr. Pullman's opposition. Still, the community remained very much an independent town within the city, and for a while it prospered. As orders and production increased in the Pullman plants, more workers settled there, and the population by 1892 included more than 20 nationalities.

Real trouble lay ahead, however. The decline of the company town began with the depression of 1893–94, following the great boom Chicago had experienced with the Columbian Exposition of 1893. Unemployment rose and wages dropped, but rents remained pretty much the same. Mr. Pullman's refusal to restore his employees' wages to their previous levels and his prompt dismissal of several members of a committee that had called on him to discuss the matter precipitated a company-wide strike.

Since some of the workers belonged to the American Railway Union headed by Eugene V. Debs, the strike quickly became a nationwide issue, with an organization called the General Managers Association coming to the support of Pullman. After considerable violence and destruction of property (none of it in Pullman), as well as the workers' refusal to run the trains, President Cleveland sent federal troops to take over and run the trains—so that the mail could go through. Although at first the president's action caused greater violence, it ultimately broke the strike. Eugene Debs was thrown in jail and his union weakened to the point of ruin. And the company's bitter, defeated workers returned to their jobs on its terms, not theirs. The only victory they won was a decision by the Illinois Supreme Court not long afterward that the Pullman company's charter did not give it the right to own and manage a town. After George

Pullman's death, the successor management made no appeal, and so ended his Utopian dream of a perfect village for his workers!

Yet the buildings remain. Times had changed by 1907, with a change from wood to steel cars and the arrival of more Polish, Italian, and Greek workers. Older residents began to move out. From 1920 to 1940 the Pullman area remained fairly stable, merely becoming an older community. In 1957 the original plant of the Pullman company moved its facilities farther east. Since then, a number of industrial plants have developed on the original factory site.

ADMINISTRATION BUILDING and CLOCK TOWER
Corner of E. 111th and S. Cottage Grove

The Administration Building complex, constructed in 1880, was originally about 700 feet in length. The red face brick structure was made up of three parts, a center section and two flanking wings. The center section contained three floors of corporate offices of the Pullman Palace Car Company.

In 1907 a large addition was attached to the southern wing. This addition, approximately 60 feet in height, begins south of the center section and continues south parallel to the old wing, the facade of which was covered with the installation of the new structure. Its architectural treatment is only vaguely sympathetic to the original appearance, and because of differing design characteristics (especially with respect to height and property setbacks), the symmetrical qualities of the original complex have disappeared completely.

Cross the street.

HOTEL FLORENCE
11111 S. Forrestville

Named after George Pullman's favorite daughter, this elaborate 4-story building of 1881, with many gables and turrets, was (and is) one of the first buildings to greet the visitor to the town when stepping off the Illinois Central train at the 111th Street Station. During the early history of the town, many persons roomed here while either studying the various aspects of the community or visiting on George Pullman's personal invitation.

Although slight changes have been made to the facade, and a large annex added to the northeast corner of the building after 1910, the hotel's fine overall appearance and pleasing qualities are readily associated with the district. The hotel closed in 1975, but lunch is still served seven days a week.

Walk south on Forrestville Avenue, through the park, and turn west on 112th Street.

PULLMAN STABLES
11201 S. Cottage Grove

According to a town rule, all residents (except the manager of the plant, who had his own stable behind his house) and visitors had to keep their horses here, apparently to prevent unnecessary clean-up tasks as well as to assure a profitable operation. The volunteer fire company was also housed in this building for a number of years, and was known for its good service.

Around the turn of the century, a popular Sunday afternoon activity was to rent a carriage team, tour the countryside, and enjoy a family picnic. The company provided for this service at the stables, and individuals could rent a horse and buggy for $3 a day.

A service station and auto repair shop now occupy the building, but interesting reminders of the past are still apparent, including two carved horses' heads located above the 112th Street entrance to the garage.

Walk east on 112th Street to St. Lawrence Avenue.

GREENSTONE CHURCH (PULLMAN UNITED METHODIST)
Corner of E. 112th and S. St. Lawrence

The Greenstone Church is perhaps the most charming building in the entire district. Its name derived from the green color of its Pennsylvania serpentine-stone facade. The massiveness of the masonry coupled with the large spire and arches suggests the Gothic Revival (of Richard Upjohn, to whom Beman apprenticed) and the Romanesque (of architect H. H. Richardson).

Because the Presbyterians had rented the church in 1885, the Catholics and Swedish Lutherans asked Mr. Pullman's permission to build their own structures. He resisted their pleas for a while, but finally leased property to them so they could build. Swedish Elim Lutheran Church (1888), and Holy Rosary Roman Catholic Church (1890), both designed by Beman, were constructed on vacant land some blocks west of the town to satisfy the needs of these congregations.

Today, the Greenstone Church is in excellent condition. Both the interior and exterior have undergone extensive restoration, under the direction of architect Charles E. Gregersen, and it remains much the same as it did when George Pullman attended services here.

Walk east.

MARKET HALL
Intersection of E. 112th and S. Champlain

By deliberate design, the building was placed in the middle of the intersection to break up the sometimes monotonous regularity of the streets' grid system. The top floor was removed in the 1930s and the remainder gutted by fire in 1972. It awaits restoration.

Now take a walk down Champlain Avenue, toward 115th Street, then west, and walk back north along St. Lawrence Avenue.

Pullman Row House
(Olga Stefanos)

PULLMAN HOUSING

The housing in Pullman is of predominantly brick construction. Much of the brick was produced in brickyards to the south of the town. There were only two freestanding houses (for managers of the Allen Paper Wheel Works). All the others were arranged in rows of 2 to 28. Although there are roughly a dozen basic housing types, variation of roof lines, general configuration, and detail produced a much greater variety in the appearance of the housing.

While the homes of Pullman's elite were generally located on the parks and boulevards, those of the poorest residents were relegated to the back streets. Between these extremes, a deliberate attempt was made to mix the quality and size of the housing. It was not uncommon to find the home of a skilled worker, or even foreman, next to a boarding house.

Unlike in other housing of the era, an effort was made to provide cross-ventilation and direct sunlight into all major rooms of the homes. One of the more advanced ideas in the design of Pullman's housing was the use of separate storm and sanitary sewers, which remains unique in Chicago.

Unity Temple interior view
(Philip A. Turner)

WALK 23 FRANK LLOYD WRIGHT IN OAK PARK AND RIVER FOREST

WALKING TIME: 2½ hours; 1 hour more for River Forest.
HOW TO GET THERE: Take a Lake Street CTA elevated train headed for Oak Park at any of the Loop El stations, and get off at Oak Park Avenue. Walk 1 block north to Lake Street and then 2 blocks west to Kenilworth Avenue, where this WALK starts. If you drive, take the Eisenhower Expressway, turn off at Harlem Avenue, go north about 1 mile to Lake Street, then 4 blocks east to Kenilworth Avenue.

---

* The Frank Lloyd Wright and Prairie School of Architecture Historic District was accepted for inclusion in the National Register of Historic Places in 1973. Two of the buildings in the district have been named National Historic Monuments: Unity Temple (1974) and The Frank Lloyd Wright Home and Studio (1976).

We are indebted to the Oak Park Public Library and W. R. Hasbrouck for developing this WALK in earlier editions. Oak Park is a community with high architectural awareness, and much restoration work has been accomplished since the 1970s. We are indebted to the Frank Lloyd Wright Home and Studio Foundation for assistance in updating and revising the information in this WALK.

The Oak Park Center (a committee of the Frank Lloyd Wright Home and Studio Foundation) coordinates many architectural tours in Oak Park and operates the Oak Park Visitors Center at 158 Forest Avenue. Before beginning your WALK through Oak Park, you may want to see the many maps and guides sold there. The center also sells a map with pictures of all the buildings included here. If you wish to have a guided tour of Unity Temple, The Frank Lloyd Wright Home and Studio, or a recorded walking tour of the area, tickets are available here. They also conduct special warm-weather tours. Call 708-848-1978 for more information.

Frank Lloyd Wright was one of three American architects who turned their backs on the accepted style of classic design and created new forms for people of the late 19th and early 20th centuries. The two others, who preceded him and doubtless influenced him in his earlier years, were Henry Hobson Richardson and Louis H. Sullivan. Each was a man of great talent and originality.

1. Unity Temple and Parish House
   875 Lake St.

2. Horse Show Fountain
   Lake St. at Oak Park Ave.

3. Francisco Terrace Apartments
   675 E. Lake St.

4. George Furbeck House
   223 N. Euclid Ave.

5. Charles E. Roberts House and Stable
   321 and 317 N. Euclid Ave.

6. Rollin Furbeck House
   515 Fair Oaks Ave.

7. William G. Fricke House
   540 Fair Oaks Ave.

8. H. C. Goodrich House
   534 N. East Ave.

9. Edwin H. Cheney House
   520 N. East Ave.

10. W. E. Martin House
    636 N. East Ave.

11. Harry S. Adams House
    710 Augusta St.

12. O. B. Balch House
    611 N. Kenilworth Ave.

13. H. P. Young House
    334 N. Kenilworth Ave.

14. Frank Lloyd Wright Home and Studio
    951 Chicago Ave.

15. R. P. Parker House
    1019 Chicago Ave.

16. Thomas H. Gale House
    1027 Chicago Ave.

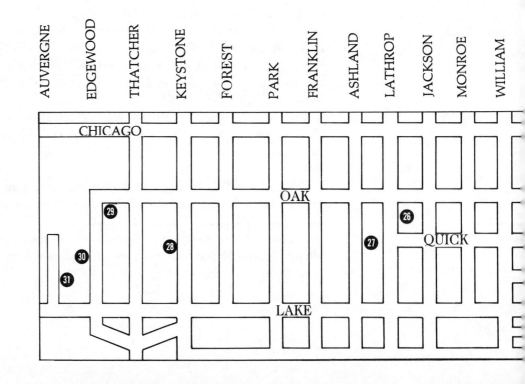

Of the three, Wright gave the most attention to domestic architecture, and over the years he developed a new style of home, now known worldwide as the Prairie House. The Robie House (1909) on the University of Chicago campus (see WALK 20) is probably the most familiar example.

The Chicago area is incredibly fortunate to have a practically complete record of Wright's progress in his early years—25 structures that he built in Oak Park and 6 additional ones in neighboring River Forest. The buildings listed for this WALK cover a period of only about 20 years in Wright's life. If you could view the homes in chronological order—which is obviously impractical!—instead of the geographical scheme offered here, you would more readily observe the changes in Wright's style.

You will be surprised at the early designs, especially those before 1900; steep gables and dormer windows have little resemblance to the style now associated with Wright's name. But the impact of the type of house he had developed by the end of that period continues to be felt today in house designs all over the world. Low roof lines, wide eaves, horizontal planes, and casement windows—all are characteristics of the Prairie House. The Prairie style was Wright's first expression of organic architecture; in it he incorporated site, material, plan, decoration, and finish into a unified whole to meet a specific functional requirement.

Unless otherwise indicated, the buildings listed here are not open to the public.

* UNITY TEMPLE and PARISH HOUSE
875 Lake

ARCHITECT: *Frank Lloyd Wright (1906); for the restoration: Unity Temple Congregation and the Unity Temple Restoration Foundation (1973, 1980)*

The Unity Temple, a Unitarian Universalist church, is Wright's only public building in Oak Park. The Temple is an esteemed international landmark. Wright was faced with three problems when designing this church: budget, urban location, and two uses. Abandoning traditional religious forms and symbols, Wright's solutions were both innovative and revolutionary—the cubic form without a steeple, the use of poured concrete, and the binuclear plan.

A common entrance unites and separates the Temple and Unity House. Drawing the eye upward, the light streaming in from the skylight and windows is the major religious element in the Temple. With the pulpit placed front and center, Wright located seats on 3 sides, so that the minister and the congregation would be close to each other. (Years later Wright used a similar floor plan for a Greek Orthodox church in Milwaukee.)

Unity House was also designed to meet the secular needs of the congregation. As in his domestic architecture, Wright made the fireplace the focal point of the room, the heart of this church "home."

Through the combined efforts of the congregation and the Unity Temple Restoration Foundation (independent of the church), Unity Temple has undergone restoration almost continually since the early 1970s. The 18-level roof was restored and in 1973 the building's exterior was resurfaced. The foyer was fully restored in 1979, including return to the original color scheme and restoration of the entryway doors. The next year both buildings were returned to their original color scheme and the lighting fixtures restored. Other maintenance goes on.

Frederick Koeper (*Illinois Architecture.* Chicago: The University of Chicago Press, 1968, p. 204), referring to Wright's design of the Unity Temple, paid special tribute to him in these words: "Like the music of Bach, the architecture of Wright develops magnificent variations on simple themes."

Unity Temple may be visited Monday through Friday between 1 P.M. and 4 P.M. and on Saturday and Sunday at 1, 2, and 3 P.M.

Walk east on Lake Street to the corner of Oak Park Avenue.

HORSE SHOW FOUNTAIN
Lake at Oak Park

This small fountain at the corner was designed by sculptor Richard Bock in 1909. It was reconstructed and relocated to this site in 1969. Wright suggested portions of the design concept.

Walk east and cross Euclid Avenue.

FRANCISCO TERRACE APARTMENTS
675 E. Lake

ARCHITECT: *Frank Lloyd Wright (1895); for the reproductions: Harry Weese and Associates (1978)*

Now a 70-unit complex called "Prairie Court," this building represents a last-ditch preservation effort. When Wright's internationally known building was razed, this portion was salvaged and reused here. The courtyard is worth a look. For more information see *A Guide to Chicago's Historic Suburbs On Wheels and On Foot* (Swallow/Ohio University Press, 1981).

Walk north on Euclid Avenue 1½ blocks.

GEORGE FURBECK HOUSE
223 N. Euclid

ARCHITECT: *Frank Lloyd Wright (1897)*

The north dormer and entire porch are additions, destroying the original proportions of this brick home with wood trim. Two conical roofs lend a slightly Oriental look.

Continue north to the next block.

CHARLES E. ROBERTS HOUSE AND STABLE
321 and 317 N. Euclid

ARCHITECTS: *Burnham and Root (1883); for the remodeling and restoration: Frank Lloyd Wright (1896)*

This 3-story wood home, designed by Burnham and Root, was built in 1883. In 1896 Wright was architect for the interior remodeling. He designed the large stable around the same time. The stable has been moved to its present site at the read and converted into a home.

Continue north to Chicago Avenue. Turn east 3 blocks to Fair Oaks Avenue, then turn north again.

ROLLIN FURBECK HOUSE
515 Fair Oaks

ARCHITECT: *Frank Lloyd Wright (1897)*

This yellow-brick house is historically important because it marks the beginning of Wright's three-year period of design experimentation. Multiple planes, denticulated eaves, corbels, and columns add up to a small but ambitious package.

Continue north to the corner.

WILLIAM G. FRICKE HOUSE
540 Fair Oaks

ARCHITECT: *Frank Lloyd Wright (1901–1902, remodeled 1907)*

This house has a stucco exterior with wood trim. Wings grow outward from a 3-story core. The garage was added when the house was remodeled.

Walk west on Iowa Street, then turn south on East Avenue.

H. C. GOODRICH HOUSE
534 N. East

ARCHITECT: *Frank Lloyd Wright (1896)*

This house has a clapboard exterior and a high roof. It was probably designed in 1895 and shows Wright's prerevolutionary phase.

Walk 2 doors south.

EDWIN H. CHENEY HOUSE
520 N. East

ARCHITECT: *Frank Lloyd Wright (1903–1904)*

Astoundingly different is this 1-story brick house that has no basement or attic. It was originally set within gardens enclosed by brick walls. There are striking resemblances to the Robie House, which Wright built in Chicago (see WALK 20).

Backtrack north on East Avenue, almost to Augusta Street.

W. E. MARTIN HOUSE
636 N. East

ARCHITECT: *Frank Lloyd Wright (1903)*

This house has a stucco exterior with wood trim. The north side, with a separate door, is reminiscent of a Hopi cliff dwelling with its almost Cubist planes and portals. At one time there were extensive formal gardens on the south side.

Continue north to the corner. Turn west on Augusta Street 2 blocks to Euclid Avenue.

HARRY S. ADAMS HOUSE
710 Augusta

ARCHITECT: *Frank Lloyd Wright (1913–14)*

This is the last house Wright designed in Oak Park. It has a brick exterior with limestone trim. The long, low emphasis reveals his mature style.

Continue west on Augusta Street 3 blocks to Kenilworth Avenue. Turn south 1 block.

O. B. BALCH HOUSE
611 N. Kenilworth

ARCHITECT: *Frank Lloyd Wright (1911)*

This was one of Wright's first commissions after returning from his trip to Europe. It has a stucco exterior with wood trim and an unusual square tower.

Walk south on Kenilworth Avenue and past the school to Chicago Avenue. Continue south along one of the town's most gracious streets.

H. P. YOUNG HOUSE
334 N. Kenilworth

ARCHITECT: *for the remodeling: Frank Lloyd Wright (1895)*

This is an 1895 remodeling; it retains the old farmhouse (around which Wright built the newer home) as the kitchen area. The recess windows and elongated porch roof add interest.

Backtrack north to the corner. Turn west 1 block to reach the most important stop on the WALK.

* FRANK LLOYD WRIGHT HOME AND STUDIO
951 Chicago

ARCHITECT: *Frank Lloyd Wright (home: 1889, remodeled 1895, altered 1911; studio: 1898, altered 1911); for the restoration of both: The Frank Lloyd Wright Home and Studio Foundation (1975–86)*

The Frank Lloyd Wright Home and Studio is a costewardship property of the Frank Lloyd Wright Home and Studio Foundation and the National Trust for Historic Preservation. Restored by the foundation to the last year Wright lived and worked in Oak Park, 1909, the building is significant both architecturally and historically. It was here that Wright for 20 years designed the now-famous buildings of his Oak Park years.

The residence, facing Forest Avenue, began as a small Shingle-style house. Wright experimented with so many design concepts in this building that it can be viewed as a working laboratory of his stylistic growth. His growing family—he and Catherine had six children—precipitated the first major alteration, the addition of the barrel-vaulted playroom to the east and the enlarging of the south facade to allow for a larger dining room.

Wright integrated his work and family life by adding the attached studio, facing Chicago Avenue, in 1898. Radically different from build-

Frank Lloyd Wright Home exterior and playroom
(courtesy Frank Lloyd Wright Home & Studio Foundation)

ings of its time, the exterior is an expression of the interior and includes many features that anticipated the Prairie style. In the eleven years that Wright worked in the 4-room studio, he produced one quarter of his total life output. The home in particular fulfills Wright's effort to "make it graciously as one with external nature."

Tours are given weekdays at 11 A.M., 1 P.M., and 3 P.M. and weekends from 11 A.M. to 4 P.M. every 15 minutes. (See the WALK introduction for fees.) Call 708-848-1978 for information.

Continue west on Chicago Avenue to see three examples of Wright's early work.

R. P. PARKER HOUSE
1019 Chicago

ARCHITECT: *Frank Lloyd Wright (1892)*

This is known as one of the "bootleg" homes because Wright began supplementing his income by moonlighting, against the terms of his contract with Sullivan. This home is designed in the Queen Anne style.

THOMAS H. GALE HOUSE
1027 Chicago

ARCHITECT: *Frank Lloyd Wright (1892)*

This is another of the "bootleg" homes, very similar to the first especially in the two high-peaked circular roofs on the east. (Two very different "bootlegs" can be seen in WALK 19.)

WALTER GALE HOUSE
1031 Chicago

ARCHITECT: *Frank Lloyd Wright (1893)*

This clapboard-sided house, a flowering of the above models, was completed shortly after Wright had left the employ of Adler and Sullivan.

Continue west and turn south on Marion Street, then turn east on Superior Street.

FRANCIS WOOLEY HOUSE AND STABLE
1030 Superior

ARCHITECT: *Frank Lloyd Wright (1893)*

The original surface of narrow clapboards has been restored after a period under imitation brick siding. The porch is notable.

Continue east to the corner.

NATHAN G. MOORE HOUSE AND STABLE
333 Forest

ARCHITECT: *Frank Lloyd Wright (1895); remodeled and reconstructed (1923)*

This spectacular house is one of few that Wright designed in a historical style—English Tudor. Nevertheless, it is composed of many materials and stylistic features bearing Sullivan's and Wright's ideas. Wright reconstructed it after a fire had destroyed the upper floor.

Cross Forest Avenue to 400.

DR. W. H. COPELAND HOUSE
400 Forest

ARCHITECT: *Frank Lloyd Wright (1909)*

Set grimly on a deep lawn, this house was later remodeled not entirely according to Wright's plans. It looks heavier than his work.

Now look next door to the south.

ARTHUR HEURTLEY HOUSE
318 Forest

ARCHITECT: *Frank Lloyd Wright (1902); remodeled and reconstructed (1923)*

This house is one of the finest examples of Wright's Prairie style. Darker and lighter red brick interact effectively in breaking the surface plane. The main living area is on the second floor, and the children's playroom and laundry facilities were originally on the ground floor.

On the other side of the street is 313 Forest Avenue.

E. R. HILLS HOUSE
313 Forest

ARCHITECT: *for the remodeling: Frank Lloyd Wright (1902); rebuilt (1976–77)*

This was a reconstruction of an existing house by Wright. The transitional style utilizes stucco with wood trim. The second story burned in 1975 and the house was reconstructed, using the original plans.

Walk east on Elizabeth Court.

MRS. THOMAS H. GALE HOUSE
6 Elizabeth

ARCHITECT: *Frank Lloyd Wright (1909)*

The combination of the flat roofs and cantilevered balconies is not typical of the Prairie style. This small home became extremely influential with European architects in the 1920s.

Backtrack west to Forest Avenue and turn south.

P. A. BEACHY HOUSE
238 Forest

ARCHITECT: *for the remodeling: Frank Lloyd Wright (1906)*

Incorporating an earlier house, the combination of brick, stucco, wood, and cement is not typical of Wright's style. The lines and colors, however, are.

Continue to walk south.

FRANK THOMAS HOUSE
210 Forest

ARCHITECT: *Frank Lloyd Wright (1901); restored (1975)*

Built of stucco on wood frame, this was the first Prairie style house in Oak Park. It has features typical of Wright's early years—leaded-glass windows, arched entrance, and Sullivanesque beaded moldings. Across the street is a bronze bust of the architect by Egon Weiner.

If you are tired and wish to end the WALK here, continue south on Forest Avenue to Lake Street and turn east 1 block. You will have returned to Unity Temple.

There are, however, 6 more Wright buildings to be seen. They are a 20- to 25-minute walk away in River Forest. To continue the WALK, proceed west 2 blocks on Ontario Street. Cross Harlem Avenue, jog a step north, and continue west on Quick Avenue. When it ends at Lathrop Avenue, turn north.

RIVER FOREST TENNIS CLUB
615 Lathrop

ARCHITECTS: *Frank Lloyd Wright, Charles E. White Jr., and Vernon S. Watson, associate architects (1906); for relocation and enlarging: Vernon S. Watson (1920)*

The exterior is of stained wood and battened sheathing. White and Watson were associate architects. Originally located on another site, the clubhouse was moved here and enlarged under Watson's supervision. It has been extensively altered.

Continue north to the corner and walk west on Oak Avenue 1 block to Ashland Avenue. Turn south to about midblock.

E. ARTHUR DAVENPORT HOUSE
559 Ashland

ARCHITECT: *Frank Lloyd Wright (1901)*

The building materials here are very similar to those at the tennis club—horizontal stained wood board and battened sheathing—and very different from those of the Thomas house (our last stop in Oak Park) of the same year.

Return to Oak Avenue. Walk west 4 blocks to Keystone Avenue and turn south. Walk about halfway down this long block.

J. KIBBEN INGALLS HOUSE
562 Keystone

ARCHITECT: *Frank Lloyd Wright (1909); remodeled (1926, 1981)*

This house has a cruciform plan with cantilevered balconies. Two large planters, a Wright trademark, help connect the first floor to the earth. The house has been remodeled twice, most recently to restore the delicate stained glass.

Backtrack to the corner. Walk west 2 blocks to Edgewood Place, and turn south.

ISABEL ROBERTS HOUSE
603 Edgewood

ARCHITECT: *Frank Lloyd Wright (1908, 1955)*

This house, built in the form of a cross, is especially distinguished by a 2-story livingroom. Wright remodeled the house in 1955, when he was 88 years old. Leaded glass dominates the front, as in a church.

To the south, the house of stucco and blue trim house bears much influence of Wright.

Continue south.

CHAUNCEY L. WILLIAMS HOUSE
530 Edgewood

ARCHITECT: *Frank Lloyd Wright (1895)*

This house has Roman brick below the window sills and stucco above. The entry arch is ornamental, and the two dormers' projecting eaves resemble visors, but otherwise the styling is restrained yet elegant.

From the corner, walk west on Lake Street 1 block. Enter the stone gates of Auvergne Place.

WILLIAM H. WINSLOW HOUSE AND STABLE
515 Auvergne

ARCHITECT: *Frank Lloyd Wright (1893)*

Brightness distinguishes this home from many above. The exterior is Roman brick and stone, with a long terra-cotta frieze above, carried to the porte-cochere. The roof was replaced in the 1970s. This was Wright's first independent commission after he left the firm of Adler and Sullivan. The wide eaves, low roof lines, centrally located chimney, and plain surfaces contrasting with ornamented sections are characteristics that Wright incorporated in later houses.

The WALK ends here. To return to the El, walk east on Lake Street 12 blocks (just over a mile) to Harlem Avenue. If you look south you will see the terminus of the CTA's line.

Williams House
(Philip A. Turner)

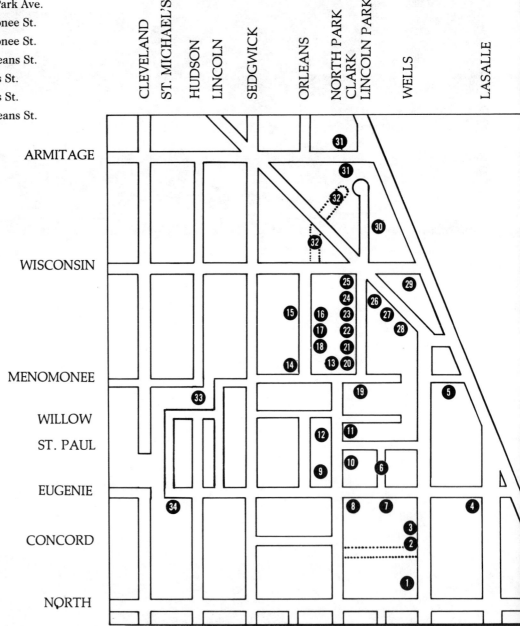

WALK 24 OLD TOWN TRIANGLE

WALKING TIME: 1½ hours.

HOW TO GET THERE: Take a northbound CTA bus No. 22 (Clark) on Dearborn, or a No. 36 bus (Broadway) on State Street. Get off at North Avenue (1600 N) and walk 2 blocks west to Wells Street.

* The Old Town Triangle Historic District is roughly bounded by Lincoln Park and Armitage, Cleveland, and North avenues.

This WALK starts at North Avenue and Wells Street at Piper's Alley—an early version of an indoor shopping-and-entertainment mall. This one was created from the original alley of the Piper Bakery of 1875.

PIPER'S ALLEY
1608 N. Wells

ARCHITECTS: *Stanley Tigerman and Associates (1976)*

The conversion includes a collection of shops, restaurants, and theaters. Second City, a nationally known comedy club and theater, is part of the Piper's Alley complex, at 1616 N. Wells Street. Second City's exterior ornament is from the facade of Adler and Sullivan's Garrick Theatre—rescued when that theater on Randolph Street near Dearborn was demolished in 1961.

Walk north on Wells Street past Second City.

CONCORD LANE

This semi-private lane has 20 3-story townhouses and brick paving, all of it meant to look like an original part of the 19th-century neighborhood. Yet it is distinctly late 20th century, with landscaping, security gates, even a basketball hoop.

AMERICANA TOWERS
1636 N. Wells

ARCHITECTS: *Schiff and Friedes (1972)*

By contrast, next door is a concrete condominium tower with an adjacent shopping and community center. The tower is set well back at the third-story level to preserve the low-rise quality of the streetscape here.

Walk north to Eugenie Avenue and turn east.

1660 N. LASALLE

ARCHITECTS: *Dubin, Dubin, Black and Moutoussamy (1972)*

This 42-story condominium tower was built in 1972, making it and American Towers among the first to alter the area's scale.

Walk back to Wells Street. Turn north 1 block to Kennelly Square, another large complex.

KENNELLY SQUARE
1751 N. Wells

ARCHITECTS: *Ezra Gordon and Jack Levin (1973)*

This is another unique development. It is named Kennelly Square for former Chicago Mayor Martin H. Kennelly and the Werner-Kennelly warehouse, which has been remodeled and is part of this complex. The east building is called The Warehouse.

The development includes a 25-story high-rise apartment building on Wells Street; a 10-story apartment building on Clark Street; a 54,000-square-foot commercial space, swimming pool, restaurant, and community facilities. The shopping gallery is skylighted and is accessible by a bridge over an open sunken arcade.

Now walk south on Wells Street, back to St. Paul Avenue. Walk west to Crilly Court, a famous bit of Chicago.

CRILLY COURT
Bounded by St. Paul (north), Wells (east), North Park (west), and Eugenie (south)

DEVELOPER: *Daniel F. Crilly (1885–93)*

Stephen F. Gale, Chicago's first stationer and first Fire Chief, owned 40 acres of country farm and meadowland just north of the city limits. He subdivided it in 1845. Five or six years later, Chicago annexed the land. Then Charles Canda, a Frenchman, bought the inside lots at the heart of it all. Those lots ran from Wells to Sedgwick, and from Eugenie to St. Paul.

Where Crilly Court is now, Canda owned a home and a barn with a large number of fruit trees. After he died in 1854, his widow Adele took the west half, and Florimond, his brother, took the east. (St. Paul Avenue was Florimond Street until 1936.) Colonel Florimond Canda, who had fought at the battle of Waterloo under Napoleon Bonaparte, was awarded a medal by Napoleon III and the Empress Eugenie, then came to settle in Chicago in 1843. It was Florimond Canda who sold the property to developer Daniel F. Crilly in 1884.

Daniel Crilly created a street through the middle of the block, from St. Paul to Eugenie, which he named Crilly Court. He built the 4-story buildings on the east side of North Park Avenue. He purchased the materials from the building that stood where Germania Place now stands. He also moved a 3-story brick building from that site to the southeast corner of St. Paul and North Park where it stands today.

The building that fronts on Wells Street is characteristic of one Chicago building type. In the Chicago Landmark Commission Guidelines, Twelve Typical Building Types, this building is used as a model with a caption "Store Fronts with Apartments Above." The structure is particularly handsome as an example because of the bay window and the iron columns. It truly livens up the street.

The Crilly estate over the years leased units to well-known Chicagoans. Eugene Field, poet and journalist, was one, and Cyrus DeVry, first Lincoln Park Zoo Director, was another. George K. Spoor occupied an

Crilly Court
(Olga Stefanos)

apartment there for many years. An early movie producer, Spoor was known for his Keystone Cops and movies with Ben Turpin and Francis X. Bushman, who gave our long-time zoo gorilla his name. In order to preserve the films, it was necessary for Spoor to keep them in his icebox. Commercial artist Haddon Sundbloom lived for many years in an apartment above the Wells Street stores. He was the creator of the kindly man on the Quaker Oats box as well as of Aunt Jemima. For over 35 years his Coca-Cola Santa was an annual Christmas feature all over the world.

At the end of World War II, this section of the city was overcrowded and rapidly deteriorating. The owner of several large walk-up apartment buildings decided to deconvert and rehabilitate his buildings, two of which were back to back, separated by an alley. By replacing old wooden porches with steel balconies and stairs, and transforming the yards into gardens and delightful play areas, he entirely changed the character of the buildings. The city, taking cognizance of his fine work, named the short connecting street to the west Crilly Court after its innovator.

Crilly Court established the procedure for much fine conservation and rehabilitation work that characterizes the Old Town Triangle. Many painters, sculptors, musicians, poets, authors, and architects have made this area their home, and over the years much remodeling has taken place.

There are so many late 19th-century townhouses and walk-up apartment buildings nearby you may think that when you've seen one you've seen them all. Not so; each is a pleasant surprise, sometimes found tucked in between taller buildings or set back far from the street. The rich texture of the fine brickwork and stone ornament make an architectural "find" of many of the buildings. Crilly Court itself is a private road with characteristics that suggest a quiet side street in the west part of London about the time of Sherlock Holmes!

225 W. EUGENIE   ARCHITECT: *Unknown (1874)*

Facing Crilly Court from the south is a remodeled 3-story frame house, with a new stucco wall and patio that make for privacy, and a charming entrance and facade. It is a well-preserved example of a wood frame cottage. The windows are crowned with keystone pediments and surrounded by rope moldings. It has a denticulated bracketed cornice under the eaves. There is a habitable rear building, which may have survived the Chicago Fire.

Continue west.

235 W. EUGENIE   ARCHITECTS: *Harry Weese and Associates (1958)*

This is a delightful contemporary structure of seven maisonettes. These comprise fourteen dwelling units of 2 stories each, the architect having placed two "layers" of 2-story townhouses in a row of seven.

Walk to the northwest corner of Eugenie and North Park avenues.

ORLEANS HOUSE
1700 N. North Park

ARCHITECTS: *Harry Weese and Associates (1960–61)*

First called the Old Town Apartments, these were designed to blend into the surrounding community through the use of similar building height and characteristics reminiscent of older buildings. The apartments in the complex have high ceilings, Franklin stoves, and hardwood floors. The conventional construction technique used masonry bearing walls and party walls. The exterior is of Chicago common brick, painted standing seam sheet metal, and painted millwork. Parking is at grade, partially under the building.

Cross to the east side of North Park Avenue.

**1701-1705,
1707-1709, and
1711-1713 N.
NORTH PARK**

ARCHITECT: *Unknown (1893)*

Built for Daniel Crilly in 1893, these courtyard apartments are early examples of a Chicago building type that became popular in the 1920s. They have slender denticulated crowning cornices, in a motif matched by the stonework over the doors.

**1717-1719 N.
NORTH PARK**

ARCHITECT: *Unknown (pre-1888)*

Although the architect and date are unknown, we do know that the building was moved to the site in 1888. It is without bays, but the relatively plain facade contrasts with a magnificent, richly carved, bracketed front porch, which is its only decoration.

On the west side of the street you will see a charming old church building, tucked away behind trees, with a patterned brick walk.

1718 N. NORTH PARK

ARCHITECT: *Unknown (1880s); for the adaptive reuse: Ast and Dagdelen (1982–86)*

This was originally St. Jacob's Lutheran Church and later the Church of the Three Crosses. More recently it became the home of the Old Town Players, a repertory theater group—oldest of many small theater groups in the city. The interior was most successfully remodeled into a delightful arena for classical as well as modern drama.

After testing several schemes for this particular site, it was decided that the church be subdivided to allow for the conversion into 3 townhouses, each oriented east and west. The design respects the existing fabric of the community. The front of the building, which has exposure on Orleans Street, is restored to its original condition with the exception of three understated doorways that provide entry. The east exposure, once the entry to the Old Town Players and set back half a block from North Park Avenue, is punctuated with protruding bay windows where originally there was a blank brick wall.

Stroll east along St. Paul Avenue, to view the charming townhouses, trees, shrubbery, and windowboxes there. Then return to North Park Avenue. The beautifully restored Menomonee Club for Boys and Girls, at the corner of Willow Street, demonstrates how children and urban living need not be incompatible.

Continue north to Menomonee Street.

314 and 334 W. MENOMONEE

At 314 you see a successfully preserved single-family wood-frame home of the 19th century. By comparison, across Orleans Street is an example of successful rehabilitation, this one a brick apartment building with offsetting brick window hoods.

At Orleans Street, walk north. You will pass many homes—some preserved, others updated in modern styles.

1838-40 N. ORLEANS

ARCHITECT: *Unknown (1886)*

Originally the C. F. W. Schmidt residence, this very handsome double-fronted apartment building has wonderful terra-cotta liberally placed on the facade and stained glass at the top of every bay window.

1835 N. ORLEANS

ARCHITECT: *Unknown (1879)*

Note too, across the street, the charming old townhouse of orangish-red brick. The house, patio, and decorative ironwork have been well maintained.

Now walk back south on Orleans Street.

1817 N. ORLEANS

ARCHITECT: *Unknown (1883)*

Note this rehabilitated, 3-story, red-brick house. Originally the Bertha Ehman house, it was built in 1883. The front stoop has been removed, but the lively line of the arched windows at the 3rd story gives this building distinction and a Moorish flavor.

Continue south.

1801-1805 N. ORLEANS

The Orleans apartment building is a rather poor facsimile of a New Orleans facade.

Walk east two very short blocks on Menomonee Street.

235 W. MENOMONEE

ARCHITECT: *Unknown (pre-1930)*

Farther east on Menomonee stands a daring rehabilitation of an apartment building: the 3rd story has been removed in order to give the 2nd-floor living room a ceiling 2 stories high. Excellent!

Turn north on Lincoln Park West.

1802 N. LINCOLN PARK WEST

ARCHITECT: *Unknown(1874)*

Originally the Henry Meyer house, this is a rare example of an extant farmhouse. It has keystones in carved wood arches, a light decorative element added to gentrify the house. On the north end a brick wall and ivy make a delightful contrast.

A few doors north you come to two red brick, high-ceilinged houses.

1814 N. LINCOLN PARK WEST

ARCHITECT: *Unknown (1878, 1886)*

Originally the Samuel Anderson apartment building (Mr. Anderson was a merchant), this was built in two stages: the rear third of the building in 1878, and the front two-thirds in 1886. The facade of this 4-story walk-up is appointed with the plastic artistry of terra-cotta. These include the lunette at the top of the bay and the window spandrels. The house is in fine condition—surely the result of tender loving care.

1826 N. Lincoln Park West
(James Cornelius)

1832–4 N. Lincoln Park West
(James Cornelius)

1816 N. LINCOLN PARK WEST

ARCHITECT: *Unknown (1890)*

Little information is available about this building, which is attached to its apartment neighbor yet is now a single home. It is in fine condition and has also received tender loving care.

Continue north.

1826-1834 N. LINCOLN PARK WEST

ARCHITECTS: *Adler and Sullivan (1884, 1885)*

Originally the Ann Halsted townhouses, this row of 2-story, red brick townhouses once had five doors but now has four. The three southern units were built in 1884, and the northern two the following year. These are among the few surviving examples of Louis Sullivan's early architectural design and planning. They have a special charm, thanks partly to the terra-cotta ornamentation, and close observation will reveal that the ornaments on the two halves are not quite the same. The corbel brackets on the northern two have a more vegetative origin and are less geometric than the three to the south. Notice the south part where the debt to Sullivan's early mentor, Philadelphia architect Frank Furness, is more pronounced.

1836 N. LINCOLN PARK WEST

ARCHITECT: *Unknown (1884)*

This and the following house were known as the two Wacker houses. Charles Wacker—first chairman of the Chicago Plan Commission, for whom Wacker Drive was named—lived next door; his mother-in-law lived in this house. It has small eave brackets, intricate turned columns, and wood fretwork on the entrance canopy in a floral motif with delicate metal filigree on the canopy roof. The large front bay window has incised, fluted exterior casings in the classic manner on a base with capitals. They extend on the ground floor in a way sympathetically emulated by the sloping fascia of the entrance canopy.

1838 N. LINCOLN PARK WEST

ARCHITECT: *Unknown (1874)*

The showpiece in this group is this brick-and-frame house, which has unusually heavy wood ornament above the first floor. This was the home of Charles Wacker (see above), and it combines characteristics of a Swiss chalet, an Italianate feeling, and a fairy tale quality. There is a wide overhanging veranda supported by curved brackets, open-work hoods above the windows, and carved wooden spindle railings flanking the broad stairway. In a garden at the rear are two more brick houses, coach houses that Wacker had built at the turn of the century.

Make a short detour by turning to your right at Lincoln Avenue and walking southeast.

1834, 1836, and 1838 N. LINCOLN

ARCHITECT: *Unknown (1876)*

These rowhouses with triangular projecting bays have unified stonefronts. Note the decorative elements above the windows, the fully bracketed cornice, and the broad frieze. The newer stairways harmonize nicely with the sidewalk.

1832 N. LINCOLN

ARCHITECT: *Unknown (1880)*

This and the next building were known as the Thekla Koch residence. Now a multiunit residence, it is still a fine example of the Second Empire style. The mansard roof has the original fishscale slate. The large-paned glass it once used was technologically progressive for its time.

1830 N. LINCOLN

ARCHITECT: *Unknown (1878)*

A generation after this building was constructed, it was embellished in the then-popular Italianate style, seen in the brackets under the eaves, the dentils, and the projecting Chicago bay. A walk in the alley to the rear is most rewarding, for the houses all have delightful rear patios. At the time of the Old Town Art Fair, usually held the second week in June each year, some of these patios are opened to the public.

Across the street is a large new complex.

HEMINGWAY HOUSE
1825 N. Lincoln Plaza

ARCHITECTS: *Solomon, Cordwell, Buenz and Associates (1971)*

The Lincoln Park community has become world renowned for the efforts of its citizens in restoring the charm of this late 19th-century area. Interspersed among the restored old houses are new developments in a variety of forms. Hemingway House is one such new development: on an unusually shaped site overlooking Lincoln Park, the challenge was to provide space for an apartment tower, attractive shops, and parking without interfering with the charm of the neighborhood.

Hemingway House contains 260 apartments and 20,000 square feet of shops and offices. All parking is below grade. The tower on the north end of the site was sited to minimize sun shading of adjacent yards and structures. The height of the 2-story commercial structure was scaled to correspond to the predominant height of the cornice line of existing structures on Lincoln Avenue, thus preserving the vertical scale of the entire block.

Return to Lincoln Park West, crossing the tricky six-way corner, and continue north.

1915-1923 N. LINCOLN PARK WEST

ARCHITECT: *Unknown (1880)*

These fascinating rehabilitated townhouses were built by Adolph Olsen in 1880. Although the two buildings near the center are plainer, this group stands out for individual as well as unified character. An interesting feature is the way in which the cornice outlines the dormer windows and the triangular pediments above them. The original slate imbrications on the mansard roof remain.

LINCOLN PARK TOWER
1960 N. Lincoln Park West

LINCOLN PARK TERRACE
2020 N. Lincoln Park West

ARCHITECTS: *Dubin, Dubin, Black and Moutoussamy (1967; 1972)*

The south apartment building has a first-rate design, although it has not aged well and its height causes a wind shear around the base on many days. A raised pool occupies the southwest plaza. On its cousin across Armitage Avenue the semicircular balconies give an individual appearance that does not in any way echo Lincoln Park Tower.

By the raised pool you are on the northern end of the former Ogden Avenue—now the Ogden Mall.

OGDEN MALL

The Ogden Mall was an important phase of the Department of Urban Renewal's plans for rehabilitating the Old Town and Lincoln Park Conservation areas (see WALK 26). Ogden Avenue, a diagonal thoroughfare, which formerly ended at Clark Street on the northeast, was closed to vehicular traffic southwest to North Avenue and converted into a pedestrian mall in 1970. The Mall was an early part of a green belt connecting Lincoln Park to the residential areas to the west. The persistence of Lewis W. Hill, former Commissioner of Urban Renewal and Development and Planning, is largely responsible for the apparent success in implementing the plan.

Follow the alignment of the Mall, continuing in a southwesterly direction to Wisconsin Street. First, pass two small apartment buildings with shops at grade level. The urban renewal plans allowed a combination of residential, commercial, and institutional development along the Mall.

Walk west on Wisconsin to Sedgwick, then turn south to Menomonee Street. Walk ½ block west.

MIDWEST BUDDHIST TEMPLE
435 W. Menomonee

ARCHITECT: *Hideaki Arao (1972)*

From a distance of 2 or 3 blocks, the Midwest Buddhist Temple—also known as the Temple of Enlightenment—appears to be set on a high plateau. It is on flat ground, but the illusion persists until one is almost next to it. The explanation is the unusual method the architect used in setting the chapel high above the main portion of the structure.

The chapel has a shingled, modified gable roof, which at a distance gives the appearance of a pagoda. The base of the temple is a concrete wall that is striated by a rough, bush-hammered technique. The first floor wall continues beyond the first floor ceiling line to become the parapet wall for a deck that surrounds the chapel.

The rectangular floor plan places a large social room directly beneath the chapel. The social room is set a few feet below grade, with an open corridor at grade level on the two long sides. The corridor gives access to classrooms and offices.

The chapel's main entrance consists of an impressive concrete stairway leading to heavy iron gates. One first reaches the deck, which is actually the roof over the corridors. It provides the means to hold ceremonial processions as well as a place to accommodate crowds waiting to enter. The exterior walls of the chapel are stucco-finished with windows of translucent glass. Upon entering the chapel, which has white walls and ceiling and heavy timber trusses, one is aware of its simple character. There is an altar at the south end consisting of a gold-leaf sanctuary and shrine that contains a small gold, standing Buddha.

The exterior remains the boldest part of the temple. It has the strength and vitality of the ancient Japanese shrines along with the simple straight lines of contemporary architecture. The parsonage to the west was built after the temple was completed, and the lovely Japanese garden was also added later. Parking is well hidden at the rear.

Walk south alongside the parsonage, emerging on St. Michael's Court.

Midwest Buddhist Temple
(Chicago Department of Urban Renewal)

ST. MICHAEL'S CHURCH
1633 N. Cleveland

ARCHITECT: *August Wallbaum (1866–69, 1872–73)*

Roman Catholic St. Michael's, a complex of buildings extending south to North Avenue, includes the enormous church at Eugenie Street as well as a convent, rectory, elementary school, gymnasium, high school, and community center. The brick and stone church was originally built in 1866–69 and partially destroyed by the Great Fire of 1871. It was restored in 1872–73 and expanded over the intervening years to its present size. The urban renewal program has made St. Michael's a part of the Ogden Mall, with a large pedestrian masonry court, or square, at the entrance facade.

The semi-Gothic-Romanesque–German Baroque character of the exterior and interior of the church comes as a pleasant surprise, if one is not an architectural purist. The interior has an enormously high ceiling with Gothic-type vaulting supported by slender columns with semi-classic capitals.

The great monumental altar is carved wood with many sculptured figures. It is capped by a figure of St. Michael with a great sword and great jeweled crown overhead, above which stands a jeweled cross. There are murals on either side of the altar. All in all, it is a fascinating Baroque setting.

Originally, St. Michael's was a large German-speaking parish. Today, one mass on Sunday is given in Spanish; the others are in English. This reflects the changing character of the neighborhood. The bells still toll the quarter hour, and the spire can still be seen from most Old Town corners.

To return to the Loop, walk east on Eugenie Street. Stop to read the plaque on the cottage at 407; it commemorates Joseph J. O'Connell, a telephone pioneer who lived in this house for almost 100 years.

Continue east to Clark Street to board a southbound CTA No. 22 or 36 bus.

Old Town Apartments
(Bill Engdahl, Hedrich-Blessing courtesy Harry Weese & Associates)

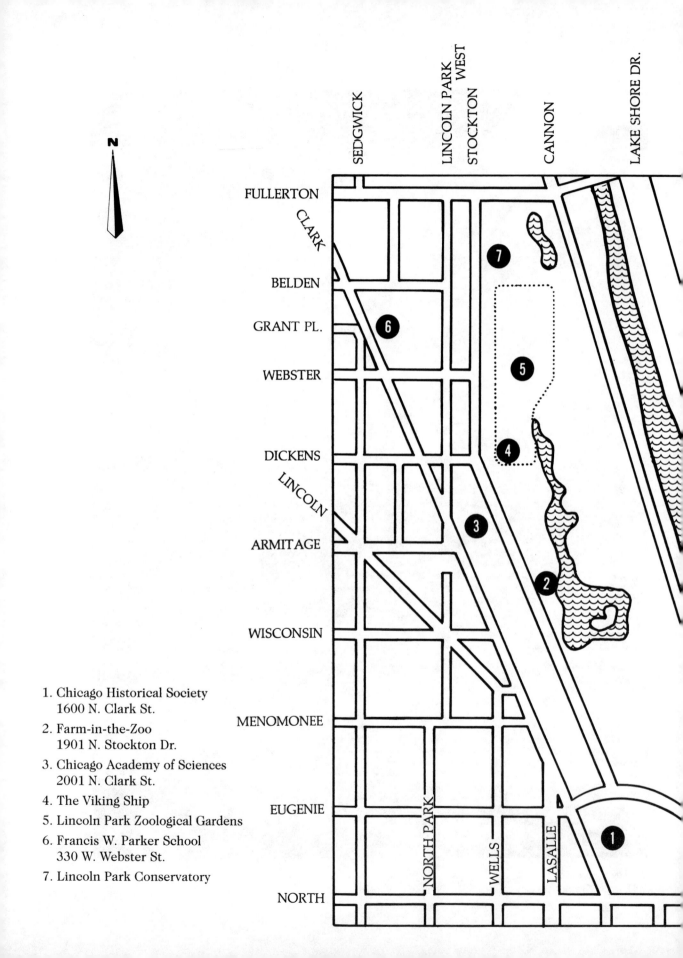

N

SEDGWICK

LINCOLN PARK WEST
STOCKTON

CANNON

LAKE SHORE DR.

FULLERTON

CLARK

BELDEN

GRANT PL.

WEBSTER

DICKENS

LINCOLN

ARMITAGE

WISCONSIN

MENOMONEE

EUGENIE

NORTH PARK

WELLS

LASALLE

NORTH

1. Chicago Historical Society
   1600 N. Clark St.

2. Farm-in-the-Zoo
   1901 N. Stockton Dr.

3. Chicago Academy of Sciences
   2001 N. Clark St.

4. The Viking Ship

5. Lincoln Park Zoological Gardens

6. Francis W. Parker School
   330 W. Webster St.

7. Lincoln Park Conservatory

WALK 25 LINCOLN PARK: MUSEUMS, ZOOS, CONSERVATORY

WALKING TIME: 1–2 hours (does not include entering museums).

HOW TO GET THERE: Take a northbound CTA bus No. 36 (Broadway) on State Street or No. 22 (Clark) on Dearborn Street (1 block west of State Street), and get off at North Avenue (1600 N) and Clark Street.

Lincoln Park was named for President Abraham Lincoln. It is Chicago's largest park, covering some 1,000 acres of land just off the lake all the way from West North Avenue (1600 N) to West Hollywood Avenue (5700 N). This WALK, however, will take you only through the southern part of the area, no farther than Diversey Avenue (2800 N). In this section you are in the old Lincoln Park, as it was before the various northern extensions—on land redeemed from the lake—were added. And here you will find most of the park's special attractions.

Near the southern end, where Dearborn Street meets Lincoln Park, a rugged bronze figure of Abraham Lincoln stands to greet you—ignoring the bench, designed by Stanford White, behind him. This Lincoln statue, by Augustus St. Gaudens, is only one of about thirty large statues in the park of such disparate personages as Garibaldi, Hans Christian Andersen, Beethoven, Shakespeare, John Peter Altgeld, Native Americans, and Sir Georg Solti. Perhaps the most unexpected in this locale are the large unclad figure symbolic of Goethe and the conventional equestrian statue of Ulysses S. Grant—who appears not at all in Grant Park, where St. Gaudens's seated Lincoln is a main attraction!

Only a few steps away from the Lincoln statue is—appropriately—the Chicago Historical Society, especially famous for its Lincoln and Civil War materials.

CHICAGO HISTORICAL SOCIETY
W. North and N. Clark

ARCHITECTS: *Graham, Anderson, Probst and White (1925);*
for new wing: Alfred Shaw and Associates (1972);
for the addition: Holabird and Root (1986–88)

The Chicago Historical Society has occupied its building—a 2-story brick structure with a well-proportioned Georgian facade—since 1925, but the Society was organized in 1856. (The previous building stood at 632 N. Dearborn Street.)

Chicago Historical Society
(Leslie Schwartz)

An imposing gray limestone west wing was completed in 1972. This wing makes it possible for the society to exhibit many important items that heretofore had to be stored in the basement.

In referring to the building addition, Andrew McNally III, president of the society, told the trustees, "The planned addition to our building will provide space for our collections, space for new exhibits, space for handling school children, and space for us to conduct lively and exciting programs."

To anyone interested in this country's history, a visit to the museum is already a lively and exciting experience. The past comes vividly to life through dramatic displays, period rooms, costumes of famous Americans, and a collection of early autos and horsedrawn vehicles, as well as through the exhibits of manuscripts, paintings, prints, and maps.

A new west entrance and an additional 28,000 square feet of space have been built, mostly for storage. A restaurant occupies the glass and steel rounded projection at the south end, along with a bookstore behind large display windows Half of the front has a sheltering sidewalk arcade. The somewhat unfinished-looking steelwork over the entrance hints at the postmodern view that our study of history is ongoing and our knowledge impermanent.

The museum is open daily 9:30 A.M. to 4:30 P.M.; Sunday and holidays noon to 5 P.M. For information, call 642-4600.

Just north of the Chicago Historical Society, with its records of the City by the Lake and of the people who made the records, is the tomb of one of those historic people, Ira Couch. Ironically, the rather small Couch Mausoleum is often overlooked, though its presence is proof that the Couch family won a lawsuit against the city to keep it here when the city cemetery was discontinued and the graves moved to private cemeteries. Ira Couch, originally a tailor, in 1836 became one of Chicago's pioneer hotel owners as the proprietor of the Tremont House, then located at the northwest corner of Lake and Dearborn streets.

From the Lincoln statue behind the historical society walk through the underpass and proceed north.

FARM-IN-THE-ZOO
1901 N. Stockton

ARCHITECTS: *Chicago Park District (1964); for the renovations and additions: John Macsai and Associates (1986–87)*

Lincoln Park Zoo, a favorite haunt of thousands of Chicago's young at heart, includes the main zoo, a children's zoo within it, and this, the Farm-in-the-Zoo, which is spread out along the west side of the South Pond. The Farm-in-the-Zoo originated as a way to familiarize city children with the farm animals they never see, and it has proved equally fascinating to children coming in from the country. You will find here not only the smaller farm animals—chickens, goats, pigs, sheep—but horses and cows as well. In the dairy barn are cows for milking and in another are beef cattle. In still another barn, horses are on display. The milking parlor in the dairy barn with all its modern equipment may not seem natural to a generation old enough to remember watching the "hired hand" squirt the milk from the cow into a big open pail (now considered unsanitary), occasionally aiming a stream into the mouth of a waiting cat beside him. But recent generations, of course, find the farm machinery—milking machines and tractors and all the rest—more natural and more interesting.

In the main barn are many exhibits and demonstrations. There you can see samples of what is actually produced on a farm and learn how many ways they are used. You can also watch the process of manufacturing a number of things that are made from farm products or especially needed on the farm—fertilizer, butter, or soap, for instance.

The Farm-in-the-Zoo is open daily 9:00 A.M. to 4:30 P.M. Free.

Chicago Academy of Sciences
(Olga Stefanos)

Across the road from the Farm-in-the-Zoo, near the corner of Clark and Wisconsin streets, is the David Kennison Boulder. This, along with the Couch Mausoleum, is a reminder that a cemetery once occupied this ground. The boulder was placed by the Sons and Daughters of the American Revolution to mark the grave of the last survivor of the Boston Tea Party group, who died in Chicago in 1852 at the age of 115 years.

Walk north on Clark Street one block to a compact museum of natural history right in the park, the Chicago Academy of Sciences.

CHICAGO ACADEMY OF SCIENCES
2001 N. Clark

ARCHITECTS: *Patton and Fisher (1893); for Auditorium: Skidmore, Owings and Merrill (1953); for Gallery: Environ, Inc. (1984); for exterior rehabilitation: Environ, Inc. (1986)*

Founded in 1857, only one year after the founding of the Chicago Historical Society, this is the city's oldest museum—in fact the oldest scientific museum in the American west. It housed Chicago's first planetarium. Here, too, Chicago's past is brought vividly to life—a past, however, long antedating anything you may have seen in the Chicago Historical Society's exhibits. For here you may walk through a section that reproduces Chicago of 300 million years ago—when it was a coal forest! And a series called "Chicago Environs" presents dioramas showing animals and plants that flourished here when the area was still open prairie, swamp, forest, and beach. There are also changing exhibits and special education programs.

Officially the Matthew Laflin Memorial, this building is a real tribute to one of Chicago's early businessmen. Laflin came to Chicago in the 1830s, having sold out his business in the east to a man by the name of du Pont! He started one of the first stockyards in Chicago, near enough the hotel he had built to manage both businesses. Another of his ventures in Chicago was a bus line. This restless innovator shared an ambition with many other early Chicago leaders: to rest at last in the city's cemetery with an imposing monument above him. Like many others, he was distressed when the graves and monuments there were moved and Lincoln Park substituted. But though he couldn't be buried where he had hoped to be, he could have an impressive monument, the Chicago Academy of Sciences building. Laflin provided $75,000 for it, and the Chicago Park District added $25,000 from its own budget.

The interior has undergone remodeling, and the Romanesque exterior has been cleaned, including replacement of the stairs and damaged stonework, in an effort to return the structure to its previous grandeur. It stands as a worthy memorial indeed for one of Chicago's earliest successful businessmen.

The Academy is open 10 A.M. to 5 P.M. every day but Christmas. Call 871-2668 for information on exhibits and lectures.

Back in the park, several structures dot the green spaces. One of the best is Cafe Brauer, between the Farm-in-the-Zoo and the main zoo. It was designed in 1908 by Dwight Perkins and was restored in 1990 after many years of disrepair. A snack bar occupies the waterside ground level, while upstairs the Great Hall, a lovely room exhibiting Perkins's Prairie school ideas, is used for special events. The building's two wings, balconies above arcades, seem to embrace South Pond.

Just to the north is one entrance to the main zoo. Inside, veer left and walk about 100 yards for an unexpected sight.

THE VIKING SHIP This astounding vessel, recently removed for repairs, is a reminder of the 1893 World's Columbian Exposition. This is the very boat—a copy of a 10th-century Viking ship—that was built in Norway and sailed across the Atlantic by a crew of 12 men. They brought official greetings from their country to the Exposition and the citizens of Chicago.

Now, on to the main exhibit.

Lincoln Park Zoo
(courtesy Chicago Park District)

LINCOLN PARK ZOOLOGICAL GARDENS

Between Stockton and Cannon drives from about 2100 N to 2300 N Lincoln Park Zoo is the park's biggest attraction. America's second-oldest zoo, it was founded in 1868. It occupies 35 acres of the park's total acreage and is maintained by the Chicago Park District, which has modernized the site while keeping its 19th-century flavor.

Traditionally, a zoo tried to keep the largest possible variety of animals, usually displayed in small, easy-to-clean cages. Beginning in the 1960s this philosophy began to change, when it was thought that a more natural setting benefits the animals and gives the visitor a more positive and instructive experience. In the 1980s Lincoln Park Zoo addressed itself to new thinking once again, focusing its collection on endangered species. Unfortunately, most of the animals we think of as traditional zoo attractions are now endangered; the casual visitor might enjoy the presentation while missing the message.

The Lincoln Park Zoo and the Children's Zoo were consolidated in an ambitious expansion and remodeling program, the first phase of which was completed in 1971. Harry Weese and Associates were the chief planners and architects. The Lincoln Park Zoological Society, a private nonprofit organization, has been active in the zoo's expansion. A second major phase was completed in the 1980s by various architects. The zoo now has scores of species among its 1,600 mammals, birds, and reptiles.

Great ingenuity is necessary because Lincoln Park Zoo, resting in the heart of the city, has a limited site. Natural habitats were created by remodeling interiors and exteriors of the old buildings, yet their wonderful character was retained. The 1980s construction consists of unique, multifunctional structures that burrow into the ground and are covered with a blanket of landscaping. This reduces their visual impact on the park and creates a terrain of winding paths and gentle hills. The Small

Mammal House of 1889, the zoo's oldest building, was razed in 1993 to make room for yet more parklike natural setting.

The grounds are open daily 8 A.M. to 5 P.M.; some buildings have shorter hours. Free.

THE PRITZKER CHILDREN'S ZOO
ARCHITECT: *Chicago Park District (1959); for the renovations and addition: Hammond Beeby and Babka (1986)*

KROC ANIMAL HOSPITAL
ARCHITECT: *Chicago Park District, Maurice Thominet Chief Architect (1976)*

SEA LION POOL
ARCHITECT: *Chicago Park District (1969)*

REPTILE HOUSE
ARCHITECT: *Edwin Clark (1922)*

This was originally Chicago's only aquarium, remodeled into the present reptile house in 1936.

HELEN BRACH PRIMATE HOUSE (formerly Small Animal House)
ARCHITECT: *Edwin Clark (1927); for the renovations: John Macsai and Associates (1984)*

LESTER E. FISHER GREAT APE HOUSE
ARCHITECTS: *Brenner, Danforth and Rockwell, Daniel Brenner consulting architect (1976)*

This amazing habitat acquired its name in 1992 upon the retirement of the zoo's director of 30 years, who made this zoo the "Gorilla Capital of the World" through a dedicated breeding program.

ANTELOPE AND ZEBRA HABITAT
ARCHITECTS: *Welton Becket Associates (1982)*

REGENSTEIN LARGE MAMMAL HABITAT
ARCHITECTS: *Skidmore, Owings and Merrill, Myron Goldsmith chief architect (1982)*

FLAMINGO DOME AND WATERFOWL LAGOON
ARCHITECT: *Chicago Park District (1978)*

Waterfowl fly uncaged at this attractive site. The U.S. Department of Commerce, along with local donors, helped develop it.

KOVLER LION HOUSE

ARCHITECT: *Dwight Perkins (1912); for the remodeling: Hammond Beeby and Babka (1986–87)*

Be sure not to miss the brick and tile Lion House, winner of a Gold Medal from the American Association of Architects. Note the delightful dancing lions above the entrance arch.

CROWN-FIELD CENTER

ARCHITECT: *Brenner, Danforth and Rockwell (1979)*

The Crown-Field Center is an amazing multipurpose building. Mixed into one, dug-in, unobtrusive building are the zoo's offices, a gift shop, an auditorium, two classrooms, and, at one time, an indoor apartment for a large family of lemurs! The upper level is ringed with an outdoor walkway where two koalas reside.

BLUM-KOVLER PENGUIN AND SEABIRD HOUSE

ARCHITECTS: *Danforth Rockwell Carow (1981)*

McCORMICK BIRD HOUSE

ARCHITECTS: *Jarvis Hunt (1900); for Bird of Prey Habitat: Skidmore, Owings and Merrill (1983); for the renovations: Schmidt, Garden and Erickson (1986–87)*

ZOO ROOKERY

ARCHITECTS: *Alfred Caldwell (1936); for the renovation: Chicago Park District, Ira M. Berke (1968)*

The Zoo Rookery is at the extreme north of the Lincoln Park Zoo. Here land and water birds make their home in a large attractive rock garden, and are free to come and go as they like.

Emerging from the zoo's grounds will put you near Webster Avenue. Walk west on it one block to our next stop. Or, you can proceed north to the Lincoln Park Conservatory.

FRANCIS W. PARKER SCHOOL
330 W. Webster

ARCHITECTS: *Holabird and Root (1962, 1986)*

This U-shaped, 3-story, hard-burned red brick structure replaced an ancient 4-story half-timber Tudor Gothic building constructed in the early 1900s. Note the metal sculptured figures of children at the main entrance facing Clark Street. They were produced by Abbott Pattison, an alumnus.

An outstanding independent private school (prekindergarten through 12th grade), this was one of the first progressive schools in the country, following the creative teaching concepts of John Dewey and Francis Parker. This is the school that brought a cow to graze in the front yard so city children could have some touch of experience with the country.

(The cow arrived long before the Farm-in-the-Zoo did at Lincoln Park.) Visitors sometimes question the wisdom of the overall architectural plan—placing the building on the Clark Street side of the property and leaving the side facing the park, which is very valuable land indeed, for a play field. The school's board of trustees, however, agreed to allow the green belt from the park to continue to Clark Street as its contribution to the community.

In a delightful courtyard facing south you will see a reflecting pool, flower garden, and stainless steel sculpture by John Kearny. This charming setting is often the background for school functions, such as plays, receptions, and other ceremonies. The brick wall separating the courtyard from the play field contains some original terra-cotta plaques from the Garrick Theatre Building designed by Adler and Sullivan—first known as the Schiller Building, which stood at 64 W. Randolph Street until its demolition in 1961. (The Second City theater group also used stones from this building. See WALK 24.)

In 1986 a third floor was added to the east wing, to match the west wing; a connecting corridor was added at that level between the wings; and the art studios were expanded on the lower level to the east. The science rooms were updated and the library enlarged. The little school was expanded to the west with a brick to match the main school, and the kindergarten rooms enlarged; all windows were replaced with double glazed insulated glass.

LINCOLN PARK CONSERVATORY
W. Fullerton and Stockton

ARCHITECTS: *J. L. Silsbee (1892, 1902); addition (1904);*
for the main entry modification: Chicago Park District (1950);
for rebuilding of propagating houses: Chicago Park District (1985–86)

The greenhouse, constructed of copper glazing bars with clear glass side windows and translucent wire-glass for the roof, protects a seemingly infinite collection of plants. The show houses, some of which date back to 1892, display a large collection of potted palms, a fernery, and a bit of real tropics where tropical fruit trees are propagated. (The Conservatory has 18 propagating houses, closed to the public.)

Four annual exhibits have become traditional: a show of azaleas in February and March; lilies and spring plants in April; chrysanthemums, of course, in November; and poinsettias and Star of Bethlehem in December and January.

This is considered one of the finest conservatories in the country. Incidentally, many of the flowers that appear in Chicago's numerous parks are started in the greenhouses connected with this conservatory. Don't overlook the park's outdoor gardens near the conservatory— Grandmother's Garden, water-lily ponds, fountains, and formal gardens.

Open daily 9 A.M. to 5 P.M. During their 4 major annual shows: 10 A.M. to 6 P.M. Free.

Lincoln Park's Casting Pond lies along Stockton Drive north of Fullerton Parkway. The casting pond can be used by anyone interested in developing that particular fisherman's skill. And about ½ mile north of Fullerton stands a golden statue of Alexander Hamilton, erected in 1952, designed by the architect Samuel Marx. (See also WALK 29.)

This is the northernmost point in your WALK. If you walk to the Hamilton statue and up onto its plaza, you will have a rewarding view. The Elks Memorial stands to the west. To the north, the direction that Hamilton himself is facing, and slightly east, is a bronze figure of John Peter Altgeld, the governor of Illinois who lost his political career but gained eternal fame for his courage when he freed the men he was convinced were unjustly convicted of throwing a bomb during the Haymarket Riot in 1886. To the east you will see the Diversey Yacht Club, and to the south (if you are willing to turn your back on the great gentleman!) a panoramic view of Chicago's always impressive skyline.

Lincoln Park Farm-in-the-Zoo
(Sean O'Neill)

1. 1943–45 N. Hudson St.
2. Pickwick Village
   515–29 W. Dickens Ave.
3. 540 W. Dickens Ave.
4. Dickens Square
   542–554 W. Dickens Ave.
5. Walpole Point
   2140 N. Lincoln Ave.
6. 2110–12 N. Hudson Ave.
7. Policeman Bellinger's Cottage
   2121 N. Hudson ave.
8. 2134–38 N. Hudson Ave.
9. 2111–21 N. Cleveland Ave.
10. 2114–16 N. Cleveland Ave.
11. 2118 N. Cleveland Ave.
12. 2124 N. Cleveland Ave.
13. 2129–31 N. Cleveland Ave.
14. 2137–41 N. Cleveland Ave.
15. Grant Hospital
    550 W. Webster Ave.
16. Contemporary Art Workshop
    542 W. Grant Pl.
17. 455 W. Grant Pl.
18. 2215 N. Cleveland Ave.
19. 2234–36 N. Cleveland Ave.
20. 515 W. Belden Ave.
21. 534–536 W. Belden Ave.
22. 538–544 W. Belden Ave.
23. 2310 N. Cleveland Ave.
24. 2314 N. Cleveland Ave.
25. 2325 N. Cleveland Ave.
26. 2328 N. Cleveland Ave.

WALK 26 LINCOLN PARK CONSERVATION AREA

WALKING TIME: 1½ hours.

HOW TO GET THERE: Take a northbound CTA bus No. 11 (Lincoln) on State Street. Get off at Armitage Avenue (2000 N) and walk west on the south side of the street.

---

* Portions of the WALK are in the Mid-North Historic District roughly bounded by Armitage, Fullerton, and Lincoln avenues and Clark Street.

You are now on one edge of the Lincoln Park Conservation area, where many improvements have been made and are still taking place. Until the 1960s there was little grass or other greenery here. The city through urban renewal and the citizens through active participation in planning and cooperation with the city have produced an outstanding program for the rehabilitation of the entire 3-square-mile area (Dickens Street to Fullerton Parkway, Larrabee Street-Geneva Terrace to Clark Street). The little sign "LPCA" that you see on windows or doors stands for Lincoln Park Conservation Association. Its members might say, "We believe in the future of our area and are willing to work and fight for it if necessary." Call 477-5100 for information.

The WALK will take you around a number of streets in the area where you can see interesting results of the conservation efforts. Selected because they are in close walking distance of each other, the streets offer outstanding examples of architectural rehabilitation. So many houses have been remodeled successfully—either restored or updated to a newer fashion—that comment cannot be made on each. What is significant is that so much good remodeling has been done that a whole area has been upgraded to show enormous new charm, grace, and vitality.

1943-45 N. HUDSON

ARCHITECTS: *Nagle and Hartray (1969)*

This group of 50 townhouses was built on a small site surrounded by 3- and 4-story turn-of-the-century townhouses and walk-ups. The project demonstrates that a high density low-rise solution in scale with the neighborhood is possible even in a site zoned, and sold originally, for a high-rise project.

Walk west on Armitage and turn north on Cleveland Avenue. Turn left on Dickens Avenue.

PICKWICK VILLAGE
515-29 W. Dickens

ARCHITECT: *Stanley Tigerman (1965)*

The complex of eight 3-story townhouses is built on an open court enlivened with shrubbery. The rear patios, arranged in a sawtooth line, are screened off from neighbors and passersby. An off-street parking area is provided. This is a well-planned housing group, which blends with its older neighbors but still has the advantage of newer facilities.

Cross to the north side of Dickens Avenue and walk west.

540 W. DICKENS

ARCHITECT: *for the remodeling: Arthur Carrarra (1959)*

The exterior of this house (painted white) has been remodeled, with its entrance placed at grade instead of at the former 2nd-floor location. The architectural style of the 1870s has been retained outside, complete with elaborate fretwork and turned pilasters on the balcony. The interior has been made contemporary with new lighting, new fixtures, and a new central fireplace. Charming gardens are tucked behind the old iron picket fence.

Next door is an example of fine rehabilitation, not only of individual buildings but of a whole development.

DICKENS SQUARE
542-54 W. Dickens

ARCHITECT: *for the restoration: Seymour Goldstein (1963)*

Six old structures (one is behind the others), which had been in deplorable condition for years, were successfully restored to the original appearance of their exteriors and rehabilitated inside. At 544 the center of the first 2 stories is effectively treated with glass from floor to ceiling. Gardens, patios, and open courts have been grouped around the buildings. The entire development is fronted by a red brick wall in a series of arches, providing rhythm—as well as privacy—to this enclosure of 19th-century gentility.

Continue west to Larrabee Street. Along Larrabee Street from Armitage Avenue north to Webster Avenue and extending back southeast along Lincoln Avenue to Dickens Avenue is the huge Walpole Point complex.

WALPOLE POINT
2140 N. Lincoln

ARCHITECT: *Seymour Goldstein (1973)*

Here, in the heart of the Lincoln Park Conservation Area, a new kind of neighborhood has been developed. On a rather tight site, the architect has successfully planned a series of play yards, gardens, green areas, tot lots, and patios in between structures and open parking areas. There are many inviting open terraces, sunken courtyards, and walks that together make Walpole Point a pleasing experience.

There are two types of dwelling units, townhouses and apartments. Eighty of the townhouses were intended initially for ownership by moderate-income families. The remaining 76 townhouses were retained by the developer for renting. The 96 apartments are rental units also. Combinations of the red brick, peaked, cantilevered roofs with angled double windows and arched openings give the effect of variety and distinctive character.

Now you are back at Lincoln Avenue and Cleveland. Continue east 1 block to Hudson Avenue and turn north.

2110-12 N. HUDSON

ARCHITECTS: *Booth and Nagle (1968)*

On this quiet short block of charming, old, well-maintained houses, this group of six modern townhouses adds a contemporary character. Many professional writers and artists live on the block, including here. All six homes face an off-street courtyard, yet even the backs you see here have trim, clean lines.

Continue north.

POLICEMAN BELLINGER'S COTTAGE
2121 N. Hudson

ARCHITECT: *W. W. Boyington (before 1871)*

On the east side of the street, a plaque on the building states: "This is Policeman Bellinger's Cottage, saved by his heroic efforts from The Chicago Fire October 1871." It is clear that even heroic efforts could not save many houses, for the majority in this area were built after 1871. One feature here is the modified Ionic columns upholding the porch. This architect designed the Water Tower Pumping Station—which also survived the fire!

Note how well maintained most of these houses are. Across the street at 2120-2122 Hudson is a dramatic classical revival facade over an old walk-up. At 2127 and 2131 are examples of charming and successful rehabilitation.

2134-38 N. HUDSON

On the west side of the street are some restored and remodeled town-houses with porches of random stone, grouped around an expertly landscaped courtyard.

Now retrace your steps 2 blocks to the northeast corner of Dickens and Cleveland avenues and walk four doors north.

2111-21 N. CLEVELAND

These townhouses have been successfully converted into apartment buildings. The below-grade patio at 2111-15, with marble floors and stone walls, adds charm to the exterior. The original entrance doors and roof cornices have been refinished. New glass panels at the below-grade apartment give the structure an air of modernity.

Policeman Bellinger's Cottage
(Leslie Schwartz)

2114 and 2116 N. CLEVELAND

Right across the street are two red brick townhouses constructed about 1880. Wooden bay, turret windows, and a mansard roof make these remodeled homes very attractive.

2118 N. CLEVELAND

Despite the hodgepodge of styles, this house has solidity and personality. The heavy stone grille seems to defy its own weight, while the wealth of other ornament conjures up mid-Victorian exuberance.

2124 N. CLEVELAND

This red brick, mid-Victorian house, built about 1880, has delightfully slender white Doric columns at the entrance and balcony overhead, and a mansard roof with fascinating iron picket work at the roof peak. Once remodeled into apartments, it has been restored as a single dwelling of original charm.

2129-31 N. CLEVELAND

ARCHITECT: *for remodeling: Richard Barringer (1958)*

These two townhouses of the 1880s are of red brick, with bay windows and entrances at grade instead of at the 2nd floor as they were before remodeling. The facades retain most of the original dour appearance, but the interiors have been done over successfully.

2137-39-41 N. CLEVELAND

Here is still another series of old townhouses successfully remodeled into apartments—three very distinct houses of brick and/or stone. Here too, new entrances at grade replace the former 2nd-floor entrances; yet the charm and general character of the old facades have been retained.

Walk north to Webster Avenue and proceed one block west.

GRANT HOSPITAL
550 W. Webster

ARCHITECTS: *Holabird and Root (1975); Solomon, Cordwell and Buenz (1982); for northwest wing: John Jacoffee (1983)*

Note the rebuilding process whereby the original mediocre structure has given way to a pleasant contemporary design that fits with its neighbors.

The exterior of the latest addition was designed to blend with the hospital's existing buildings by matching the adjacent building's heights, materials, and window placement. The addition, connected to the two existing structures, houses general offices, laboratories, multipurpose meeting rooms, and an auditorium.

Walk around the hospital and proceed north on Geneva Terrace. Turn right on Grant Place.

CONTEMPORARY ART WORKSHOP
542 W. Grant

ARCHITECTS: *Unknown (c. 1885, c. 1925)*

Originally the Borden-Wheelen Dairy, the rear building was built in a decade of much growth in the neighborhood. The front building dates from some 40 years later. This is now an artists' workshop where painters work and sculpture is taught. John Kearney, a well-known Chicago sculptor, founded and heads the workshop. A tour can be arranged by calling 472-4004.

Walk east to the corner.

455 W. GRANT

At the corner of Cleveland Avenue and Grant Place is a 3-story apartment building of hard-burned brick, built around an open court. The court entrances are below grade in a patio facing Grant Place. This is a well-planned complex of the late 1960s, blending with the surrounding, older structures.

Walk south on Cleveland Avenue.

2215 N. CLEVELAND

ARCHITECT: *Bruce Graham (1969)*

Here is an example of an urban townhouse meant to blend in only by its scale. It is 2 stories of monolithic concrete, including a walled garden to enclose the site. There are travertine marble walks and a black steel bar gate.

Walk north on Cleveland Avenue.

2234–36 N. Cleveland
(Sean O'Neill)

2234-36 N. CLEVELAND   This is a 3-story frame duplex townhouse. The brick face on the grade level and wood siding at 2nd- and 3rd-floor levels are painted over. Black and white trim around the windows and white Corinthian columns at the entrance complete this charming old structure, built around 1874.

Walk north to Belden Avenue and turn west to view a complex of townhouses.

515 W. BELDEN   Built in 1968, this complex of about 20 2-story townhouses focuses around an open court. Fairly well designed in brick and buffed stone and generously landscaped, it presaged the later higher-density development of some nearby streets.

Continue west.

534-536 W. BELDEN   On the other side of the street are two red brick townhouses remodeled into apartments. From the white limestone and glass entrances to the new balcony at the former entrance, this is a most successful enterprise.

538-544 W. BELDEN Here is a marvelous old red sandstone apartment building, joined to its pale-gray neighbor. The remodeling includes metal grillwork on the balcony, black trim around doors and windows, and a black cornice on the ornate roof—for a most attractive effect.

Backtrack to Cleveland Avenue and turn north.

2310 and 2314 N. CLEVELAND Here you see two well-restored Victorian brick houses with mansard roofs. The second has a fanciful iron weathervane on top.

Cross the street.

2325 N. CLEVELAND This is a 3-story red brick house of 1880 with limestone at grade, set back from the street behind an iron picket fence. A square bay window with roof turret, Gothic-style dormer windows topped with finials, and a 2-story bowed addition at the back give a definite stamp of individuality.

2328 N. CLEVELAND Here is a 3-story limestone-faced house that is embellished by Romanesque revival columns and ornaments. The addition of frame stairs and balustrade fit rather than detract from this well-restored old house.

Back at Belden Avenue, walk east to Clark Street. On the far corner note the delightful square with landscaping and a limestone sculpture attributed to Lorado Taft. Just south on Clark note how Grant Place has been closed to through traffic. This is a good spot to rest.

From this point you can board a southbound No. 22 or 36 bus to return to the Loop.

1. 646 W. Fullerton Pkwy.

2. St. Paul's Church and Parish House
   2335 N. Orchard St.

3. Childern's Memorial Hospital
   2300 Children's Plaza

4. DePaul University—Lincoln Park Campus

5. Chalmers Pl.

6. Arthur J. Schmitt Academic Center
   2323 N. Seminary Ave.

7. Stuart Center
   2324 N. Seminary Ave.

8. Munroe Hall
   2312 N. Clifton Ave.

9. University Hall
   2345 N. Clifton Ave.

10. Richardson Library
    2350 N. Kenmore Ave.

11. Church of St. Vincent DePaul
    1010 Webster Ave.

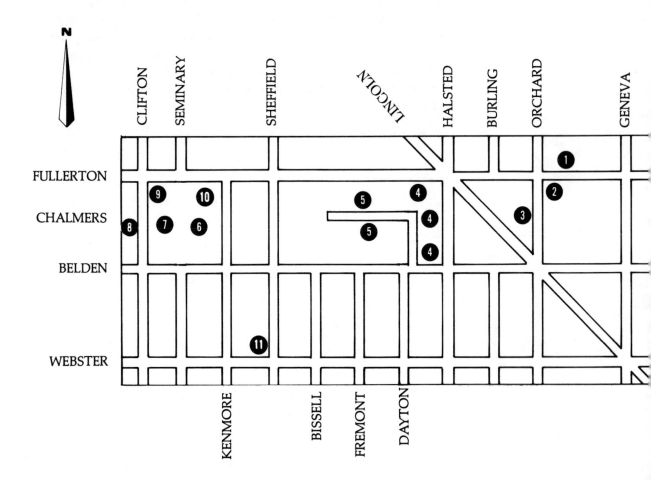

WALK 27 DePAUL UNIVERSITY: LINCOLN PARK CAMPUS

WALKING TIME: About 1½ hours.
HOW TO GET THERE: Take a northbound CTA bus No. 36 (Broadway) on State Street or a No. 22 (Clark) on Dearborn Street (1 block west of State). Get off at Fullerton Avenue (2400 N). Walk west 2 blocks to Orchard Street, where this WALK starts. (On the way you will pass churches and townhouses featured in the next WALK, 28.)

This WALK will take you primarily on a tour of DePaul University's Lincoln Park Campus. En route you will encounter many well-kept old townhouses. A stroll through the area will quickly demonstrate the pride with which its people and institutions regard their community—a factor essential to success in almost any community conservation effort.

646 W. FULLERTON

This is a pleasant 2-story brick house with a deeply recessed door suggesting privacy, as well as a dominating bay of carved wood that suggests both elegance and openness.

Across the parkway is an imposing church.

ST. PAUL'S CHURCH AND PARISH HOUSE
2335 N. Orchard

ARCHITECT: *Benjamin Franklin Olson (1951, 1959)*

The parish house was erected in 1951. After a large fire had destroyed the earlier church of St. Paul's (a United Church of Christ congregation), the new church was built in 1959. The design is modified Spanish Romanesque, with red brick and stone trim.

Continue west to the nationally known Children's Memorial Hospital.

CHILDREN'S MEMORIAL HOSPITAL
2300 Children's Plaza

ARCHITECTS: *Schmidt, Garden and Erickson (1961);*
for the addition: Perkins & Will (1981–82)

This is one of the various hospitals served by Northwestern University's Medical School. The design of the hospital building, which was developed at various stages by the same architects, is strong but not too severe. As the hospital expands beyond its original block, harmonizing with the community is a concern.

The Children's Memorial Hospital modernization program by Perkins & Will was done in two phases. First a high-rise elevator core and a triangular-shaped diagnostic/treatment wing were constructed. This

Children's Memorial Hospital
(Bill Engdahl, Hedrich-Blessing courtesy Perkins & Will)

consolidated the hospital's emergency, surgery, radiology, anesthesiology, laboratories, and pharmacy departments in expanded, modern space. In the second stage, four floors were added to the main hospital to consolidate in patient services, and existing buildings were renovated. Perkins & Will received the Merit Award of the Chicago Building Congress in 1982 "for blending of the latest technology with the tradition of a century of care for the children on the historic landmark site of Children's Memorial Hospital."

Just west of the hospital are the buildings formerly occupied by McCormick Theological Seminary and now part of DePaul University's 25-acre Lincoln Park Campus. Cross Halsted and continue west on Fullerton to the 1976 addition, an area stretching from Fullerton Avenue south to Belden Avenue and from Halsted Street west to Sheffield Avenue.

DePAUL UNIVERSITY, LINCOLN PARK CAMPUS

Although the official address is 2323 N. Seminary Avenue, the Lincoln Park Campus of this fine university occupies much of the area bounded by Halsted Street (800 W) and Racine Avenue (1200 W), Fullerton Avenue (2400 N), and Belden Avenue (2300 N).

Enter at the first gate with an opening for pedestrians on Fullerton Avenue and take a little time to enjoy this eastern part of a beautiful campus. Note especially the brick and concrete School of Music (1968) and McGaw Hall, a classroom building first used as a library (1963)—both contemporary in design—and the Concert Hall, built as the James

G. K. McClure Memorial Chapel (1963), a Georgian structure. All three buildings were designed by Holabird and Root. There is no jarring effect in the contrasting architectural styles.

Turn west and stroll around Chalmers Place, a private square.

* CHALMERS PLACE

In this pleasant green area, comparable to Louisburg Square in Boston, are privately owned 3-story townhouses of 1885–89 in the Queen Anne style. They face the north and south sides of the square. Stained glass adds character to some of the doorways.

On the west side of the square is the University's limestone Commons building of 1929, in collegiate Gothic. West of the Commons is a second large green, faced by Francis V. Corcoran Hall and Francis X. McCabe Hall, student residences, and the Hayes-Healy Athletic Center, also of 1929.

Go to the west side of Chalmers Place and turn south to Belden Avenue. Proceed west under the El tracks to reach the newer part of DePaul's Lincoln Park Campus. The first point of interest you pass is Alumni Hall, at 1011 W. Belden, a huge limestone building with black granite base.

Walk west 2 more blocks. At Seminary Avenue turn north into the pedestrian mall.

ARTHUR J. SCHMITT ACADEMIC CENTER
2323 N. Seminary

ARCHITECTS: *C. F. Murphy Associates (1967)*

On your right is an early anchor for the new campus, an imposing, 5-story concrete building with classrooms, faculty and administration offices, and seminar rooms. By raising the Belden Avenue entrance well above the street, the architects gave this structure an imposing approach and the effect of great height. The cantilevering of the upper level will remind you of the building at 222 N. Dearborn Street, designed by the same firm. Schmitt's more-used entrances, however, are at street level from the mall and Kenmore Avenue.

STUART CENTER
2324 N. Seminary

ARCHITECTS: *C. F. Murphy Associates (1971)*

Directly across the mall is the Stuart Center, designed by the same architects in the same theme of great masses of concrete planes and surfaces. Although not nearly as overpowering a structure, it manages to maintain its individuality. It does so because only a portion is higher than 1 story, thus presenting a strong horizontal mass that extends from a 3-story windowless section.

The interior holds a pleasant surprise: the reception hall, cafeteria, lounge, and snack room wrap around a garden atrium, updating the idea of a medieval cloister.

Walk through the building, heading west.

MUNROE HALL
2312 N. Clifton

ARCHITECTS: *Freidstein and Fitch (1970)*

The campus extends west to Clifton Avenue, and there on the opposite side is a compact yet spacious-looking student residence hall. Again, concrete forms vertically and horizontally frame the large windows of each room. Although DePaul is primarily a commuter university, there is demand for on-site housing by a substantial number of students.

UNIVERSITY HALL
2345 N. Clifton

ARCHITECTS: *Lohan Associates (1986)*

To the north, a newer residence turns toward an older architectural style. The easily visible, raised entries face both the street and the new quad the building helps to define. Four stories of attractive red brick are accented by a limestone belt course and window hoods.

On the quad's east side is our last stop on campus.

RICHARDSON LIBRARY
2350 N. Kenmore

ARCHITECTS: *Lohan Associates (1992)*

Completing the sense of an enclosed quad is the structure that sets a tone of scholarly dedication. DePaul's library was formerly crowded into two floors of the Schmitt Center but now rests in this spacious, inviting 4-story building of brick, named for the retiring president. Pairs of 2-story windows, one atop the other, give the illusion of a setback supported by buttresses, when in fact the brick piers are flush throughout. Spandrels bear the school's symbol, a modified tree and cross. Students enter through Kelly Hall, a cloister-like 2-story arcade featuring a stained-glass window that won a prize for American glass at the 1904 World's Fair. The library interior, including a 2-story reading room, joins Prairie style red and white oak with noise-reducing carpet.

Before returning east on Belden Avenue, if you are interested in seeing the church built by the Vincentian Fathers who founded DePaul University, you might walk east to Sheffield Avenue and turn south to Webster Avenue.

CHURCH OF ST. VINCENT DePAUL
1010 Webster

ARCHITECT: *J. J. Egan (1895–97)*

This very large edifice is constructed with gray limestone skin in a French Romanesque style. The nave has a high, barrel-vaulted ceiling supported by the ribs that extend from the freestanding columns. At the transept are two large arches that are sprung from opposite corners to form an X in the ceiling.

The semicircular apse contains a white marble sculptured altar and two small altars on either side. As you turn to leave, note the stained-glass

Richardson Library Reading Room
(DePaul University)

windows, especially the great rose window in a circles-within-circles pattern. The blues, reds, and vermilions are quite lovely when the sun is shining.

Now walk back to Belden Avenue and east to Lincoln Avenue. There are several fascinating restaurants, bars, and theaters in the vicinity.

1. Columbus Hospital
   2520 N. Lake View Ave.
2. Francis J. Dewes House
   503 W. Wrightwood Ave.
3. 466 and 468 W. Deming Pl.
4. 470–480 W. Deming Pl.
5. St Clement's
   Roman Catholic Church
   642 W. Deming Pl.
6. 2461 N. Geneva Terrace
7. 535–541 W. Arlington Pl.
8. Lincoln Park Presbyterian Church
   600 W. Fullerton Pkwy.
9. 618 W. Fullerton Pkwy.
10. 626 W. Fullerton Pkwy.

11. 638 W. Fullerton Pkwy.
12. Church of Our Savior
    530 W. Fullerton Pkwy.
13. Cenacle Retreat House
    513 W. Fullerton Pkwy.
14. 345 Fullerton Apartments
    345 W. Fullerton Ave.
15. 2400 N. Lake View Avenue Building
16. Wrigley Mansion
    2466 N. Lake View Ave.
17. 426 W. Arlington Pl.
18. 425 W. Arlington Pl.
19. 440 W. Arlington Pl.
20. 418 W. Arlington Pl.

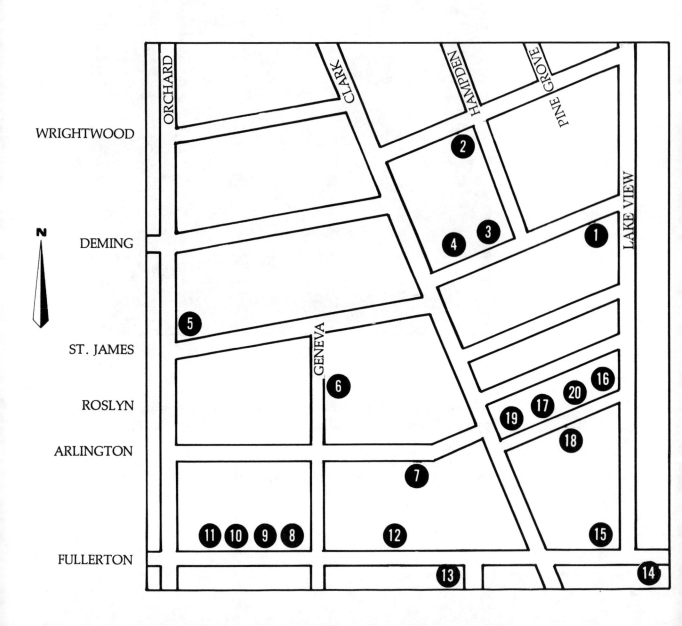

WALK 28 DEMING PLACE AND NEARBY STREETS

WALKING TIME: 1 hour.

HOW TO GET THERE: Take a northbound CTA bus No. 151 (Sheridan) on State Street. Get off at Roslyn Place (2500 N) at the edge of Lincoln Park, and walk 2 blocks north to Deming Place (2534 N).

---

* Part of this WALK is in the Lake View Historic District, roughly bounded by Wrightwood Street, Lake View Avenue, Sheridan Road, Belmont, Halsted, and Wellington streets.

Deming Place at Lake View Avenue consists primarily of high-rise buildings. Later in this WALK, you will enjoy the pleasant surprise of seeing charming residential 19th- and early 20th-century townhouses. You will also have the pleasure of following streets on which houses are set back on spacious lawns with great and handsome old trees. Some of the streets bend, adding to the element of surprise. Walking here is a delight.

The first stop is the corner of Deming Place and Lake View Avenue.

COLUMBUS HOSPITAL
2520 N. Lake View

ARCHITECTS: *DeSina and Pellegrino; Consulting Architects: Albert Schunkewitz and S. Chan Sit (1973)*

The 10-story north wing is formidable in comparison with the main hospital building of 1950. The precast-stone panels against the tinted glass windows with their anodized aluminum trim give a strong emphasis to the vertical lines of both facades. The entrance and portico on the corner has additional strong vertical lines in the striated bronze columns.

Columbus Hospital has expanded to the extent that it now covers almost the entire south side of Deming Place to Clark Street. Architecturally, the hospital unfortunately lacks unity, reflecting the fact that each phase was a separate design function.

Directly across the street, at 400 West Deming Place, is the genteel Marlborough Apartments of 1912, making quite a contrast with the hospital. The Indiana limestone facing on the two lower floors, along with the brickwork and bay windows of the twelve upper floors, make this charming building a pleasant sight.

Now walk west on Deming Place to Hampden Court, then 1 block north to Wrightwood Avenue (2600 N).

* FRANCIS J. DEWES HOUSE
503 W. Wrightwood

ARCHITECTS: *Adolph Cudell and Arthur Hercz (1896)*

Francis J. Dewes, like the architects, was born in Europe. This fact may explain why the limestone structure celebrates the baroque style, with enormous male and female figures supporting the upper balcony of wrought iron (A departure from the exclusively female caryatids of ancient Greek sculpture!). Heavy ornament surrounds the entrance and upper window. A mansard roof tops off the building.

Walk back south on Hampden Court to Deming Place. At 2600 you will pass a contemporary 6-story red-brick building with Cor-Ten steel balustrades on the balconies. Cor-Ten steel was used on the Daley Center building and Chicago's Picasso sculpture (see WALK 4).

Next, walk west on Deming Place. Although many of the comments that follow may sound repetitious, you may be sure that the buildings referred to will not look repetitious, for all have a most welcome individuality.

466 and 468 W. DEMING

The twin townhouses, ivy reaching up their red-brick facades, are a joy to behold—the huge bay windows with their black painted wood trim; the playful dormer windows and brickwork at the 3rd floor, crowned with a delightfully curved and graduated brick wall. It is a reminder of 19th-century Boston or Philadelphia. (Chalmers Place on WALK 27 has some similar houses.)

470-480 W. DEMING

These are five 2-story connected townhouses with red brick facades and individual bay windows—and tidy little gardens.

Now walk west to Clark Street and note that you are in the midst of a 2-mile strip of ethnic restaurants, art galleries, night spots, boutiques, and health-food stores. This phenomenon began in the 1960s, the result of several former Old Town merchants moving here and attracting new merchants to what is sometimes known as New Town.

Cross Clark Street (which runs southeast-northwest in this part of the city) and continue west on Deming Place. Here the street starts to curve and the buildings are set back farther from the street. The lawns seem actually greener and the trees bigger and shadier! Continue west to Orchard Street.

ST. CLEMENT'S ROMAN CATHOLIC CHURCH
642 W. Deming

ARCHITECT: *George D. Barnett (1917–18)*

At the corner of Deming Place and Orchard Street stands St. Clement's Roman Catholic Church, just beyond Ronald McDonald House at 622 W. Deming Place (formerly a convent). The church, French Romanesque with limestone facade and a rose window over the entrance, has a

Opposite:
Francis J. Dewes House
(Allen Carr)

pleasant surprise awaiting visitors who go inside. Above the spot where the apse and transept meet is a dome lined with mosaic tile figures that give the viewer a feeling of being in the 11th or 12th century.

Retrace your steps back east to Geneva Terrace, and turn south ½ block. Here again, unexpectedly, are some 19th-century townhouses with gardens and trees.

2461 N. GENEVA   Note the small house at the rear of the garden—built in pre-Civil War style.

Continue south on Geneva Terrace. When you reach Arlington Place, walk east about 100 yards.

535-541 W. ARLINGTON   These four connected houses are set well back in their yard, all in good scale. Note the pristine red brick and stone facade; only one of the original white wooden Ionic-column porticos remains. The site reflects the style of the period before the Civil War.

Return to Geneva Terrace and continue south to Fullerton Parkway. At the corner you come to a church.

LINCOLN PARK PRESBYTERIAN CHURCH
600 W. Fullerton   ARCHITECT: *Clinton J. Warren (1888)*

The limestone structure is built in the Romanesque style. It is old but well maintained. The sanctuary itself forms most of a circle.

Continue west on Fullerton Parkway, an entire block of 19th-century townhouses. Note in particular these examples.

618 W. FULLERTON   This 3-story house is mostly covered with ivy.

626 W. FULLERTON   The arresting tower at the corner has interesting brick supports, as does the east wall of the house. Note the ornamental glass above the door.

638 W. FULLERTON   This is a typical 19th-century house with a 2-story bay window.

Turn and walk back east on Fullerton Parkway past Geneva Terrace and several more 19th-century townhouses, set back 25 feet, with well-kept lawns and trees. Continue east.

CHURCH OF OUR SAVIOUR
530 W. Fullerton   ARCHITECT: *Clinton J. Warren (1889)*

This Episcopal church is a charming structure of the late 19th century, in English Romanesque design. The interior walls are of unglazed terra-cotta, an unusual early use of that material.

Across the street is a more recent religious structure.

**CENACLE
RETREAT HOUSE**
513 W. Fullerton

ARCHITECT: *Charles Pope (1965–67)*

This large convent building, set behind its parking lot, was constructed of hard-burned brick. It is a sedate and well-maintained addition to the community.

Now cross Clark Street and walk one block east.

**345 FULLERTON
APARTMENTS**
345 W. Fullerton

ARCHITECTS: *Harry Weese and Associates (1973)*

These striking 30-story concrete twin towers, located on a corner site overlooking Lincoln Park, have a particularly powerful base and entrance. In order to minimize the effect of the new development on the park, and to maintain the tall, narrow scale of the other buildings nearby, a twin-tower design was chosen. The two towers are situated along the south and west lot lines, increasing the feeling of openness at the base and minimizing the effect of one tower upon the other. They share a common lobby of glass. While each facade is parallel to the street, the setback of one tower from the other allows equal views of Lake Michigan, the city, and the park.

At the northwest corner of Fullerton and Lake View avenues is a single high-rise.

**2400 W. LAKE
VIEW AVENUE
BUILDING**

ARCHITECT: *Ludwig Mies van der Rohe (1963)*

This building was planned by the famous architect Ludwig Mies van der Rohe. The handsome structure is sheathed in aluminum, with columns exposed at the base and the vertical lines carried by mullions. The luxurious character of the apartments is indicated by the exterior plate glass and the marble walls of the lobby, to say nothing of the swimming pool in the adjoining courtyard.

Walk north 1 block. At the corner of Lake View Avenue and Arlington Place is the Wrigley Mansion.

*** WRIGLEY
MANSION**
2466 N. Lake View

ARCHITECT: *Richard E. Schmidt (1896)*

Hugh Garden may have collaborated on the design, which unfortunately has many resting places for pigeons. Otherwise the fine old building has been well maintained in its late Italian Renaissance style. The exterior has limestone base and brick facade, with brick and terra-cotta quoins at the four corners and abundant ornamentation at the 3rd-floor level. The rooms have high ceilings. A greenhouse graces the west front.

Walk a few steps west on Arlington Place to see another 19th-century townhouse, also well preserved.

Wrigley Mansion
(Leslie Schwartz)

426 W. ARLINGTON Observe the brick-and-limestone facade with arches over the wooden bay windows.

On the other side of the street is 425 Arlington Place.

425 W. ARLINGTON This 3-story house has a facade of rusticated stone, stout Romanesque columns, and a fine carving under the pediment.

Back on the north side of the street is another 19th century house.

440 W. ARLINGTON This is a 3-story Gothic revival of the late 19th century, in stone and blond brick.

418 W. ARLINGTON Back to the east is a pleasant rusticated stone house in a lovely shade of reddish-brown. It also has been well maintained.

The next WALK begins where this one did, 2 blocks north of the corner.

View of Fullerton Avenue
(Philip A. Turner)

1. 2626 N. Lake View Ave.

2. 2650 N. Lake View Ave.

3. 2700 N. Lake View Ave.

4. 2704–2710 N. Lakeview Ave.

5. Elks National Memorial Building
   2750 N. Lake View Ave.

6. Commonwealth Plaza
   330 and 340 W. Diversey Pkwy.

7. 2800 N. Lake Shore Drive West

8. St. Joseph Hospital
   2900 Lake Shore Drive West

9. Stone Medical Center
   2800 N. Sheridan Road

10. Brewster Apartments
    2800 N. Pine Grove Ave.

11. Britton I. Budd Apartments
    and Green Senior Center
    501 W. Surf St.

12. The Green Brier
    559 W. Surf St.

13. The Commodore
    550 W. Surf St.

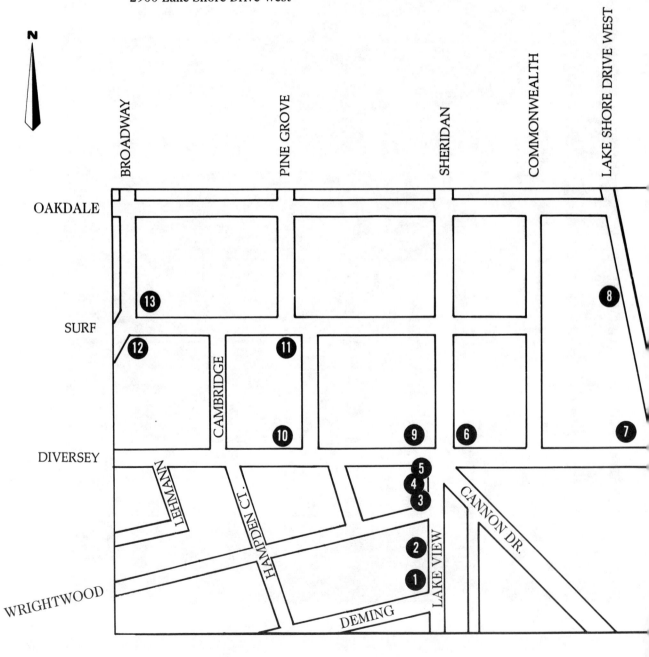

WALK 29 LAKE VIEW, DIVERSEY, SURF

WALKING TIME: 1 hour.

HOW TO GET THERE: Take a northbound CTA bus No. 151 (Sheridan) on State Street or Michigan Avenue and get off at Deming Place (2534 N).

* Part of this WALK is in the Lake View Historic District, roughly bounded by Wrightwood Street, Lake View Avenue, Sheridan Road, Belmont, Halsted, and Wellington streets.

2626 N. LAKE VIEW

ARCHITECTS: *Loewenberg and Loewenberg (1970)*

This 40-story apartment building and its handsome Y-shaped neighbor—also a 40-story apartment building—are excellent examples of two owners and their architects cooperating so that nearly every apartment in each building enjoys excellent sight lines.

2650 N. LAKE VIEW

ARCHITECTS: *Loebl, Schlossman, Bennett and Dart (1973)*

The tinted glass and anodized aluminum window frames against the striated vertical lines of the concrete give the 40-story building a delicate and slim line. The bay windows are well placed and go toward creating a domestic appearance, in spite of the great height of the structure.

Walk north on Lake View Avenue.

2700 N. LAKE VIEW

ARCHITECT: *David Adler (1920)*

This handsome structure is the former Ryerson Family Mansion. (The Ryersons also owned homes on Astor Street. See WALK 15.) The house here is said to be a replica of an 18th-century London townhouse. It is now occupied by a community-service organization.

2704-2708-2710 N. LAKE VIEW

Attached to the north of the Ryerson Mansion are 3 townhouses, all in the same style and tied together with a common roof and party walls—a characteristic seen in so many of our modern rows of townhouses. A stone base, dark red brick facade, wooden columns painted white, and slightly different ornamentation and details at each entrance give these houses an effect of special charm and grace. Note the delicate transom tracery over the doorways.

Next door is the monumental Elks National Memorial.

2710 N. Lake View
(James Cornelius)

**ELKS NATIONAL
MEMORIAL
BUILDING**
2750 N. Lake View

ARCHITECTS: *Egerton Swartout (1926); for the Magazine Building:
Holabird and Root (1966)*

The building was constructed in memory of Elks who had died in World
War I. The Memorial building consists of a great central rotunda—75
feet in diameter, 100 feet high—and 2 main wings. The base and columns
support the huge dome, which is made up inside of pieces of marble from
all over the world. The entrance is—of course—adorned by two bronze
elks! The Magazine Building to the west is a later addition, to provide a
place for the many documents of the society. Indiana limestone is used
throughout. The main building is open free to visitors, weekdays from
9 A.M. to 4 P.M.

At the northeast corner of West Diversey Parkway and North Sheridan Road, diagonally across from the Elks Memorial, are two aluminum-
sheathed tower apartment buildings.

**COMMONWEALTH
PLAZA**
330 and 340 W.
Diversey

ARCHITECT: *Ludwig Mies van der Rohe (1957)*

The two towers are expertly sited so as to give each apartment a
spectacular view. The columns are exposed at the ground level; mullions

divide the windows and carry the vertical sweep upwards. The two structures have a sculptured, almost poetic quality.

Walk east on Diversey Parkway.

2800 N. LAKE SHORE WEST

ARCHITECTS: *Solomon, Cordwell and Buenz (1970)*

As you approach this imposing apartment structure, note the buff color of the reinforced concrete exterior. The rugged columns and spandrels spaced in a rhythmic pattern give the block-long exterior an interesting facade.

This building is a classic example of a Chicago residential high-rise. The concrete structure is simply and clearly expressed on the exterior, with bronze-tinted glass infilled. The slight exterior bays express the internal unit layout and break down the facade into humanly scaled pieces. Occupying a choice piece of land with views of the park and lake in two directions, the complex includes full recreational facilities with a heated swimming pool, saunas, private plaza and roof decks, and hospitality rooms at the building's top.

If at this point you are feeling palpitations, go directly north behind the 2800 building to St. Joseph Hospital.

ST. JOSEPH HOSPITAL
2900 N. Lake Shore West

ARCHITECTS: *Belli and Belli (1963)*

This complex of buildings contains the main 3-winged, 12-story structure, parking decks, and nurses building. The hospital serves the entire north side of the city. The design, unfortunately, is eclectic and does not achieve what the designers set out to accomplish.

SCULPTURE

Before returning to Sheridan Road, you will be rewarded by looking south into Lincoln Park to see three important pieces of sculpture. First is a standing figure in bronze of John Peter Altgeld, governor of Illinois during the Haymarket Square riot and bombing of 1886. His courage and liberalism in pardoning three of the men convicted of murder drew him both condemnation and fame.

Next is an allegorical bronze of Johann Wolfgang von Goethe. It is a figure of heroic scale, holding an eagle. The piece was dedicated in 1913 to this great poet and thinker by the German-speaking community of Chicago.

About 100 yards south of the Goethe statue is a sculptured memorial to Alexander Hamilton, the first Secretary of the Treasury of the United States. The upright figure of Hamilton, though made of bronze, is appropriately painted gold. It is mounted on a red-granite cube, itself mounted on a huge black-granite structure, making a dramatic contrast. The memorial, designed by Samuel Marx, was erected in 1952 from funds supplied in memory of Kate Sturges Buckingham—the person who herself had left funds for the Buckingham Fountain in Grant Park in memory of her brother. (See WALK 1.)

Next is the building at the northwest corner of West Diversey Parkway and Sheridan Road.

STONE MEDICAL CENTER
2800 N. Sheridan

ARCHITECTS: *E. F. Quinn and Roy T. Christiansen (1951); for the renovation: Loebl, Schlossman and Hackl (1983)*

Stone Medical Center demonstrates the outcome of adaptive reuse in architecture. This 6-story light gray limestone building, formerly a union headquarters, now serves as a health-care center. With limited new building options, imaginative rehabilitation was the most practical choice. A new glass and metal frame entrance, interior atrium, and signage graphics were created to establish a strong visual identity from both streets and from Lincoln Park. The interior was completely gutted for the construction of the atrium, physicians' suites, laboratory facilities, conference rooms, and a coffee shop, which also serves the general public. A pair of Egon Weiner statues, entitled *Peace in Unity* and *Brotherhood*, were commissioned by the labor union and now flank the entrance. Each group consists of four kneeling figures, representing the four races of mankind (often identified as African, Native American, Asian, and European). All are kneeling in a sign of man's dependence on a higher power and on community unification.

Walk 1 block west on Diversey Parkway.

* BREWSTER APARTMENTS
2800 N. Pine Grove

ARCHITECT: *E. H. Turnock (1893); for remodeling: Mieki Hayano (1972)*

The original name was Lincoln Park Palace. Red polished marble appears at the entrance moldings and window columns of the first floor. By all means obtain permission to enter. Once inside, you will see the delightful open grillwork and cage of the elevator, the light court, skylight, and metal grillwork of the stairways. It seems strange that the architect, who once worked with William LeBaron Jenney, should have produced so remarkable a building only once in his lifetime.

The remodeling work and design have been handled with sensitivity and good taste. Indeed, the architect for the remodeling deserves the kudos of a grateful city. He has even added a fine touch of drama by constructing the metal faux-entry gate that is set in the parkway by the Pine Grove entrance.

The apartments have been tastefully remodeled and now have modern wiring and plumbing. Nevertheless, this 9-story structure with its high ceilings and bay windows—rugged, rough-faced with dark gray granite—seems out of place, something like a sleeping giant right on Diversey Parkway with all its noise and movement.

Walk north on Pine Grove Avenue to Surf Street.

BRITTON I. BUDD APARTMENTS AND GREEN SENIOR CENTER
501 W. Surf

The Britton I. Budd Apartments and Green Senior Center, though no great architectural masterpiece, are worth noting because of their function. This remodeled structure, operated by the Chicago Housing Authority, is a mecca for many of the older citizens of the area.

Walk west along Surf Street to the corner of Broadway. Here, on opposite sides of the street, stand 2 huge apartment buildings, constructed near the turn of the century.

THE COMMODORE
550 W. Surf

ARCHITECTS: *Edmond R. Krause (1897); for the rehabilitation: Nakawatase, Rutkowsky, Wyns and Yi (1985)*

THE GREEN BRIAR
559 W. Surf

ARCHITECTS: *Edmond R. Krause (1904); for the rehabilitation: Architects International (1985)*

These dignified brick structures have open courts, high ceilings, and smooth brick walls. The design of each facade is modified Georgian. Entrances are from Broadway as well as from the courtyards facing West Surf Street. When the sun is in the west, it shines through the lobbies into the courtyards. Louis Sullivan lived in The Green Briar for eight years.

Both buildings have been recently rehabilitated, including the restoration of the lobbies, the replacement of all mechanical systems, and the restoration of the woodwork. They became condominiums in 1992.

This WALK has shown you, among other things, quite a variety of apartment buildings: examples of modern architecture from Mies van der Rohe's to the Chicago Housing Authority's, and buildings dating back to the 1890s, the Brewster and the Commodore.

You are at Surf Street and Broadway, in the center of a strip of interesting boutiques, restaurants, taverns, and art galleries. It is called New Town. You crossed a portion of it in the previous WALK. Stroll a couple of blocks north and enjoy some of the fascinating sights and rhythm of this section of the city.

To return to the Loop, take a No. 36 CTA bus on Broadway or return east to Sheridan Road for the No. 151 bus going south.

1. 3801 N. Alta Vista Terrace
2. 3805 N. Alta Vista Terrace
3. 3802 N. Alta Vista Terrace
4. 3812 N. Alta Vista Terrace
5. 3814 N. Alta Vista Terrace
6. 3819 N. Alta Vista Terrace
7. 3824 N. Alta Vista Terrace
8. 3826 N. Alta Vista Terrace
9. 3830 N. Alta Vista Terrace
10. 3847 N. Alta Vista Terrace
11. Graceland Cemetery
    4001 N. Clark St.

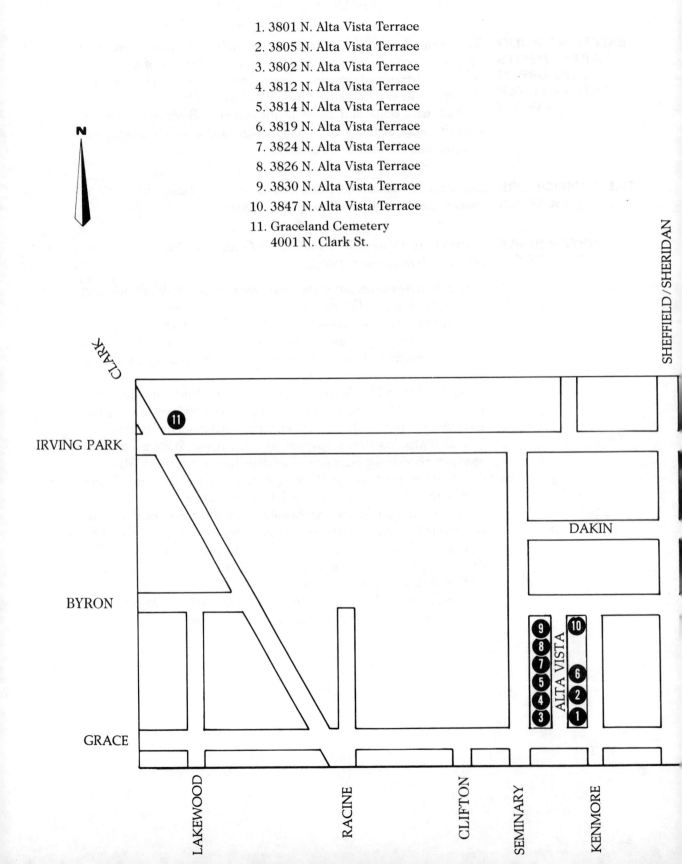

WALK 30 ALTA VISTA TERRACE–GRACELAND CEMETERY

WALKING TIME: 1 hour or less.
HOW TO GET THERE: Take a northbound CTA bus No. 22 (Clark) on Dearborn Street. Get off at Grace Street (3800 N). Walk 2 blocks east, past the House of the Good Shepherd Convent, to Alta Vista Terrace (1054 W).

* ALTA VISTA
East of N. Seminary
between W. Byron and
W. Grace

This short block has 40 townhouses on both sides of a narrow street, which might be in Boston or Philadelphia or London. It seems to belong to a past century; it is definitely not a street of today. The well-maintained old houses were constructed in 1900–1904 by one builder, who gave each house an individuality in design—almost certainly J. C. Brompton, who worked for Samuel Everly Gross, the developer of the street.

The two sides of the street are almost mirror images; that is, the house at the northwest corner is nearly identical to that at the southeast corner, and so on, with the two facing each other at midblock being a pair.

Alta Vista Terrace was designated in 1971 as an Architectural Landmark District. The designation was made by the Chicago Historical and Architectural Landmarks Commission with the consent and approval of the Chicago City Council. This action will prevent encroachment or destruction of the district. The owners volunteered the action and enthusiastically participated in all the public hearings.

3801 N.
ALTA VISTA

In this house, on the east side of the street, limestone columns surround a wooden entrance in a pleasant eclectic design.

3805 N.
ALTA VISTA

An attempt at classic detail in the facade makes this another eclectic design. Note the stained-glass transom.

3802 N.
ALTA VISTA

On the other side of the street is a classic Georgian facade. The large wooden cornice at the roof line and over the entrance relate well with the bay window of the living room. The scale is good.

3812 N.
ALTA VISTA

Here is another stained-glass transom over the entrance doorway—clearly one of the architect's favorite elements.

Some doorway treatments at Alta Vista
(Allen Carr)

**3814 N.
ALTA VISTA**

This house has a Greek revival facade, with Doric pilasters at the entrance and windows. A wooden cornice at the roof level gives the facade a sense of good scale.

**3819 N.
ALTA VISTA**

On the east side again is still another stained-glass transom. The house has Ionic wood columns at the entrance and 2nd-floor windows, and a bay window at the 1st-floor level.

**3824 N.
ALTA VISTA**

Back on the west side of the street, you see a limestone facade and bay window. A doorway in natural finish completes this interesting townhouse.

**3826 N.
ALTA VISTA**

An English half-timber facade gives variety to the facades here near midblock. Ornamentation above the door is reduced now from the original design.

**3830 N.
ALTA VISTA**

This house has an old brick facade of good scale and workmanship. The rounded entryway and stained glass are also well executed.

3847 N. ALTA VISTA On the east side again, the last house on the street has a 2-story bay topped by a turret and a finial. This nicely punctuates the end of this part of the WALK.

On your return to West Grace Street, walk behind the houses on the west side of Alta Vista Terrace. You may catch a glimpse here and there of some attractive patios and gardens.

Now walk west along Grace Street to the stoplight at Clark Street. Turn north to the next stoplight. Cross Irving Park Road to the entrance of Graceland Cemetery.

GRACELAND CEMETERY
4001 N. Clark The cemetery is open every day from 8:00 A.M. to 4:30 P.M. Tour groups must check in at the office. A map is available for 25 cents.

After entering the gate, proceed in a northerly and easterly direction about ½ mile until you reach a small lake near the northeast corner of the cemetery. By walking around the lake you will see some of the most incredible monuments ever built for one place. They are of every size, shape, and style, yet within certain areas there is a flow of continuity. Where else but at a museum would one find an assemblage of such eclectic forms—the ancient pyramid, the obelisk, the classic columns, and Gothic turrets?

The names on the various tombstones and sculpture read like a Who's Who of early Chicago. Such names as Ryerson, Field, Armour, Pullman, Palmer, Wacker, Glessner, and McCormick serve to remind us of the stability of that era. Along with Governor Altgeld and mayors Harrison and Busse, the distinguished architects Louis Sullivan, Daniel Burnham, and Mies van der Rohe are included. For more detailed information see *A Guide to Chicago's Public Sculpture* (University of Chicago Press, 1983).

* GETTY TOMB ARCHITECT: *Louis H. Sullivan (1890)*

You will find the Getty Tomb in the northeast section of Graceland Cemetery, on the northwest side of the lake. The lower half of the structure is plain, unadorned stone. The ornamentation of the upper half and of the bronze doors is exquisite, with two designs well harmonized. The tomb was proclaimed an Architectural Landmark in 1971:

> In recognition of the design which here brings new beauty to an age-old form: the tomb. Stone and bronze stand transformed in rich yet delicate ornament, a requiem for the dead, and inspiration to the living.

After leaving Graceland Cemetery, you will undoubtedly agree that the Getty Tomb transcends in beauty all other monuments there.

Louis Sullivan's tombstone
(Sidney Kaplan, M. D.)

Getty Tomb designed by Louis Sullivan
(Philip A. Turner)

1. 806 W. Buena Ave.
2. 822 W. Buena Ave.
3. 4230 N. Hazel St.
4. 4234 N. Hazel St.
5. 4243 N. Hazel St.
6. 839 W. Hutchinson St.
7. 840 W. Hutchinson St.
8. 832 W. Hutchinson St.
9. 826 W. Hutchinson St.
10. 814 W. Hutchinson St.
11. 817 W. Hutchinson St.
12. 803 W. Hutchinson St.
13. 808 W. Hutchinson St.
14. 800 W. Hutchinson St.
15. 750 W. Hutchinson St.
16. 740 W. Hutchinson St.
17. 730 W. Hutchinson St.
18. 726 W. Hutchinson St.
19. 716 W. Hutchinson St.

20. 706 W. Hutchinson St.
21. 654 W. Hutchinson St.
22. 650 W. Hutchinson St.
23. 4230 N. Marine Dr.
24. 645 W. Hutchinson St.
25. 651 W. Hutchinson St.
26. 657 W. Hutchinson St.
27. 703 W. Hutchinson St.
28. 707 W. Hutchinson St.
29. 713 W. Hutchinson St.
30. 715 W. Hutchinson St.
31. 721 W. Hutchinson St.
32. 727 W. Hutchinson St.
33. 737 W. Hutchinson St.
34. 747 W. Hutchinson St.
35. 757 W. Hutchinson St.
36. Boardwalk
    4343 N. Clarendon Ave.
37. Pensacola Place
    4334 N. Hazel Pl.

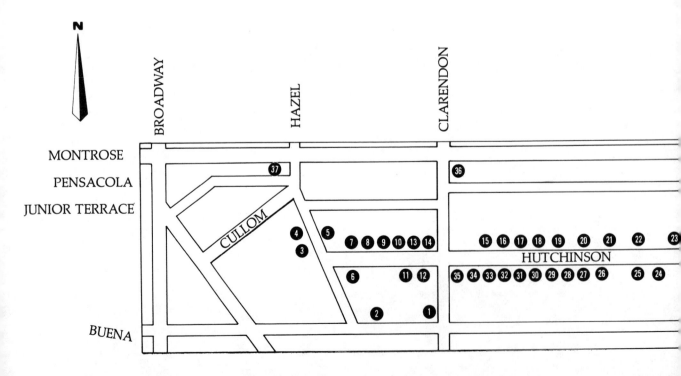

WALK 31 HUTCHINSON STREET DISTRICT

WALKING TIME: 1 hour.

HOW TO GET THERE: Take a northbound CTA bus No. 145 on State Street. Get off at Buena Avenue (4200 N) and walk to the northwest corner, to 806 W. Buena Avenue.

* Portions of this WALK are in the Buena Park Historic District, roughly bounded by Graceland Cemetery, Marine Drive, Irving Park Road, and Montrose Avenue.

West Hutchinson Street is located in the community of Uptown, an area on the North Side that began as the Town of Lakeview in the mid-19th century and was incorporated into the city in 1889.

Most of the houses along West Hutchinson Street were built during the last decade of the 19th century and the first two decades of the 20th century. The unique character of the street derives from the large concentration of houses designed by architect George W. Maher and from complementary styles.

A variety of architectural styles prevailed during the years that West Hutchinson Street was being developed. Much of the 19th-century residential architecture was characterized by revival of historical styles. The Queen Anne style is represented here, as is the Romanesque. Altogether, the houses along Hutchinson Street present a capsule history of American residential architecture from their era. It is important to know that George Maher was a contemporary of and also worked with Frank Lloyd Wright and George Grant Elmslie. All of them were as young as they were talented. They soon became leaders in the development of an indigenous American architecture—known as the Prairie school design and the Chicago school.

806 W. BUENA ARCHITECTS: *Doer Brothers (1917–18)*

This Renaissance revival mansion, now a day school, was built for C. Zimmerman. The main body is constructed of red common brick. The 2-story sun porches flanking the street facade are of limestone, as is the front portico. This large, formal portico, centered on the symmetrical facade, is supported on paired columns and frames the front entrance. The large rectangular windows of the 1st floor are topped by arched panels of limestone and decorated by simple roundels; wrought iron railings form mock balconies. The windows of the 2nd story are simply framed in brick, though cornice-like sills of limestone above the window frames are supported by brackets. An elaborate belt course, similar to the cornice in its design, marks the top of the 2nd floor. The treatment of the 3rd story is similar to that of the attic story of Renaissance palaces. Decorative brickwork is a basic element of the design here; headers of brick project from the surface, forming frames for the small windows and the panels between. The double hip roof is covered with green mission tile.

Walk west on Buena Avenue.

822 W. BUENA   ARCHITECT: *Unknown (1907)*

Claude Seymour built this house and lived here for about six years, then moved into the larger house at 817 W. Hutchinson Street. This smaller yet handsome 2-story home is constructed of warm orange brick. The two large round bays project from the street facade; rising a full 2 stories, they are topped by shallow conical roofs. The veranda, which once extended the full length of the facade, reflects the bay shape only on the western end of the facade, where large windows open from the living room. Heavy brick piers support the roof of the veranda and also the low fence. Simple pilasters inconspicuously frame the corners of the facade. An interlace pattern of molding supports the glass in the front door and the top lights of the 2nd-story windows. The wood frieze under the eaves is decorated with garlands. The dormer windows, modified from the Palladian type, are surmounted by volutes, which support a simple finial. The two modeled Queen Anne–style chimneys crown the simple roof line.

Now turn north on North Hazel Street and cross to the west side.

4230 N. HAZEL   This is a striking brick and stucco house of contemporary design. It is set as far back as its neighbors to preserve views.

Continue north.

4234 N. HAZEL   ARCHITECT: *Richard E. Schmidt (1904)*

There has been some question about which architect in Schmidt's office produced the design. Both William E. Drummond and Hugh M. G. Garden, young architects who were later to produce many fine Prairie school designs, were in Schmidt's employ. A similar design, labeled "L. Griffen House, Buena Park, Chicago," was published in the Chicago Architectural Club Catalog in 1902. More recently published materials have asserted Drummond's primary role in the design of this, the Wolff House.

The Wolff House is a 2-story L-shaped residence constructed of brown brick. The broadly sloping, double hipped roof and its overhangs emphasize the horizontality that is the trademark of Prairie school architecture. The top of the L faces the street. The single-story wings project from the south and east facades, sheltering the main entrance and an enclosed porch. The white limestone belt course, which forms the lower sills of the small 1st-floor windows and the coping of the front porch, binds the design together. A white concrete mud sill sloping sharply to the ground adds further horizontal emphasis.

Louis Wolff was a manufacturer of plumbing goods. In the Book of Chicagoans (1911) it is noted that he was a member of the Chicago Automobile Club, the Chicago Athletic Club, and the South Shore Country Club.

Continue north to 4243 N. Hazel Street—a combination studio, atrium, and residence.

4243 N. HAZEL   ARCHITECT: *Unknown (1909); for renovation and addition: Anthony Frigo (1975)*

This house was constructed about 1909 and a new kitchen wing has been added at the rear. The art gallery was constructed for the use of the owners—the husband being a talented painter and the wife, a weaver of wall hangings.

Walk back to the corner of Hutchinson Street.

839 W. HUTCHINSON   ARCHITECT: *George W. Maher (1909)*

Despite the rather awkward handling of certain elements in the design of this house, it is the work of George W. Maher. The house probably dates from 1909, when Maher was beginning to work with a new type of design, one that was inspired by English architects such as C. F. A. Voysey and the Viennese architect Joseph M. Olbrich. The long 2-story facade of the house is covered by a steep hip roof, which conceals a ballroom. The emphasis on horizontality, so basic to the Prairie school style, is evident in the long sill that joins the three small windows on the 2nd floor and the copper striations in the roof surface. In this design, Maher's concern for the role of the wall as enclosing surface is apparent. The cream-colored common brick is laid in a stretcher bond and the joints are not raked; thus, the flatness of the wall plane is emphasized. The windows are set deeply into the surface of the wall and are asymmetrically arranged, reflecting the arrangement of the interior spaces.

Maher's motif-rhythm theory of design called for the repeated use of the same decorative motif as a unifying element in the design. This theory is carried out by the repeated use of the low arch with short lateral flanges; the basic form is most apparent in the pediment over the main entrance. It is reflected many times: in the flower boxes at either side of the stair,

839 West Hutchinson
(Charles Brooks)

in the coping on the chimney, and even in the catch basins of the downspouts.

840 W. HUTCHINSON

ARCHITECT: *George W. Maher (1894)*

The oldest in the area, this house was built for John C. Scales. At the time, George Maher was still producing designs that displayed the influence of his ten-year stay in the office of Joseph Lyman Silsbee. This house is typical of the Queen Anne style in the irregularity of its massing and the variety of color and texture of the materials used.

A rubblestone base firmly anchors the 2-story house to the earth. The broad eaves of the veranda add horizontal emphasis while enclosing much of the south and east facades. Rubblestone walls extend above the 1st floor in the round elements of the design and in the chimneys. The 2nd story is decorated with elements suggesting medieval half-timber construction; dark brown molding is set off by the white stucco that covers the wall. The round bay on the south facade is topped by a conical roof surmounted by a large gable. Here Maher chose to work with medieval motifs: the bargeboard of the gable is cut in a trefoil shape.

Behind this is a leaded glass window that is nearly flamboyant Gothic in style. Under the window is a terra-cotta cartouche.

The Hazel Street facade is much more complex in its massing. The door, which is tucked under a deep overhang, is rounded at the top. Over this door is a tripartite Gothic-style window having wooden tracery at the top. On the west facade a 2-story rubblestone turret is surmounted by a faceted conical roof. There are few square corners in the plan of the Scales house; the design is held together by the heavy masonry base and by the repeated horizontals of the roof lines.

Walk east.

832 W. HUTCHINSON

ARCHITECT: *Unknown (1921)*

This brick house of 2½ stories was built in 1921. The entrance is on the east side of the low ground story and the principal rooms are on the 2nd story. The main features of the handsomely composed Hutchinson Street facade are the wide 2nd-story window and the gable directly above it. The window, occupying most of the width of the facade, is set into an opening with a pointed segmental arch; this arch echoes the configuration of the gable above. The Dutch-type gable is trimmed in stone, capping the Hutchinson Street facade. Projecting to the west is a small wing with a blank brick wall on the ground floor and an enclosed porch above.

Continue east.

826 W. HUTCHINSON

ARCHITECT: *George W. Maher (1904)*

W. H. Lake was a grain broker and senior partner in the firm of W. H. Lake and Company, which was located in the Board of Trade Building. Lake, following the lead of his neighbor John Scales, chose to commission George Maher as architect for his home, too.

In the Lake House, Maher developed his final version of the Farson House (1897) type. In this type of design Maher made his most significant contribution to the indigenous American architecture he worked so hard to develop. Unity is achieved by formal arrangement of elements within the design. The basic form of this house type is a massive rectangle with horizontal elements dominating the composition and drawing it together.

The 2-story rectangular facade of the Lake House is overshadowed by the deep overhang of the double hip roof, creating the most striking horizontal element in the design. The low rectangular dormer breaks the broad plane of the roof at its center. The three large windows are symmetrically arranged at the 2nd floor level; two panels containing simple art glass designs frame the central double-hung window. The west windows, above the main entrance, are enhanced by a simple bowed limestone sill supported by a decoratively carved bracket. The main entrance below is framed by a simple wide band frame and two low, thick walls. A deep veranda extends from the center of the front facade to the east, adding another strong horizontal element to the composition.

Continue east.

814 W. HUTCHINSON

ARCHITECT: *Unknown (1948)*

This 2-story red brick house was built in 1948. Decorative elements in the design include limestone keystones over the windows, simple white shutters, and wrought iron.

Across the street is 817 W. Hutchinson Street.

817 W. HUTCHINSON

ARCHITECT: *George W. Maher (1913)*

This house was constructed in 1913 for Claude Seymour. Drawings of the front facade were published in the Chicago Architectural Club Catalog for 1913. Seymour was a vice-president of Otto Young and Company, a jewelry concern. Like many of his neighbors, Seymour was active in the Chicago Automobile Club and a member of many other fashionable clubs.

In his design for the Seymour House, Maher borrowed heavily from English country houses by C. F. A. Voysey and the firm of Parker and Unwin. The 2-story house is basically H-shaped, though a 1-story porch (not an addition) does break the symmetry of the facade. The many windows and their arrangement here are typical of Parker and Unwin's designs, but the geometric pattern in the leaded glass is distinctly the work of Maher. This design and its variations are used consistently in all decorative elements to lend a measure of continuity; Maher called it his motif-rhythm theory. A motif similar to that used in the window glass is also found in the balustrades, which enclose the front terrace. The large front door, containing a leaded glass window, is sheltered by a low arched canopy supported by four large, classically inspired brackets. The entrance to the property is a simple iron gate in a fence supported by large brick piers. Both the steps and the walkway leading to the house are of the same red brick as the structure itself.

Continue east.

803 W. HUTCHINSON

ARCHITECTS: *Schmidt, Garden and Martin (1910)*

This 2-story house is a handsome, well-proportioned example of Richardsonian Romanesque design. The heavily rusticated limestone of the exterior walls emphasizes the massiveness of the structure. The simple forms are handled with great care; relationships between solid and

817 W. Hutchinson
(Charles Brooks)

void and the proportions used are evidence of the work of a good architect or an excellent contractor. The Clarendon Avenue facade contains two systems of complementary symmetry: under the double hip roof four windows are symmetrically arranged. The surrounding porch is divided by three broad arches, each springing from a thick pier; these piers are aligned with the window voids above. Entry to the house is by way of the porte-cochere on the Hutchinson Street facade or through the large door on the Clarendon Avenue side.

On the other side of the street is 808 W. Hutchinson Street.

808 W. HUTCHINSON

ARCHITECT: *W. F. Pagels (1908)*

This 2-story Prairie school style house is constructed of red brick, complemented by details of blond brick and carved limestone. The design of an arch flanked by rectangles (seen in the limestone details and the large 2nd-story window) may be due to the influence of George Maher. A wood frame porch, now removed, once sheltered the main entrance and balanced with the large window area on the eastern half of the street facade.

The next house east is the residence of former Governor James Thompson.

**800 W.
HUTCHINSON**

ARCHITECTS: *Huehl and Schmid (1906)*

This house was constructed for A. E. Pyott. The large, 2-story Prairie school style residence has a 1-story base of blond Roman brick. The 2nd story is of mock half-timber construction; here cream-colored stucco contrasts with brown wood. Limestone is used for the window sills and the capstones of the 1-story front porch on the Hutchinson Street facade.

Cross Clarendon Avenue and continue east on the north side of the street. The WALK will return on the other side.

**750 W.
HUTCHINSON**

ARCHITECT: *George W. Maher (1902)*

The design of this 2-story house, especially the west facade, is a fine example of Maher's Farson House style. The west facade is symmetrical. A low double hip roof is broken at the center by a classically styled dormer typically found in Maher's designs. The base of the roof is bordered by a shallow, classically inspired cornice. Below this cornice, a pattern of alternating arrows perforate the decorative molding, which is supported by a row of dentils. The smooth surface of the cream-colored brick is broken by the main entry on the west facade. The entry is set in a large stone frame (reminiscent of Louis Sullivan's Wainwright Tomb in St. Louis) projecting from the center of the 1st story. Above this, a small window is set behind a large frame supported by two colonettes. The capitals of the columns used throughout this design are very similar in style to those designed by Sullivan. The facade is also broken by four large, simply treated windows.

The Hutchinson Street facade is broken by a rounded 1-story sun porch, the roof of which projects to form a porte-cochere. The sun porch is very similar to those found in the designs of English country houses built at the end of the 19th century. The long wooden cornice is supported by the same unusually styled Sullivanesque colonettes. Today the owners of this house use the entrance off the porte-cochere as the main entry.

**740 W.
HUTCHINSON**

The entrance to the house is set back from the street to provide privacy for the owners. Trim (such as the capstones surrounding the front porch and the window sills and lintels) is of limestone, which contrasts with the deep red color of the brick walls.

730 W. HUTCHINSON

Built in the late 1950s during the last period of development on the street, the 2-story red brick house has details of Indiana limestone.

726 W. HUTCHINSON

ARCHITECT: *Unknown (1898)*

Though it has recently been remodeled, the 2-story house retains its 1st-floor base of blond Roman brick. The front entrance and the 2nd story have been completely remodeled.

716 W. HUTCHINSON

ARCHITECT: *John R. Stone (1901)*

This classical revival style house stands in striking, yet instructive, contrast to the other homes along the street. The boldness with which the classical elements of the design have been executed in wood negates the basically simple brick volume of the house. The pedimented roof is supported by brackets and decorated with rows of dentils and egg-and-dart moldings. A simple tripartite window is surmounted by a richly modeled floral ornament. The pediment is supported by a colonnade of modified Ionic columns 2 stories in height. A matching white frame sun porch fills the 2nd story, breaking at its center to form a bay window; both are set in frames derived from the classically inspired Palladian style.

This house was the home of William F. Monroe, who founded a well-known tobacco shop shortly before the turn of the century. Though ownership of the shop has changed, it still bears his name.

706 W. HUTCHINSON

ARCHITECTS: *Huehl and Schmid (1905)*

This 2-story residence was built for Dr. John A. Robison. Constructed of cream-colored Roman brick complemented by limestone detail, it is topped by a steeply pitched roof of red tile. Though the influence of the Prairie school of architecture is apparent in this design, many of the details are taken from classical architecture. The tripartite window in the attic dormer is divided by stout neoclassical columns. The windows are framed in limestone, which is also used in the belt course above the second story. The porch, which extends two-thirds of the length of the south and east facades, is supported by eight neo-Ionic columns. The carriage house alongside has been converted to a separate residence.

654 W. HUTCHINSON

ARCHITECT: *Unknown (1940)*

This 2-story red brick house has a 1-story projection to the east where the brick has been laid in a simple diaper, or diamond, pattern.

650 W. HUTCHINSON

ARCHITECT: *Unknown (1937)*

The design of this 2-story red brick house is enhanced by the use of limestone in the coping, belt course, and the 1st- floor window frames. Colonial details, such as the front door frame, also add interest to the design.

At the northwest corner is 4230 N. Marine Drive.

4230 N. MARINE

The massing of this 2-story residence is simple and functional, and the diamond-shaped pattern in the brickwork of the Hutchinson Street facade adds interest to the design.

Cross Hutchinson Street to the south side of the street. The WALK now continues westward.

645 W. HUTCHINSON

ARCHITECT: *George Kingsley (1914)*

This 2-story house is a fine, early example of the residential architecture of the 1920s and 1930s. The design is enriched by the careful use of high-quality building materials. The rich color of the red brick facade is matched in the tile roof. The roof is framed with broad but simple gutters of copper, which have now acquired a green patina. Limestone is used for the window sills and in the plain entablature-like band under the eaves. The elaborate portico over the main entrance is suspended by chains anchored to the facade by limestone rosettes.

651 W. HUTCHINSON

ARCHITECT: *Unknown (1914)*

This 2-story house has a 1st floor of red brick, while the 2nd story and the attic dormers are of wood frame construction, covered with dark stucco. The 1-story porch on the street facade has been filled in and a large picture window added.

657 W. HUTCHINSON

ARCHITECT: *Unknown (1914)*

This 2-story red brick house has recently been tuckpointed with white mortar. The entrance on the tree-shaded east facade provides privacy.

703 W. HUTCHINSON

ARCHITECT: *Unknown (1940)*

The limestone trim above the 1st-floor windows contrasts with the exterior walls of pink common brick in this 2-story house.

707 W. HUTCHINSON

ARCHITECT: *Unknown (1912)*

This 1-story bungalow has been remodeled; a 2-car garage now occupies the basement of the house, which has been faced in white permastone.

Some elements of the original design remain: the main entry on the east facade is unchanged, yet the scale of the picture window is not the same as that of the original window.

713 W. HUTCHINSON

ARCHITECT: *George Garnsey (1907)*

This 2-story frame house was constructed during the 1st decade of this century. Narrow horizontal siding on the 1st floor contrasts with the shingle-covered 2nd floor. A Palladian window (a classically-inspired window divided into three parts) is set into the dormer, which is centered on the attic story of the street facade.

715 W. HUTCHINSON

ARCHITECT: *Unknown (1911)*

The sloping roof and broad eaves of the 1-story house tend to diminish its size, making it appear to hug the ground. Actually this cream stucco house is quite large, for the gentle slope of the roof allows for a spacious attic story.

721 W. HUTCHINSON

ARCHITECT: *Unknown (1951)*

This 2-story red brick house was constructed during the last period of development on the street. Here the sandstone stair and understated portico above the front entry add interest to the design.

727 W. HUTCHINSON

ARCHITECTS: *Jenney and Mundie (1897)*

The randomly laid limestone base of this house lends it an air of informality; the character of the house emphasizes the suburban beginnings of Hutchinson Street. One of the first houses constructed on the street, it is 2½ stories in height. A large polygonal porch, supported on neoclassical columns, frames the main entrance.

737 W. HUTCHINSON

ARCHITECT: *George Kingsley (1911)*

This 2-story red brick residence is a very fine example of Prairie school domestic architecture. The design is based on a balanced system of proportion. Though the 1-story enclosed porch on the Hutchinson Street facade does not extend the width of the house, axiality is maintained in the alignment of the four windows below the tripartite bay window of the 2nd floor. The recessed front entrance, containing a large double door flanked by two modified Corinthian columns, corresponds in the original design with the void of the 2nd-story sleeping porch, now enclosed. Indiana limestone has been used extensively as a unifying element in the design.

747 and 757 W. HUTCHINSON

ARCHITECT: *C. Whitney Stevens (1909)*

These 2-story residences, identical except for certain secondary elements of design, were built for John H. and William H. Powell. They are constructed of common brown brick; the front facades are symmetrically arranged and dominated by a wide porch. The double pitch roofs are broken by rounded dormers on the front facades, but horizontality is stressed by the broad overhangs surmounting the roof and porch. The limestone belt courses, sills, and coping (of the front porch) reflect the white plaster used to highlight the overhangs. Decorative brickwork plays an important role in the overall design, breaking up massive elements (such as the piers that support the front porch) and accenting the horizontality of the second-floor facade.

Walk north on Clarendon Avenue. If time permits, walk 1 block north to Junior Terrace, a short street, and note the first house at 805 W. Junior Terrace (part Prairie school and part Mediterranean design), as well as 811 W. Junior Terrace (of the George Maher period). Both houses, along with others in the block, are superb examples of excellent maintenance.

Next you will see a pair of new high-rises. At the corner of Clarendon and Montrose avenues is Boardwalk.

BOARDWALK
4343 N. Clarendon

ARCHITECTS: *Stanley Tigerman and Associates (1974)*

This 28-story apartment complex is of reinforced concrete glazed with solar bronze float glass. The base of the building contains commercial space, a swimming pool with bath house, tennis court, and a landscaped plaza deck.

Walk west on Montrose 2 blocks to Hazel Street.

PENSACOLA PLACE
4334 N. Hazel

ARCHITECTS: *Stanley Tigerman and Associates, Associate in Charge: Robert Fugman (1978–81)*

The Janus piece to Boardwalk, this middle-income housing and commercial complex struggles with its schizophrenic site. In one direction are Marine Drive and the well-off; in the other are rooming houses and tenements full of immigrants. Thus imbalanced, the complex denies resolution, the difference between the two facades becoming even more pronounced when they are juxtaposed. Walk around to see the west side of the building to compare the facades.

For a bus to the Loop, return east to Clarendon Avenue.

INDEX

Page numbers in *italics* refer to pages on which illustrations appear.